GREED TO GREEN

*Solving Climate Change
and Remaking the Economy*

CHARLES DERBER

Paradigm Publishers
Boulder • London

To Elena

And to climate change activists everywhere

Copyright © 2010 Paradigm Publishers

Published in the United States by Paradigm Publishers, 3360 Mitchell Lane, Suite E, Boulder, CO 80301 USA.

Paradigm Publishers is the trade name of Birkenkamp & Company, LLC, Dean Birkenkamp, President and Publisher.

Library of Congress Cataloging-in-Publication Data

Derber, Charles.
  Greed to green : solving climate change and remaking the economy / Charles Derber.
    p. cm.
  Includes bibliographical references and index.
  ISBN 978-1-59451-811-9 (hbk. : alk. paper) — ISBN 978-1-59451-812-6 (pbk. : alk. paper)
  1. Environmental policy—Economic aspects. 2. Climatic changes—Economic aspects. 3. Capitalism—Environmental aspects—United States. I. Title.
  HC79.E5D454 2010
  363.738'7460973—dc22

2009026416

Printed and bound in the United States of America on acid-free paper that meets the standards of the American National Standard for Permanence of Paper for Printed Library Materials.

Designed and Typeset by Straight Creek Bookmakers.

14 13 12 11 10 1 2 3 4 5

Contents

Introduction

Capitalism's Time Bomb
and the Fierce Urgency of Now

The dictionary defines a time bomb as "something that threatens to have an abruptly disastrous outcome in the future."[1] Climate change—the largely imperceptible rise in our greenhouse gas emissions and earth temperature—is a time bomb, and this book suggests how we can defuse it.

Humanity has confronted other time bombs—such as the threat of all-out nuclear war. They make up two of a broader special category: existential threats that could potentially end human civilization. During the cold war, the editors of the *Bulletin of the Atomic Scientists* regularly printed its famous Doomsday Clock, putting the minute hand at one minute to midnight during the Cuban missile crisis. The *Bulletin* now sets the clock to monitor the threats to human survival from both nuclear war and climate change, setting the clock at this writing at five minutes to midnight.[2]

It makes intuitive sense that changing our perceptions of time is important in defusing a time bomb. The very idea of a time bomb—especially one whose tick-tock, tick-tock we can hear but ignore—hints at ignorance or indifference to the future and a time horizon shorter than the period in which the time bomb will explode. The climate time bomb is moving potentially out of our control because we are living in a socioeconomic system that relentlessly shrinks our time horizons and paralyzes our will to act on future common needs.

A solution to climate change has to help us change our current experience of time as part of a broader remaking of our economy and culture. Our perceptions of time are one part of our culture and mind-set, with deep roots in our capitalist order. Climate change—and the pathology of our short-term mind-set—is so intertwined with our crisis-riddled economy that solutions to global warming cannot happen without rapid systemic changes in our capitalist order, a defining theme of this book.

The reality of climate change as a long-term systemic social crisis with a short-term action window shapes the solutions I offer here. All of us, ordinary citizens and world leaders, must recognize climate change as an urgent existential threat organically linked to our economic model and way of life. *I propose here that the threat is so grave and urgent, and the U.S. responsibility so central, that the president invoke his powers—prescribed carefully and judiciously in the Constitution for periods of "extraordinary crisis"—to bring all of us together in partnership to create decisive emergency action now.*

I focus this book on solutions. Such solutions must (1) meet the new time constraints of nature and (2) transform our political economy because climate change is, indeed, capitalism's time bomb, a reflection of inner contradictions in the workings of our markets, politics, and consumerist culture. I show how the president and the rest of us can act just fast enough to avoid catastrophe.

In the pages that follow, I offer a brief map to the rest of the book. In Part I, I focus on the truth about climate change and the denial regime obscuring that truth. In Part II, I show how emergency solutions must start in the United States itself, with fundamental changes in our economic model and mind-set. In Part III, I show the changes in the world as a whole that can lead us away from climate change catastrophe. And in Part IV, I show that grassroots action must lead change both at home and abroad.

Truth and Denial

In an age of climate change, the consequences of fudging, distorting, spinning, or denying truth are more serious than in other eras. This is the era in which we can least afford to disrespect truth. The scientific consensus is that climate change is a threat to human civilization and that the window of opportunity to prevent catastrophe is rapidly closing.[3]

The very idea of truth has been weakened in our new postmodern capitalist era. Princeton philosopher Harry Frankfort argues that we live in a culture of "BS," where powerful corporations and political leaders use advanced electronic technologies to spin or fudge truth for their own interests.[4] Millions of Americans believe that contempt for truth—not only among politicians but also among ordinary people—is the most disastrous legacy of the Bush administration, notorious for its denial of science and climate change.[5]

Disrespect for the truth about climate change is creating a tragedy. In Part I, I explore a set of issues about the truth of climate change itself. But these chapters also raise broader questions about varieties of cognitive and psychological truth, about who creates the truths that the public accepts in capitalist societies, and how and why various groups and generations of ordinary Americans now accept or deny the truth of climate change. Because this is also a book about solving an urgent crisis, I focus on the psychology and politics that lead people to deny and ignore certain kinds of truth and move like wildfire to act on others. *In our short-term culture, long-term truths that we cognitively accept as valid become abstract and disconnected from our urge to act.* Our economic and political systems create short-term, ego-centered myopia—and we urgently need to help people act on long-term truths that lose electric charge in a short-term culture and are often subject to powerful forces of denial in capitalist and other societies.

In Part I, I look closely at the battle between truth and the denial regime on the climate change issue. The denial regime is an interconnected network of corporations, politicians, and opinion-makers with vested economic interests and ideological perspectives shaping their—and our—climate change views. It plays a major role in framing the public discourse and subordinating truth and in recent years has evolved into a "stage 2" model of denial that rhetorically embraces the reality of climate change while undermining the public will to create the emergency action required. The denial regime is part of a larger "ideological apparatus" that is organized to protect our current form of capitalism while claiming to operate in the service of truth rather than power.

The president has a key role to play in resurrecting truth and combating the denial regime. His voice has special authority to invoke and act on both short- and long-term truths. The president's truth-telling has never been more important than in the age of climate change, where the scientific truth about future civilizations and generations has been denied and overwhelmed by shorter-term crises. We are blessed with a new president who respects science and truth and a public long waiting to hear both.[6]

Capitalism, Climate Change, and the Greening of the Globe

A biologist trained in environmental science directs a new environmental studies program on my campus, Boston College. Such programs are spreading quickly at universities across the country. Those taking the lead are usually natural scientists with the disciplinary and technical skills necessary to understand many of the key issues.

But we need quickly to create and spread knowledge about climate change across the entire curriculum. Climate change is too important to be left to scientists, environmental groups, or any other specialized group. If the crisis of climate change does not become rapidly integrated into the social sciences and humanities courses of universities—as well as become a leading topic of conversation in churches, workplaces, and town halls across the country and world—we may lose the battle.

Scientific discovery and technological breakthroughs in our energy system are obviously crucial to finding a solution. But social, economic, cultural, and political breakthroughs are just as important. Societies created the climate change crisis, and they must now lead social change to deal with the Frankenstein elements of their own creation.

C. Wright Mills, a leading U.S. sociologist of the twentieth century, wrote of "the sociological imagination."[7] He was talking about the responsibility of sociologists to create critical thinking about our socioeconomic-political system that can help solve simultaneously personal troubles and societal crises. If Mills were alive today, he would be championing a "green" sociological imagination, focusing on the intertwined themes of climate change, corporate power, consumerist lifestyles, militarism, and the power elite.[8] A green sociological imagination shows that climate change is a toxic *symptom*, rooted in and caused by deep design problems in our socioeconomic order and way of life. Solutions require examination of capitalism as much as of climate. Mills would urge sociologists and all intellectuals to help conceive solutions based on social justice and light a fire to create citizen action before it is too late.

A new field of environmental sociology is emerging that is helping create a twenty-first-century green sociological imagination.[9] Max Weber, Karl Marx, and Emile Durkheim are the towering giants who founded modern social theory, and they created a prophetic analysis of capitalist economies and cultures.[10] They sketched the way industrial capitalism regiments and shrinks our time horizons, as short-term profit and consumption appetites quicken the pace of work and everyday life. They also hinted that contemporary capitalism, run by huge monopolistic global corporations at the expense of workers and local businesses, combats tendencies toward stagnation by turning itself into a casino luring the entire population into debt, credit, and endless consumption.[11] The green sociological imagination leads us today to question with ever greater urgency capitalism's morality, which holds that by pursuing our own selfish interests in the marketplace, we ensure the common good.

The task of the green sociological imagination is to use the critical analyses of the founders of social science to transform urgently corporate capitalism in the United States and the world, based on a clear understanding of the relation between capitalism and climate change. The great early social theorists foresaw the capitalist erosion of the unprofitable "social commons," such as public education, public transit, and health care. But they gave only hints of what the green sociological imagination must now highlight: how our new turbocharged, debt-based, and globalized capitalism is propelling us at frightening speed toward the ultimate tragedy of the atmospheric commons—a tragedy of the air, sky, oceans, rainforests, and thousands of species, including our own.[12]

American Capitalism and Global Warming

If climate change is a symptom, we can solve it only by looking at the underlying disorder. Part II looks at how the U.S. model of capitalism creates a particularly virulent model of climate change crisis in America itself and how we must create systemic change to save ourselves. Part III extends the argument to the world as a whole.

There are many models of capitalism, and Part II focuses on the U.S. model because it leaves the heaviest footprint on the planet and is also the most influential in the world. Any prospects of solving the climate change problem will require quickly changing key systemic elements of our economy. Even though this is a daunting task, it is becoming more possible because the 2008–2009 Great Recession has created widespread suffering in the United States itself and raised deep questions at home and abroad about the U.S. economic system.

In looking at capitalism, we are not focused on economic issues alone. Capitalism has economic, political, and cultural (including social-psychological) subsystems. All are crucial in giving rise to climate change, and all require change. Together, they create a society that is materialistic, profit driven, consumerist, competitive, short-term focused, and inclined toward excess. All are toxic for the environment and are at the heart of the climate change crisis.

Capitalism is not the only system that can cause climate change. Soviet communism was worse. So was communist China in the twentieth century. But capitalism is the dominant economic system in the world today, absorbing most of the collapsed communist economies and lying at the heart of the global warming crisis. The Chinese economy has evolved into a hybrid today and is a leading contributor to the crisis, largely because it has incorporated many capitalist ideas of growth and consumerism driving climate change. The same is true of most other leading world economies, including the European Union and India. But the most ecologically dangerous forms of capitalism are embodied in the U.S. model, and globalization has diffused these U.S. elements into most of the leading world economies.

In the United States, the view of climate change as a symptom of capitalist disorder is rejected or ignored. True, there are factors other than capitalism driving climate change, perhaps most important the unsustainable growth of the world's population. Journalist Chris Hedges warns that "all measures to thwart the degradation and destruction of our ecosystem will be useless if we do not cut population growth. By 2050, if we continue to reproduce at the current rate, the planet will have between 8 billion and 10 billion people, according to a recent U.N. forecast."[13] Hedges argues that this population growth is already ravaging planetary resources and destroying thousands of species annually and will ultimately devastate, through climate change, our own species. And Hedges is right: We must collectively act globally to curb this growth.

But rapid population growth—although essential to stop in the age of global warming—functions largely to speed up climate change that is structurally rooted in a rapidly globalizing U.S. model of capitalism. The failure to focus on capitalism reflects the power of capitalists themselves and their political allies in the United States. In addition, the ideological apparatus in capitalist societies has successfully promoted the idea in the United States that there is no alternative to capitalist systems.

Thomas Friedman, perhaps the most influential establishment journalist in America, argues that "the historical debate" over viable economic systems "is over. The hands-down winner," he says, is U.S. "free market capitalism," which he calls "free market vanilla."[14] Friedman dismisses any other economic possibility: "There is no more mint chocolate chip, there is no more strawberry swirl and there is no more lemon-line."[15] But even Friedman, in his new call for a green revolution propelled by massive government incentives, has begun to change his tune.[16] I show that the popular notion of TINA ("there is no alternative") is utterly wrong.

TINA is a suicidal but seductive philosophy, especially alluring in the United States, based as it is on the truth that capitalist economies can be powerful engines of seemingly unlimited growth, profit, and individualism. But these very capitalist attributes—and the rejection of limits in itself—are part of what make the U.S. capitalist model systemically dangerous for the environment and a leading cause of climate change.

The U.S. approach to solving climate change, embodied in the works of many environmental thinkers, regards capitalism as the solution rather than the problem.[17] I show that the prevailing U.S. idea that it is *only* the "magic of the market" that can spawn the technological and entrepreneurial energy breakthroughs we need is wrong. Moreover, technology itself cannot solve the climate crisis. The technological focus—leading Friedman and others to equate the green revolution with a government-aided but capitalist-driven ET (energy technology) transformation that will dominate the twenty-first century as the IT (information technology) revolution did in the late twentieth century—causes most Americans to support a capitalist solution to what is a symptom of capitalist disease.[18]

What this view ignores is that climate change requires a social revolution as well as a technological one. The social dimension means we must focus attention on those economic, political, and lifestyle, or cultural, elements of the U.S. capitalist model that are incompatible with sustaining human civilization. Solving climate change does not require changing all elements of capitalism or the entire U.S. model, because, in fact, it has some democratic values and a culture of innovation and entrepreneurship that can be helpful in a solution. But many of the core attributes of the U.S. capitalist model are the toxins that explain why the United States carries a per capita carbon footprint at least double that of highly developed economies in Europe and as much as thirty times more than that of developing nations.

Because the time frame for solutions is short, as the Doomsday Clock ticks at five minutes to midnight, it appears nearly impossible to imagine systemic change in the period necessary. But as already indicated, even though the task is formidable, we are seeing dramatic historical changes, beginning with the economic crisis and the 2008–2009 recession, that make improbable solutions more probable. I argue throughout this book that the current devastating economic crisis is an opportunity to create unexpected changes that can simultaneously deal with our economic problems while solving our climate change challenge. Fortunately, we have a president in Barack Obama who has an approach to the economic crisis that targets climate change as a lever for remaking the economy. Obama is not seeking to transform capitalism as a system, but in the depths of the current crisis, he has targeted some of its most toxic elements and may open up space for the new public conversation about capitalism and climate change that I propose.

Is System Change Possible?

The idea of change in any large-scale societal system seems alien to many Americans, who focus on their own lives and dreams. They have absorbed the capitalist notion that if we each focus on ourselves, the common good will take care of itself. Many in the United States lack any sense of what a "social system"—whether capitalism or social democracy or fascism—really means. Just as importantly, they have no sense of possibility that systems can be changed or that they have the power to make a difference (except in their own lives). As a sociologist, I use a teaching tool to help awaken students to a "systemic" way of thinking, and I share it here hoping that it may help and empower readers as it does my students.

In classes and workshops, I have sometimes given students the Russian dolls called *matryoshkas* specifically as a teaching tool for enriching the sociological imagination. Each small doll is nested into the next largest one. When I give students the dolls and ask them to play around with them, take them apart, put them back together, and reflect on them, students come up with interesting observations. One is that the structure of the largest societal doll shapes all the smaller ones. Each smaller doll has to "fit" the larger doll's mold. Otherwise, it will not survive or sustain itself; it will be crushed by the larger "system."

This quickly makes clear that social systems are real and shape us. To some degree, we are all stamped in the mold of the larger society, a useful lesson especially for U.S. students who have been taught that we invent ourselves and are masters of our own destiny. Sometimes, students note with some surprise that what we individuals, the smallest dolls, imagine to be our own free choices—such as to shop at the mall or work long hours—are not so free after all. The U.S. societal doll has created a transportation grid, suburban-exurban sprawl, and partially coerced consumption that leave many of us few options.

Students observe that the structure of the dolls I give them—made of brightly colored hand-painted wood—is strong. It is not easy to bend or twist or change the structure of the dolls. This tells them, they say, that social structures are powerful and not easy to change. But the fact that there is some give—you can move one small doll around a bit within the space where it fits into the larger one—also leads to the core sociological idea of "agency." It shows, say the students, that despite the ways in which the larger social structures mold the smaller ones, there is room for individuals and groups to act back on the larger structures and change them.[19]

A green sociological imagination adds a new doll, the biggest one of the natural world or environment. Its structure and needs set limits on the sustainability of all the smaller dolls. The climate change crisis is about the growing radical disconnect between the largest doll—the natural environment—and all the smaller dolls. The second largest doll—representing global capitalist society—is in turbo-speed, radically shortening our time frames and moving us toward an extreme "invisible hand" morality at precisely the moment when the environmental doll cries out for long-term wisdom to prevent a catastrophic tragedy of the commons.[20]

How to realign the shape of each doll—especially our capitalist societal doll—to make it consistent with the sustainability of the largest environmental doll is the biggest question for the green sociological imagination. Realigning the dolls in the spirit of stewardship and social justice is the greatest challenge to the U.S. president, other world leaders, and ordinary people around the world.

Action and the Grass Roots

The majority of people who are doing something about climate change are trying to change their lifestyles by, for instance, recycling, turning down heating and wearing more sweaters, taking shorter showers, insulating homes or putting up solar panels, and/or buying a hybrid or an electric car. These are important changes, and I can testify that they are exciting and rewarding to make personally. But for reasons that I discuss in the final chapters, these changes will not, alone, solve the climate change crisis.

Because climate change is a symptom of pathologies in our capitalist system, solutions can be accomplished only by large-scale global and national changes in the "rules of the game."[21] But our power elites vigorously defend a system that rewards them. That is why change requires citizen action and grassroots movements on a global scale and in an emergency time frame to help move the president and other world leaders toward the awesome responsibilities they now face.

As this must be done very quickly, it raises questions about whether our current politics and grassroots movements are up to this new challenge. My own background makes this a very personal question for me. I have spent most of my life not just as an academic but also an activist in progressive movements. These include movements for peace, social justice, human and civil rights, and democracy, as well as environmental causes. These movements—and their larger liberal base in the general U.S. public—are the groups most aware now of climate change truths, most sensitized to the pathologies of capitalism, and most likely to participate in or support green social change. I feel these are "my movements"—and because I know something about them and feel responsibility, I devote much of Part IV to their crucial role in leading change from below.

These progressive movements can use many of the same visions and strategies to stop climate change that they have used with some success on other issues. An argument I make repeatedly here is that the "pregreen" progressive issues and solutions—ones focusing on social justice—are intimately intertwined with the rising green ones. This reflects the reality that climate change is a symptom of the capitalist systemic problems that these movements have long been fighting. Climate change impacts, for example, are already hurting the must vulnerable poor people in the United States and the world, and the global poor are most at risk, which explains why the new "environmental justice" movement and climate change solutions must tightly link environmental policies with larger capitalist and social justice concerns.[22]

Only drastic systemic change in capitalism itself can solve the problem, and movements are the main repository of such radical vision. But existing social movements cannot do the job as they are now structured. Liberal, labor, and Left movements have become fragmented and disconnected from the larger public in recent years. Even though millions of Americans have progressive values, many of them do not identify with any social movement and have been turned off by what they see as the polarization, political correctness, anger, or adversarial style of the movements themselves. Beyond the need of these movements to reorganize themselves and reconnect with their base, a topic I explore in detail, deeper political changes are needed, mobilizing a nation of exhausted workers and indebted consumers to the politics of people-driven change that President Obama has rhetorically championed.

Obama Nation and the Perfect Storm

I write this book as the United States has taken a dramatic political turn. The governing corporate capitalist regimes in Washington tied to the Reagan Revolution and the Bush-Cheney administration faced a crisis of legitimacy as the Wall Street meltdown spread to Main Street and created the most serious economic crisis since the Great Depression. Voters elected Obama president because the economic meltdown had hit them hard personally and had created a heightened awareness of all the simmering crises bred by the current regime—from health care to jobs to wars to the environment.

Obama and the economic crisis come, then, as a kind of package, mingling economic disaster with political hope. Together, they create a perfect storm that heightens but in no way guarantees the prospect for systemic change in both the United States and the world. Turning points may occur on many important political issues, but climate change could emerge as a key tipping point issue creating major system change in Obama Nation. With Obama's election during an economic meltdown, prior prognoses about the political prospects for solving climate change have become outdated. We are witnessing history in the making and the possibility of unexpected system transformation that I call "regime change at home."[23] At this writing, as Obama moves into his first term and the economy falls deep into a hole of unknown depth, we can still not fathom whether regime change in the United States will occur or what form a new regime might take.

Nonetheless, this book is an early effort to peer intensively into the future contingencies that the present storm makes possible. There remains the strong possibility that we will keep spinning our wheels in the current fossil fuel corporate capitalist regime. Obama may be a transformative president, who understands climate change as an existential threat, but he has not yet shown the radical boldness required for system change. Yet this is a president who has a sense of history, an appreciation of the sweep of time, and he has already invoked hope for change as the heart of his mission. Moreover, Obama is ready to call for necessary sacrifices while also recognizing that many of the green lifestyle shifts and political changes we need will reduce our work time, enhance our communities, and make us personally happier.

Hope then rises in the shadow of the climate storm. The Great Recession has caused political elites—as well as new leaders—to change their thinking about government, markets, and energy, if not about capitalism itself. More importantly, the public is wired to act in a way we have not seen for decades and has greater needs for systemic change than U.S. elites and leaders do. This means that Obama Nation's most important colors might turn out to be not only black and white but also green.

Obama's race immediately defines the historical character of his presidency. But in the long run, green systemic change, driven by the public and social movements, as well as by the most enlightened business and political elites, may become his and our most important legacy. It could help save the world.

PART I

Truth and Denial

1

Brain and Belly

Scientific, Popular, and Gut Truths

The frog who survived learned the truth. It was 212 degrees in the bubbling teacup he called home, and it was too hot to think about anything else. This survivor frog—let's call him Al—felt the heat, jumped out, and decided to tell the world. He devoted his life to rousing his fellow frogs.

The boiled frog, let's call him George, never saw the truth and remained in denial until the end. He was too cool. Any possible threat seemed abstract and far in the future. He kept warming up, slowly and pleasantly, until he was cooked—and all the rest of us frogs boiled with him.

The lessons for humans are clear. We need to be Als, not Georges. Everyone must learn and act on the truth about climate change. Climate change is an existential truth, a one-of-a-kind truth that will determine whether we survive or we boil.[1] But I should say "truths," because truth comes in at least three different varieties, the subject of this chapter. One is scientific, the second is popular, and the third is gut.

The Three Truths

1. Scientific truth: a theory or finding established by scientific methods on which the overwhelming majority of scientists agree.
2. Popular truth: the knowledge on a subject that the majority of people in a society believe to be true.
3. Gut truth: knowledge that is so visceral that it cannot be ignored and spurs personal or collective action.

These three categories of truth help identify us as people who can see and act on truth in our lives—or deny and refuse to act. The brain shapes what we see and believe, but the belly makes us activists or couch potatoes. Because climate change is an existential emergency requiring action now, absorbing the science is not enough. The survival of human civilization as we know it will be ensured only when the popular majority sees climate change as common wisdom or "popular truth," and we must also quickly come to view climate change as the kind of gut truth catapulting us into action.

We face a climatic time bomb. Without experiencing all three climate change truths, we could all end up like the boiled frog. Unfortunately, too many of us are obsessed with the short term and desensitize ourselves to long-term dangers. We leave tomorrow's problems for another day or another generation. If we do not change this short-term mentality, we may all end up cooked.

Scientific Truth and Science Fiction: How to Tell the Difference

Al Gore is clearly a man on a mission. Gore views climate change as the most important challenge faced by humans. His assessment grows out of his respect for science, which has established warming as a scientific truth.[2] Many Americans, however, doubt that scientists have got it right. Simmering just under the surface are deep ambivalence about science itself and a lack of clarity about how scientists themselves distinguish scientific truth from fiction.[3]

Americans have long had a love/hate relation with science, unclear about the nature of the enterprise and the credibility of its truths.[4] Many of us have an internal dialogue between our own internal scientist and internal antiscientist:

INTERNAL SCIENTIST: Science is the basis of all our wonderful technology. I love it.

INTERNAL ANTISCIENTIST: It also created the nuclear bomb. Science is destructive.

INTERNAL SCIENTIST: The nuclear bomb proves how powerful scientific truth is.

INTERNAL ANTISCIENTIST: It is playing with fire. It is arrogant and substitutes its own truth for higher truth we can know only by our faith or intuition.

INTERNAL SCIENTIST: Scientific truth is only about the physical world. It does not claim to create values or meaning. But it is the real thing when it comes to nature.

INTERNAL ANTISCIENTIST: Scientists are like everyone else. The funders corrupt their research—and so does their own careerism. Their values shape their research goals and their findings.

INTERNAL SCIENTIST: Yes, but in the end the rigorous method of science will get us to the truth.

INTERNAL ANTISCIENTIST: But scientific truth—and even the big theoretical paradigms—keeps changing. Doctors used to bleed us based on an absurd medical science. Now we pop pills that may be proved dangerous.

INTERNAL SCIENTIST: Yes, but you take the pills, don't you?

INTERNAL ANTISCIENTIST: Yes, but I am not certain they work. And I think all your theories, especially the big ones about the universe like climate change, are just speculation—or truth that can be proved wrong.

INTERNAL SCIENTIST: Now on that scientific truth, you ignore us at your great peril.

INTERNAL ANTISCIENTIST: Yes, but if we blindly believe you, that is at our peril too, for it may lead us to the most extreme and costly action to solve a problem that may be a hoax or just dead wrong.

And so on and on.

This debate goes on in many societies, and it is healthy in some respects. Science itself views skepticism as a high value and makes it part of its own approach. Science is not absolute truth. It is "socially constructed" just as all forms of knowledge are, and it is inherently permeated with its own metaphysics and value biases.[5] As philosopher Michael Polanyi argues, scientific methods are never perfectly objective, and as postmodernist and social constructionist theorists argue, scientific knowledge always reflects underlying assumptions that cannot be proved.[6] Science can assume an arrogance about the superiority of its own claims, even in areas of values and meaning where it has no legitimate privileged claim. And even where scientific consensus exists, as on climate change, there are many uncertainties on very important details.

But in the United States, the internal antiscientist is often more than a skeptic or a reasoned social constructionist: angrier, more doubtful, and often just bigoted, closed-minded, or fundamentalist. This is reflected in Americans' attitude toward the scientific truth of climate change, dismissed by more Americans than people in almost any other country. Willful closed-mindedness or ignorance about scientific truth—whether in the United States or in other nations—may become suicidal for all of humanity.

There are many causes for the generalized distrust of science and the specific denial of climate change in America, one being the continued power of fundamentalist religion in American life. Scientific truth is often seen as contradicting the Bible. Witness the everlasting debate about evolution, and the millions of Americans who see science as a sacrilege.[7] The negative tinge of science in America also reflects the anti-intellectualism that Harvard historian Richard Hofstadter described as decisively coloring American culture.[8] The Americans who elected and reelected George W. Bush, a man who cultivated anti-intellectualism and was proud of never reading books, were happy to claim him as one of their own.

This is depressing, because the future of humanity may quickly come to turn on whether Americans join the rest of the world in paying close attention to the science of climate change. And that depends on a clear-eyed view of science, how scientists establish truth, and what distinguishes it from science fiction.

Despite our ambivalences, most of us actually act something like scientists in our everyday lives. Scientific truth arises from hypotheses subjected to careful observation. My friend and colleague David Karp, a keen observer of people, says that we are all amateur scientists because daily life requires that we constantly make hypotheses and test them. We make hypotheses about why we feel pain in our arm and test them by moving the arm in particular ways. If somebody passes us in the hallway and does not say hello or respond to our own cheery greeting, we hypothesize that the person is preoccupied with personal problems or might be angry with us; we tend to test that hypothesis, too, by asking other people about what is going on with that individual or by asking the person directly or by thinking back about whether we did anything offensive.

Of course, such daily "scientific investigation" does not have the rigor that professional scientists use and does not imply respect for science. But the fact that all of us do it hints at the value of the scientific approach. Scientists create knowledge based on hypotheses as subjective or accidental as the hypotheses we use in figuring out our daily life. But these hypotheses have to survive rigorous empirical investigations to create scientific knowledge. Not until such knowledge has been verified and accepted by the overwhelming majority of scientists—which is the current status of certain core principles about climate change—does it achieve the status of scientific truth.

The hurdles for anything moving from hunch to hypothesis to provisional knowledge to scientific truth are high. To be viewed as scientific truth, a piece of knowledge must undergo rigorous studies, must be replicable, and must achieve near unanimity of acceptance among the world's scientists, a group not known for its sheeplike or conformist tendencies (although scientists, like all professionals, can become conformists themselves in pursuing their discipline's own favored paradigms of the moment; philosopher of science Thomas Kuhn shows that theoretical scientific paradigms carry subjectivism and bias).[9]

Scientific truth is credible partly because it invites skepticism about itself. Scientists can themselves become rigidly wedded to their own pet theories, but most are professional skeptics—the skepticism is built into most versions of the scientific method and the norms of the scientific community. The burden of proof is on those claiming truth; until that high burden is achieved, scientists will consider their own findings to be provisional or perhaps even science fiction, while also recognizing that the truth itself can evolve as theoretical paradigms change and put findings in new contexts.[10]

Although still involving important uncertainties and contingencies on many details readily acknowledged by the climate scientists themselves, basic scientific knowledge of climate change has now been established as scientific truth. This is the most important starting place for any book on climate change.

The Mind of the Masses: Popular Truth, Science, and Propaganda

Popular truth is what the majority of ordinary people believe to be true. It is my label for "conventional wisdom," the truth as seen by most citizens. It is the first bridge between truth and action. There is no necessary relation between scientific and popular truth. In the United States, as just noted, we find many important areas where scientific truth and popular truth diverge. In most developed countries of the world, there is little gap between the scientific and popular truths of climate change. The gap is larger in the United States, a huge hurdle in dealing with the crisis.[11]

Popular truth is often false belief or sheer wish fulfillment. In fact, as in the case of people denying evolution, or, to take another example, those who think that African Americans are less smart than white Americans, or women less intelligent than men, it can be pure prejudice and viciously dangerous.

We are not stuck with any popular truth; it evolves, and we can play a big role in changing it. In the case of climate change, this offers hope. As I show later, popular truth about climate change has changed rapidly in the United States and the world, and this change appears to be accelerating at a surprising rate.

Looking at public polling data to discover popular truth is part of our task in later chapters, but for now we need to consider one key matter more closely. How is popular truth created? How do people come to believe in certain truths? Who shapes these perceptions and beliefs? Especially when considering the most important subjects such as climate change, how much do we know about the people and processes that shape popular truth?

The "sociology of knowledge"—a school of thought about how knowledge is created—give some good and potentially hopeful guides.[12] We know, for example, that popular truth is created through social processes. We come to learn the truth from people around us—our friends and family—and from more people more distant from us who claim to know truth and disseminate it: an "ideological apparatus" of politicians, corporate leaders, mass media, religious preachers, teachers, and the like whose role is to create culture and mold values and popular perceptions of truth.[13]

In every society, the ideological apparatus plays a central role in shaping popular truth about scientific, social, and political issues such as climate change. In monarchies, dictatorships, and even many democracies, the ideological apparatus takes its cues from a small ruling elite, the dictator or party leadership or financial oligarchy, that defines official truth on all matters. In *1984*, a classic novel about a totally propagandized society, George Orwell described a society where thought control was absolute and Big Brother, the Great Leader, completely determined popular truth. Anyone who deviated from this truth was brought into Room 101, the Guantánamo prison of 1984, where prisoners were locked in rooms crawling with snakes or spiders or whatever they were afraid of as part of a torture process to "reeducate" the heretic to the official truth.[14]

The United States is not organized in this way, but it has an ideological apparatus with great power. It includes our political and corporate leaders and mass media that are owned and managed by mega-wealthy corporations with huge stakes in what ordinary people believe. The very fact that there is considerable freedom of the press makes it more difficult to discern the overwhelming influence of our ideological apparatus. Despite our democracy and relatively free press, we live in a highly propagandized society.[15]

Our ideological apparatus aggressively influences popular views about issues such as climate change. Big money and power are in play—and the stakes are just too high to be left to chance. Managing perceptions of threats and orchestrating public fear are major parts of these "truth" campaigns. In the case of terrorism, we have seen how politicians and pundits can play fear like master musicians in shaping consent for wars. When it comes to climate change, they can be masters of denial.[16]

The ideological apparatus powerfully shapes our collective perceptions of time itself, a critical factor when we understand climate change as a time bomb. The capacity to defuse a time bomb depends on our socially conditioned capacities to see and act on both short-term and long-term threats. But the guiding ideologies, economic institutions, and political leaders in America lead us toward short-term thinking that sabotages our ability to focus on even the most catastrophic long-term dangers. Overcoming this is a matter that involves speaking truth to power but also outmaneuvering some of our own inner emotional resistances to thinking about catastrophe and acting to meet long-term crises.

Fortunately, culture itself is always malleable. The propaganda system in the United States is not all powerful, and it can be resisted. Mass movements of grassroots activists, particularly in the age of the Internet and the blog, have a growing capacity to shape popular truth and combat the dogma of the ideological apparatus.[17] On issues such as climate change, even single individuals who have moved partially outside the established propaganda system, such as Al Gore, have shown an astonishing ability to help reshape popular truth.

Truth in the Gut: Too Hot to Ignore

Comedian Stephen Colbert calls "truthiness" the product of a society where people, especially leaders, define truth on the basis of what they feel in their gut. Evidence from other sources does not count. Thus, George Bush could go to war in Iraq because his gut instinct was that Saddam Hussein had nuclear or biological weapons, even when this ran counter to what Bush's own intelligence services were saying.

But this is *not* what I mean by gut truth. I am not talking about a truth learned by instinct; it may very well be a truth learned from science. What makes it different from nongut truths is that it is so visceral—it grabs a person so powerfully in the gut—that she or he cannot ignore it.

Gut truths learned from instinct can be at odds with science and can also be dangerous, as we learned in the era of fascism and in the Bush years.[18] For purposes of discussing climate change, I am restricting my idea of gut truth to truths we learn from science, *but only those scientific truths that move us to action.*

The brain is full of so many truths, including scientific truths, that we cannot possibly pay attention to most of them. Most truths lack the electric charge necessary to focus our mind and require us to act. So our mind is much like an old attic that we rarely climb up to see; it is full of items that we may believe to be true but that do not grab our attention or change our behavior.

But a small number of truths are "hot," even burning, like a flame threatening to engulf us if we do not pay attention to it. Let us say a friend or family member gets sick with cancer. Or we ourselves do. Suddenly, the truths about cancer move from abstract knowledge to gut realities. These "gut truths" are not filed away in some dusty closet or attic. They force us to pay attention and act.

Gut truths are not the only truths with consequences. Scientific truths that get filed away by the population in the dusty attic can still have massive consequences—in the case of climate change, catastrophic ones. But gut truths are the only ones that move people to action. If climate change were to remain a nongut truth, its consequences for hurricanes, droughts, sea levels, and other unpleasant natural disasters would accelerate, but it would not have the essential consequence of mobilizing us to stop climate change.

In the world of politics, gut scientific truths are those that compel us to act in one of two senses. They mobilize us to support leaders and government or corporate policies that address our gut truth. And they light a fire under us to take personal action to align our personal lives with the gut truth.

Given that most scientific and popular truths have low electric charge, and many of these truths in America threaten established interests, politicians can afford to ignore them. This is not the case with gut truths. Political and corporate leaders will work very quickly to try to keep emerging popular and gut truths such as climate change from remaining popular truths; they will mobilize the ideological apparatus to discredit them.[19] And if they nonetheless become or stay popular truths, leaders will mobilize the ideological apparatus in an all-out manner to keep these popular truths from becoming gut truths. Leaders will fill our brains with all kinds of fears, doubts, and distractions in an attempt to push the truths back from the gut to the dustiest files of our brain.

Truths can quickly shift in our brain from the dusty to the gut type (or back the other way). For example, we may believe the truth that high levels of cholesterol-packed plaque in our arteries can kill us. But we ignore it, as we continue eating those tasty deep-fried onion rings, loaded with the worst kind of inflammatory, plaque-building cholesterol. The cholesterol-plaque truth is collecting dust in our brain's closet.

Two things could change that fast. One is a heart attack. Suddenly the cholesterol-plaque truth jumps out of the brain's closet into the gut. The same is likely to happen if a person's total cholesterol has jumped to more than 350. A doctor's message is then likely to catapult a brain truth into a gut truth.

So the *first* fact about truth is that it is likely to move from brain to gut the more personal it is. The more we see it as a truth affecting our survival, the more likely it will travel fast to the gut. That is good news about existential truths such as climate change, which have profound implications for both our personal and our collective survival.

Time is a *second* critical factor. If we believe a truth affects our personal survival, but not for a long time, that truth is likely to be thrown into the attic. The faster we think it is going to hit us, the higher the probability that this truth will move into the gut and stay there. But the time factor is not such good news regarding climate change. It can encourage us to mimic frog George rather than Al, because no climate change doctor will tell us unequivocally that climate change is going to hit and hurt us personally tomorrow. That is why so much of this book is dedicated to exploring how a short-term society can mobilize itself to ward off the long-term danger of climate catastrophe.

We have already seen that two forces are working against us here. One is that our entire economy and society—working through the ideological apparatus—have turned Americans into obsessive short-term thinkers, stripped of much of our capacity to see and act on long-term problems. This short-term conditioning is woven so deeply into the U.S. economic and cultural fabric that it generates deep pessimism about solving climate change.[20] Add to that a complex set of existential and inner psychological forces that lead us to deny death and to focus on today rather than tomorrow—and we realize just how much the crisis of climate change is a crisis in our experience of time itself.

The significance of the truth of climate change, that is, its unprecedented consequences for the survival and well-being of humans and the planet, is a *third* factor that helps determine whether truth migrates from brain to belly. In general, the greater the consequences, the more likely it is that the truth will move to the gut. But there is no linear relation. In fact, to some degree, the greater the doomsday consequences are, the less likely we are to allow the truth to hit our gut. Even knowledgeable authors who write about the extreme dangers of climate change may internally be resisting what they are writing as gut truth, because it is just too scary to let the truth in. In his book on climate change, *Heat*, George Monbiot, was brutally honest about his own tendency to deny the reality of what he was writing about—and then explained what suddenly made it gut real. Monbiot writes: "One week before this book was meant to be finished, my daughter was born.... Everything I had been thinking about became—for the first time—real for me."[21]

Monbiot had written a brilliant book about climate change truth, but it was all "abstractions," he confessed in the last chapter. It came from the brain rather than the belly, until his daughter's birth drove the overwhelming reality of mortality into his gut: "But this baby, this strange little creature, closer to the ecosystem than a fully grown human being, part pixie, part frog, part small furry animal, now sixteen days old, and curled up in my lap like a bean waiting to sprout, changes everything. I am no longer writing about what might happen to 'people' in this country in thirty years' time. I am writing about her."[22] Truth travels to the gut, it is clear, when it gets very personal and seems to be overwhelmingly, undeniably threatening to somebody close.

A *fourth* factor has to do with the certainty of the truth. The greater the certainty, offered by science or intuition, the more likely it is that the truth will hit the gut. But if science or propaganda creates significant uncertainty, a high chance remains that the truth will stay in the brain's attic. This is bad news for climate change truth, where propaganda, time horizons, and other factors create uncertainty.

Uncertainty carries with it psychologies of risk that need serious attention. As noted earlier, inaction about climate change carries huge risks of disaster, but precautionary behaviors are also risky, as they are costly and may rule out action on issues of more short-term pressing concern, such as today's poverty or wars. Awareness of the trade-offs can lead truths to move from the gut to the attic or back to the gut, depending on how the risks are perceived and shaped by the ideological apparatus. But the more the risks of inaction are perceived as disastrous and outweighing the risks of action, the more likely it is that the truth will travel to and stay in the gut.

One of the great arts of life and politics is to know when to put the truth in the attic and when to move it to the gut. The decision about where to file it has huge implications, but the decision is usually made unconsciously, shaped by external truth-tellers or propagandists and internal fears and emotional priorities.

In the case of climate change, where the costs and consequences of both action and inaction are so high, it is important that we seek more awareness and control of this personal sorting of truth. It is a very hard thing to assert control over what constitutes gut truth for us. Both rational and irrational, internal and external forces play a role. It is extremely difficult for the public to see gut truth that goes against the grain of entrenched powerful interests and challenges the subtle dogmas of the ideological apparatus. It is just as hard to conquer the powerful inner emotions and daily short-term preoccupations that cloud our ability to act on long-term threats. But that is no excuse for not thinking hard about whether we are living this issue from the attic or the gut.

Boiled frog syndrome—the mind-set of George the frog—has two roots. One is mass denial of existential scientific truth. The second is mass acceptance of the truth but the collective decision to put this uncomfortable truth in the attic. We have a responsibility to overcome both tendencies if we seek to survive.

2

Scientists United

The Climatic Consensus

Small things can sometimes make big differences. Very small changes in temperature, we are now learning, can trigger big and consequential changes. As a child, I can remember my mother taking my temperature when I did not feel well. Whenever my temperature was around 100, just slightly more than 1 degree above normal, she acted fast, usually calling the doctor and sending me to bed, while frequently putting her hand on my forehead to check how hot I was. One degree above normal made me sweat and made her sweat more, not letting me go to school. I can remember a few times when my temperature rose to 103 or even 104. My mother saw this little spike as a big deal. She put me to bed and called the doctor immediately.

From such childhood experiences, it is not hard to absorb the idea that small changes in our own body temperature can make a big difference. But it is only in the last few decades that we have had to recognize that very small changes in the earth's temperature are also very consequential for the planet. The world has what seems to be a small fever, and we need immediately to cool down.

The world's small fever is an emergency. Virtually all climate scientists and the overwhelming majority of professional scientific bodies around the world have converged on a truly consequential consensus: that global warming is real and that any further rise of temperature is dangerous.[1] This may prove to be the most important scientific consensus ever achieved, although the public, especially in the United States, has failed to fully perceive it.[2]

Unfortunately, more warming is already "in the pipeline," part of a tipping point that has already occurred. In 2009, the National Academy of Sciences reported that increased warming throughout the twenty-first century has become inevitable and irreversible, because of natural feedback cycles triggered by our burning of greenhouse gases.[3] But if we want to avoid real disaster, we must keep the fever minimal and do everything possible to prevent temperature from going up more than 3.5 degrees Fahrenheit.

According to the British Meteorological Society, a rise of 3.5 degrees could lead between 2.5 and 3 billion people to face drought and water shortages, meaning *close to one-half of the world's population could suffer thirst.*[4] The UN Food and Agriculture Organization has reported that with about the same small rise of temperature, 2 billion people in forty poor countries would suffer big crop losses that would "drastically increase the number of undernourished people."[5] James Hansen, NASA's chief climatologist and one of the world's leading climate scientists, concluded in his 2008 testimony to Congress that "the oft-stated goal to keep global warming less than 2 degrees Celsius (or 3.6 degrees Fahrenheit) is a recipe for global disaster, not salvation."[6]

In this chapter, I lay out the consensual scientific truth that needs to travel to our collective belly and become the world's most important gut truth. I focus on just the basic facts of climate change rather than the more complex interpretations of why it is happening, and why the United States has a special responsibility, a matter I take up in several later chapters.

I recently ran a three-day workshop with a group of midlevel business managers, and I told them the unvarnished global warming truth. I figured that managers are pragmatic and have to deal with tough scientific data all the time. But this was something completely out of their experience. They did not contest or reject the facts. But they found it so "overwhelming"—the word that they kept using—that they almost immediately filed it in their remote brain attics, refusing to let it go down to the gut.

Because I do not want this to happen to the readers of this book, I have divided the scientific truth about global warming into two chapters. This one summarizes a version of the scientific consensus of a climatic time bomb that understates the dangers. Because this chapter has a conservative bias, I hope that it will trigger less fear and more openness on the reader's part. In the next chapter, I lay out the view of leading scientists, who offer no sugarcoating of the unvarnished story.

The Conservative Consensus: The Bottom Line

On November 10, 2007, Rajendra Pachauri, a vivacious sixty-seven-year-old Indian scientist with wispy hair and a long white beard, received a telephone call he did not expect. A spokesman for the Nobel committee was on the line. He told Pachauri something few people ever hear: that he was being invited to Oslo, Norway, to be a corecipient of the Nobel Peace Prize.

Pachauri quickly noted that the Nobel committee was awarding the prize to a committee of more than 2,500 scientists from more than 130 countries, which he chaired. They were being collectively honored for their work together as part of the Intergovernmental Panel on Climate Change (IPCC), which published in 2007 its fourth and most definitive report on global warming. It is considered the gold standard of scientific truth on the subject.[7]

The Nobel committee saw two realities. First, the IPCC was the repository of the world's scientific truth on global warming. Second, its work was more important to peace and survival than any other scientific truth the Nobel could have honored.

Established in 1988 by the United Nations and the World Meteorological Organization, the IPCC is charged with determining the agreed-upon scientific facts about climate change, its impacts, and what can be done. This is an unprecedented enterprise and could be carried out only through the international cooperation of thousands of scientists, working long hours voluntarily, to interpret the findings of tens of thousands of climate studies. The IPCC's aim is not to make policy but to establish the basic scientific facts.

The IPCC has issued four major reports (in 1990, 1995, 2001, and 2007) compiled with the help of more than 2,500 scientific experts, drafted by more than 800 contributing scientists, and written ultimately by 400 of the world's leading climate change scientists. Each successive report has added the most recent findings, and each offers a more dire assessment than its predecessor, reinforcing the oft-stated view that the reports are conservative. Newer data, including the forthcoming 2009 report, keep showing that rates of warming, melting, extinction of species, and the like are already outstripping projections in earlier reports.[8]

The endorsers of the IPCC's work read like a Who's Who of the world's most important scientific bodies. They include the national scientific academies of Australia, Belgium, Brazil, Canada, the Caribbean, China, France, Germany, India, Indonesia, Ireland, Italy, Malaysia, Mexico, New Zealand, Russia, South Africa, Sweden, the United Kingdom, and the United States. Professional societies lending their imprint include the American Meteorological Society, American Geophysical Union, American Institute of Physics, American Astronomical Society, American Association for the Advancement of Science, Stratigraphy Commission of the Geological Society of London, Geological Society of America, American Chemical Society, and Engineers Australia.[9]

No professional climate science associations and no major scientific associations have rejected the IPCC core consensus truths, although a growing number of scientists see the IPCC as understating the dangers. In a review of 928 published papers on climate change, the prestigious journal *Science* found precisely *zero* studies that rejected the IPCC consensus that "human modification of climate is compelling."[10] It is important to emphasize this, because polls show, as we see in later chapters, that the public believes that scientists are divided not just about important details (which is true) but also about whether global warming is actually occurring and whether human action has caused it. This misperception has been fueled by a tiny number of scientific outliers and major special interests in the fossil fuel industries and in political circles linked to them.[11]

The IPCC 2007 report, the most recent and definitive at this writing, does not read like a thriller or true crime book and is not likely to become a popular best seller. But despite its dry scientific language and neutral tone, it packs a huge wallop. It states a few core scientific truths that should be nailed on every schoolhouse door.

The Unequivocal Nature of Global Warming

First, the warming of the climate system is unequivocal. The IPCC makes very few "unequivocal" statements, but here it minces no words and permits no doubt. Our small planetary fever is established scientific truth. The proof is in thousands of direct measurements of "increases in global average air and ocean temperature" as well as in rigorous observations "of widespread melting of snow and ice and rising global average sea level."[12]

The years 1995–2006, the dozen years just preceding the 2007 report, "rank among the 12 warmest years in the instrumental record of global surface temperature since 1850."[13] That was the first year that scientists directly measured global temperatures using scientific instruments. Measurements have shown unusual and irrefutable warming during those 150 years.[14] Warming increased twice as fast in the last 50 years as in the prior 50 years. The temperature is rising in the upper atmosphere as well as at the surface, in the Arctic and Antarctic, and in the oceans down to depths of 3,000 meters, which, along with rapid glacial melting, is causing sea water levels to rise unusually rapidly.[15] Because global temperature was not measured directly by scientists before 1850, the knowledge of temperatures in the planet's distant past is less certain, based on indirect assessments from sources such as tree rings, corals, and ice cores.

But the IPCC reports evidence that temperatures in the Northern Hemisphere are now hotter than at any time in the last 1,000 years. From 1000 until 1900, temperatures stayed pretty flat. Then they began to rise sharply. The IPCC states that "the rate and magnitude of global or hemispheric surface 20th century warming is likely to have been the largest of this millennium, with the 1990s and 1998 likely to have been the warmest decade and year."[16]

In 2006, the U.S. National Academy of Sciences issued its own report about our changing temperature over the last four centuries. The academy reports "a high level of confidence that global mean surface temperature was higher during the last few decades of the 20th century than during any comparable period during the preceding four centuries."[17] The National Academy, America's most prestigious scientific body, added that it is most likely hotter now than in the last 1,000 years.[18]

But what if we try to take a temperature reading going back even further? A 2006 study from climate scientists at NASA and Columbia University reports that we are now less than 1 degree Celsius short of being at the hottest temperature *in the last 1 million years.*[19]

What about even earlier? There were periods many millions of years ago when temperatures shot up even higher than those today, but they were short-lived. One happened 55 million years ago at the end of the Paleocene epoch. Scientists record a spike of 5–8 degrees Celsius for a few thousand years, when temperatures in Arctic regions heated up to about 73 degrees Fahrenheit, perhaps caused by a "methane burp," a spectacular sudden release of the potent greenhouse gas methane. It may have been pleasantly balmy in the North Pole, but it led to a massive die-off of species in the oceans and big changes in the mammals making their home on the land-covered Arctic.[20]

The Human Impact on Global Warming

Second, there is at least a 95 percent probability that human activity is contributing to global warming.[21] We have met the perpetrator and, as the cartoon character Pogo puts it, "he is us." Although bloggers and pundits still passionately argue about the perpetrator, the scientific debate is over.

This truth of human complicity is sobering because it means our current warming is unlike all prior ones. It is a byproduct of our own making, a consequence of our deeply entrenched economic, political, and energy systems. But we have reason to hope, because if humans are causing the fever, we should be able to stop it.

After looking at the rise in greenhouse gases that we humans help produce, the IPCC is telling us that science has proved beyond a reasonable doubt that (1) the rise is unprecedented, (2) we are responsible, and (3) our greenhouse gases are "forcing" temperature rises that must be "urgently" brought under control.[22] Greenhouse gases include carbon dioxide (CO_2), methane, nitrous oxide, and water vapor. They are called "greenhouse gases" because they act like a greenhouse, trapping heat. Whenever we drive our cars or use electricity generated by coal or other fossil fuels, we are producing pollutants that turn our atmosphere into a gigantic enclosed greenhouse, preventing heat from escaping and ginning up our planetary fever.

A small rise in CO_2 concentrations, as well as in methane and other greenhouse gases, can make ominous large differences. Usually calculated in parts per million (ppm) in the atmosphere, CO_2 concentrations have been rising on average about 2 ppm each year since 1975. These small changes in CO_2 (along with equally small but consequential changes in methane and nitrous oxide) are creating major changes.[23]

The rise in greenhouse gas concentrations is now established as incontrovertible scientific truth. The IPCC puts this truth starkly: "Global atmospheric concentrations of carbon dioxide, methane, and nitrous oxide have increased markedly as a result of human activities since 1750 and now far exceed pre-industrial values over the last 650,000 years."[24]

That many years are an eye-popping number. Over this vast period of years, CO_2 concentration in the atmosphere has ranged between 180 and 300 ppm. Just before Britain's industrial revolution, the CO_2 level was about 280 ppm.[25] But by 2008, the ppm level had risen to 385, a number never before experienced by humans.[26]

The IPCC, although viewed by many as conservative in its estimates, is emphatic about the importance of the current levels and rises in carbon levels. It states flatly that "carbon dioxide is the most important anthropogenic greenhouse gas," significantly forcing up global temperatures. The IPCC reports that the Industrial Age precipitated a dramatic change in carbon levels in the atmosphere, but that was just the beginning. In the last decade, from 1997 to 2007, carbon concentrations have been growing significantly faster than in the last fifty years, when they grew significantly faster than in any earlier fifty-year period.[27]

The same is true of methane. "The atmospheric concentration of methane in 2005 exceeds by far the natural range of the last 650,000 years (320 to 790 ppb [parts per billion])." It was about 715 ppb at the start of the Industrial Revolution in the early nineteenth century but rose in 2005 to an astronomical 1,774 ppb.[28] Thus, we are freely dumping massive carbon and methane pollutants into the environment with consequences beyond our imagination.

The IPCC reports that our "understanding of anthropogenic warming and cooling influence on climate has improved ... leading to very high confidence (more than 95% likely) that the global average net effect of human activities since 1750 has been one of warming."[29] Translation: We can now say with great certainty that we humans are causing our own collective fever.

The IPCC states further that "the combined radiative forcing due to increases in carbon dioxide, methane and nitrous oxide" has been increasing since the Industrial Revolution at a rate "unprecedented in more than 10,000 years."[30] Translation: We are engaged in a grand experiment of cooking ourselves at a rate never before tried in human history.

The Likely Rise in World Temperatures

Third, world temperatures will likely rise between 2 and 11.5 degrees Fahrenheit during the twenty-first century, significantly affecting our ecosystem. Even if we stabilize greenhouse gas emissions, they are likely to create continued warming for at least 1,000 years.

Now here is where the IPCC science, although still based on conservative assumptions, begins to get stranger than science fiction. The IPCC knows it cannot precisely predict the future, because it depends on what we do, as well as on feedback cycles not fully understood. So the IPCC offers several possible realistic scenarios, from a "business as usual" approach with high rises in CO_2 emissions to a world in which greenhouse gases are limited by aggressive efforts. With each scenario, the IPCC looks at how the fevered patient—the earth, the oceans, and various species—will be affected.

The scientists start by looking at how the planet has already changed as a result of the small fever it has been running. The many physical and biological impacts already observed in various regions and due partly to global warming include the following:

- more and larger glacial lakes
- shrinking glaciers
- rising sea levels, creating more flooding and disruption of coastal settlements and species
- more acidic oceans and bleaching and dying of coral reefs
- warming of lakes and rivers with damaging effects on water quality
- more droughts and drought-affected areas, influencing health and survival
- more heat waves and heat-related illnesses and deaths
- more frequent and intense tropical cyclones causing flooding, death, and property loss
- more disturbance of crops due to fire and pests
- increases in malnutrition as crop growing seasons become shorter in many regions
- increases in deserts where crops once could be grown
- more people in northern latitudes infected by tropical diseases
- disruption of human settlements in mountain regions caused by melting glaciers
- loss of coastal wetlands and increased damage from coastal flooding with sea level rise
- growing rate of heat-related species extinctions[31]

We are suffering these unpleasant effects of global warming right now, with those of us in poorer, more low-lying, and more tropical areas more severely affected than the rest of us. In the future, these same effects will worsen. The impact will be more extreme depending on how fevered we allow the patient—our planet—to become.

The IPCC classifies the harm into five areas, highlighting the temperature rise (in Celsius) at which we begin to see very significant change:

1. *Water*: At a rise of 3 degrees, "hundreds of millions of people are exposed to increased water stress." Drought increases with each additional degree, with billions of people at risk when temperatures rise 4 degrees and higher.[32]

2. *Ecosystems*: With a rise of 2 degrees, "most corals are bleached," and at a 2.5 degree rise, "widespread coral mortality" begins to occur.[33] With a rise of 1 degree, "up to 30% of species" are at risk of extinction, and with a rise of 4 degrees, 40 percent or more of the world's species may perish.[34] With a rise of 1.5–2.5 degrees, we will see "major changes in ecosystem structure and function," negatively affecting biodiversity and food and water supplies.[35]

3. *Food*: At low latitudes, and seasonally dry and tropical areas, a rise of 1–2 degrees will reduce crop productivity and increase risk of hunger for hundreds of millions.[36]

4. *Coasts and low-lying areas*: Each degree rise will increase sea rise and coastal erosion. At 4 degrees rise and more, hundreds of millions of people in low-lying and coastal areas will be flooded. The largest affected populations are "in the mega-deltas of Africa and Asia," with small islands such as the Maldives and coastal areas of nations such as Bangladesh likely to disappear and create millions of deaths and environmental refugees.[37]

5. *Health*: At 2 degrees, we will see a change in disease vectors, with new diseases affecting new populations. At just over 3 degrees, we will see "increased mortality from heat waves, floods and droughts."[38] At 4.5 degrees, we will see newly widespread malnutritive, diarrheal, cardio-respiratory, and infectious diseases.[39]

As discussed in the next chapter, the temperature points that the IPCC sees as manageable are conservative. For example, it views a CO_2 level stabilized at 450 ppm as acceptable, involving a rise of 4 degrees Fahrenheit. The IPCC asserts that there is still time to turn things around, although it warns that the afflictions and plagues discussed in the previous list are already occurring and we must change course rapidly.

To keep the CO_2 level below 450 ppm is going to take a monumental effort. If we seek to allocate carbon emissions equally on a per capita global basis, with a cap at 450 ppm, it would take a 90 percent cut in carbon emissions in the rich countries by 2030. None of the policy proposals currently under consideration in Congress or in global climate negotiations aim at anything close to this. In the United States, Barack Obama came nearest in the 2008 campaign by pledging a 80 percent reduction in emissions by 2050, sending us into the IPCC red zone.

In the book of Exodus in the Old Testament, God unleashes ten plagues on the Egyptians to induce the pharaoh to free the Jews he has enslaved. When I was a child at Passover seders, I felt creepy as we chanted the ten plagues in unison, dipping our fingers in blood-red wine with the mention of each plague:

blood
frogs
gnats
flies
livestock disease
boils
hail and fire
locusts
darkness
death of the firstborn of each Egyptian family

The list of plagues hitting us from global warming has eerie similarities to the Egyptian plagues (perhaps reflecting the speculations of some scientists that the Egyptian plagues actually resulted from real volcanic eruptions and other natural disasters spewing out methane or heightened CO_2). Are we being punished for enslaving ourselves to our modern corporate pharaohs like Exxon or for becoming addicted to capitalist pleasures? Here are ten plagues that the climate scientists, as quoted in IPCC reports, believe will almost surely strike us as hard as the plagues that hit the Egyptians if we do not liberate ourselves from current enslavements:

wildfires
crop failures
drought
floods
disease
forced migrations
livestock deaths

deaths of young, old, and sick
malnutrition
communities buried by wind and water

Perhaps everyone in the world should join together at a global seder and recite these new plagues together. It might bring the truth on temperature from our brain to our belly.

3

The X-Rated Truth

Tipping Points and Points of No Return

Stanford University climate scientist Stephen Schneider might at first glance appear to be a catastrophic thinker. Schneider discusses the possibility of catastrophes such as a meltdown of the huge Antarctic ice sheets, a shutting down of Atlantic Ocean warming currents, and a release of large amounts of the most dangerous greenhouse gases from the melting of Arctic glaciers. These could create perhaps the worst catastrophes humans have ever endured, threatening the survival of human civilization.[1]

But Schneider, a leading climate scientist, is not easily dismissed as a catastrophic thinker or a Cassandra. True, he is contemplating unthinkable catastrophes. But he is not predicting that they are certainties about to happen. Rather, he is suggesting that they *could* happen given current scientific knowledge and that the probabilities, although small, are not so low that we can safely ignore them. Other climate scientists, such as Germany's Stefan Rahmstorf of the Potsdam Institute for Climate Impact Research, agrees that these scenarios deserve our very serious attention.[2]

Schneider calls events such as the melting of the Arctic or Antarctica "the dark edge of the bell curve." At the center of the bell curve, as anyone who has studied probability theory knows, are the most probable events. As one goes farther out toward the edge of the curve, the events become increasingly less probable. When Schneider talks about the events at the dark edge of the bell curve, he is telling us about unacceptable catastrophes that might really occur and have been too quickly taken off our collective radar screen.[3]

If Schneider were the only scientist telling us to pay attention to these almost unimaginable catastrophes, we might more easily ignore him. But Schneider is just one of a host of eminent climate scientists who have expressed a concern about the conservative bias of the IPCC report and its failure to shine a floodlight on the dark edge. In fact, the IPCC itself acknowledges that there are scenarios not discussed in detail in its reports that are over-whelmingly dangerous.

Many leading climate scientists share this view and believe that catastrophic tipping points are not as far down the bell curve as even Schneider might suggest. Put differently, their concern is not just the IPCC's failure to highlight events at the dark edge, but also the structure of the bell curve itself. In these scientists' view, the tolerable margin for rises in CO_2 and temperature are smaller than those stated in the IPCC reports. For example, they see stabilizing the carbon level at 450 ppm as a recipe for "disaster, not salvation."[4]

In this chapter, I reveal what these eminent scientists regard as the un-varnished or "revisionist" story of global warming. I have titled this chapter "The X-rated Truth" because it is best suited for those who can handle very disturbing information. Unlike X-rated films, however, we all ultimately need to get this shocking truth into both our brains and our bellies.

The Revisionist Story

James Hansen, a Columbia University professor and NASA's chief climate scientist, is a mild-mannered fellow, and author of scores of major scientific research papers on climate change.[5] But even though he does not look like the Moses of Charlton Heston, listen to his 2008 testimony to Congress about tipping points on ice melting and sea rise. The first part is a prophecy on accelerated glacial melting: "Climate can reach points such that amplifying feedbacks spur large rapid changes. Arctic sea ice is a current example. Global warming initiated sea ice melt, exposing darker ocean that absorbs more sunlight, melting more ice. As a result, without any additional greenhouse gases, the Arctic soon will be ice-free in the summer."[6]

That is a lot faster than imagined in the IPCC report. And the ice-free summer Arctic is inevitable even if we magically stop emitting any more greenhouse gases today. In Hansen's view, strong "amplifying feedbacks" can create tipping points of the kind made famous by Malcolm Gladwell in his mega–best seller of the same name.[7] One small change (in this case, small temperature increases produced by humans driving more cars and burning more electric lights) unleashes an unstoppable sequel of amplifying changes (the smaller glaciers reflect back less heat into space and the ocean absorbs more sunlight, thus triggering new temperature rises and more ice melts) quite independent of what humans do. Instead of a gradual and smooth progression, abrupt turning points occur, with potentially irreversible consequences that humans have never faced before.

But who cares? we might ask in the case of Arctic melting. If the Arctic ice melts so fast, perhaps for the first time in millennia humans will be able to enjoy an exciting summer boat ride to the North Pole. Before fantasizing this adventure, we must consider that Hansen sees glacial melting as a series of tipping points that can spiral out of control into nightmarish happenings: "More ominous tipping points loom. West Antarctic and Greenland ice sheets are vulnerable to even small additional warming. These two-mile-thick behemoths respond slowly at first, but if disintegration gets well underway it will become unstoppable.... In my opinion, if emissions follow a business-as-usual scenario, sea level rise of at least two meters is likely this century. Hundreds of millions of people would become refugees. No stable shoreline would be reestablished in any time frame that humanity can conceive."[8]

After reading Hansen's testimony, I read news stories about huge ice sheets—the size of Argentina—dropping off of West Antarctica into the ocean. I also knew that the melting of the Greenland ice sheets—which are currently melting 60 percent faster than ten years ago and losing 19 billion more tons of ice than in any prior year—would *raise ocean levels 23 feet*.[9] I went back and read and reread Hansen's warnings about "hundreds of millions" of environmental refugees. I knew from other studies that sea-level rises of less than 2 meters (about 6 feet) would cover "large parts of Louisiana, Florida, and estuaries along the Atlantic Coast, especially Delaware Bay coastal cities," while wiping off the map low-lying islands and inundating Bangladeshi and Nile deltas, where million of predominantly poor people live.[10]

In 2009, new studies suggested more definitive warming of Antarctica. The National Academy of Sciences published a new report by the IPCC saying that even a 1.8 degree rise or less above 1990 temperatures could create "increases in drought, heat, waves, and floods" and that "it is now more likely than not" that global warming is already responsible for "observed increases in heat waves, intense precipitation events, and the intensity of tropical cyclones," as well as the 2003 heat wave in Europe that killed tens of thousands.[11] Another series of reports from climate scientists at Stanford and MIT, also published in the first few months of 2009, revealed an alarmingly faster rise in carbon dioxide emissions than had been anticipated in the IPCC reports.[12] Stanford climate scientist Christopher Field affirmed, "We are basically looking now at a future climate that's beyond anything we've considered seriously in climate model simulations."[13] Both the Stanford and MIT reports envisaged "surprisingly large increases in the chances of much higher temperatures" because of multiplicative interacting effects with dangerous positive "feedbacks" spiking the fever.[14] In 2007 and 2009, the National Academy of Sciences also reported that the rate of growth of CO_2 emissions accelerated more rapidly between 2000 and 2006 than in any prior period, reflecting a high percentage of carbon dioxide staying in the atmosphere and less absorbed by the ocean and forest sinks. All of these developments are a sign of accelerated positive feedback cycles with immense dangers to the human future that the revisionist story is built around.[15]

We can begin to appreciate the social and political implications of seeing global warming as a series of major tipping points. Would countries around the world reeling from many other environmental catastrophes open their borders to this greatest forced human migration of all time? How many hundreds of millions would die, either in the great floods themselves or at the hands of the armies in panicked countries prepared to engage in a globalized military triage?

An emerging line of argument—focusing on large feedback cycles and dramatic tipping points—reveals the most disturbing problem with the IPCC scientific consensus story described in the last chapter. The problem is not just the overly conservative estimates of glacial melting, drought spread, species extinctions, or rate of release of methane stored in ice sheets and deep under the oceans[16]—the conservative estimates are getting scientists' attention. The problem is also the need to change the plot line and our understanding of the story itself.

The IPCC is fully aware that global warming brings amplifying feedback cycles, which I explain shortly, but it does not tell its story in a way that puts the spotlight on the dangerous tipping points and the time bombs they can trigger. I suspect the scientists did this not out of ignorance (although they lacked some very important new data released in 2007–2009), but out of the political constraints of the governments, their own inherent scientific caution, and their desire not to be viewed as alarmist.

The revisionist story of climate change as a system of new and increasingly dangerous tipping points is quite different from the view of a world slowly heating up that we can cool down by policies of rational "mitigation," the word used repeatedly in IPCC reports. The revisionist scientific school—led by eminent scientists such as Hansen and joined now by many scientific contributors to the IPCC itself—suggests rather that we are already lurching rapidly toward a chaotic, fevered world increasingly resistant to our own intervention or mitigation. The longer we wait, the more we set in process stronger feedback cycles that turn even modest further temperature rises into big tipping points, even if we apply every cooling device that we can dream up.

The 2007 Westminster Report, delivered to a packed and hushed session of the British Parliament, issues a clarion call for a radically updated story. "Over the last two years," the authors say, "there has been a profound shift in the scientific understanding" of climate systems.[17] In the old story, there is progressive and linear warming induced by greenhouse gases, which continues relatively smoothly without mitigation until it is too hot to live on the planet. The implication of this classic story, as the Westminster Report suggests, is "that we can, at any point, reduce the rate of emissions, stabilize the concentration and prevent the temperature from rising any further."[18]

In the new story, say the revisionist scientists, human-made "emissions act as a trigger to a complex set of mutually reinforcing feedbacks, many of them activated by rising temperature. The resultant climate change is out of all proportion to the precipitating event."[19] The Westminster Report sums up the new story this way: "The implication is that climate change is non-linear. Once set in motion it is acceleratingly self-perpetuating. There is then only a small time-window within which human intervention has any (rapidly diminishing) chance of halting the process to a stable state."[20] The Westminster Report begins to make clear the very different story that revisionist scientists are now telling us.

The Revisionist Story

- Global warming is an existential emergency, threatening human civilization as we know it.
- Global warming is not a gradual linear process, but a story of abrupt and potentially irreversible changes.
- We must act decisively to curb greenhouse gas emissions immediately, in the next few years, or we may lose the battle.
- We must reduce carbon dioxide emissions beneath 350 parts per million to prevent disaster.
- It is later than we think; this is an urgent life-and-death crisis requiring drastic change now.

At the heart of the new story are three central concepts—feedback cycles, tipping points, and points of no return—that are game-changing for the climate and, interestingly, for much of social life unrelated to global warming. In the rest of this chapter, I explore each of these ideas and show how they lead to the revisionist story that few would describe as sugarcoated—a story of an unprecedented time bomb that could more quickly and decisively alter the human experiment than the dire scenarios in the IPCC reports.

Feedback We Do Not Want

Anybody who has seen Woody Allen movies can easily relate to the idea of amplifying feedback cycles. Hypochondria, a theme in most of Woody's films, is anxiety gone wild with feedback cycles. Woody gets a headache and becomes anxious, fearing that he has a brain tumor. His anxiety triggers stress hormones that race to his brain and intensify his headache, making him more anxious. He runs to the doctor, who takes brain scans that reveal a strange-looking spot and increase his anxiety further. This intensifies his headache, with Woody now awaiting test results and spinning toward a runaway panic.

Woody is the perfect embodiment of the amplifying feedback cycle. His panic is a result of several reinforcing feedback cycles intensifying anxiety. His films make these feedback cycles seem a lot funnier than the climate feedback cycles that the scientists are now worrying about. But then, again, there are many different kinds of feedback cycles—some strong and some weak, some self-perpetuating and some petering out, some positive and some negative, some hilarious and some terrifying.

All amplified feedback systems involve a change that triggers one or more other changes "feeding back" on the original change and amplifying or intensifying it. In a very "strong" positive feedback system, the feedback is like hitting a home run that triggers a big amplification of the original change. A strong feedback system is more likely to be self-perpetuating than a weak one, because "the home run" or even several home runs by different batters keep ratcheting up the level of continuous change and make it, as in Woody's sensitive nervous system, hard to calm down. In the weak variety, the feedback induces smaller new change than the original one, and the process eventually dies out and stabilizes, the outcome Woody desperately seeks but his overwrought nervous system does not permit.

Virtually all climate scientists recognize that the climate system is full of amplifying feedback cycles. Hansen describes the feedbacks involved with glacial melting.[21] Another classic one involves water vapor. As the earth warms, it creates more water vapor, the most widespread greenhouse gas that creates more warming. There are others, many of which the IPPC ignored. One is the "carbon sink" cycle. Today, 50 percent of our carbon emissions are absorbed by an essential "sink" of soil and land vegetation as well as plankton in the sea. On both land and water, our new carbon emissions are suppressing the "sink" effect and in the case of the land sink actually reversing it through feedback cycles. As CO_2 concentrations increase and the temperature warms, soil and vegetation start actually radiating out heat rather than absorbing it, which in turn depresses further the cooling effect of the carbon sink and increases the temperature even more.[22] This sounds a bit like the earth's version of Woody's panic attack as we keep loading the atmosphere with more CO_2.

The bad news in the revisionist story is that many of the feedback cycles in climate are the kind we do not want. They are the home run, "strong" variety. And even though there are both positive and negative climate feedback cycles (in this case, negative means feedbacks to warming that generate cooling rather than more warming), the positive cycles (those in which the feedback to warming is more warming) are now more numerous and stronger. In fact, some argue that *all* the core elements of the climate system are now in "a net positive feedback cycle."[23]

This takes us to the truly bad news in the climate system: There are multiple positive feedback cycles that seem mutually reinforcing. This phenomenon is called "second-order" feedback cycles. Here is where the science really begins to look like science fiction. In a second-order system of many positive feedback cycles, each "feedback mechanism generates its own specific process. The output of each feedback is an input to all other feedback, so the system as a whole constitutes an interactive set of mutually reinforcing sub-systems."[24]

Woody Allen's hypochondria is an example of such second-order interacting and mutually reinforcing cycles. All the reinforcing triggers of his own anxiety feedback cycles lead Woody into one of his runaway panic attacks.

In climate change, the warming feedbacks related to glacial melting interact with the feedback cycles related to water vapor, to the carbon sink, and to many others. In the dark edge of the revisionist story, this second-order feedback system accelerates the rate of climate change and faces us with the possibility of a "tipping point" in the entire planet.

Tipping Points in Climate

As a sociologist, I appreciate that Malcolm Gladwell has looked at "tipping points" as a sociological term. Gladwell sees a tipping point as "the moment of critical mass, the threshold, the boiling point," at which something that was unique or rare mysteriously and suddenly "infects" virtually a whole population, like an extremely contagious virus. In his famous example of the 1990s fad for Hush Puppies shoes, a small number of people began to wear them, but at a certain threshold point they almost overnight became the hot footwear for everyone.[25] A tipping point is that surprise moment when a gradual process creates a huge qualitative change, as when a solid object tilts to the point that it begins to topple or when a slowly warming cup of water, with frog in it or not, begins to boil. It creates a new reality.

But does global warming create tipping points? We should not equate amplifying feedback cycles with tipping points. The good news for the climate change story is that many amplifying feedback cycles—which we know are a big part of nature and warming—do *not* create tipping points. The bad news is that some do, a fact that Gladwell probably should have mentioned because they may be the most important tipping points in history.

A positive climate feedback such as glacial melting in the Arctic will accelerate warming, but whether it becomes a tipping point depends on many factors. Is the positive feedback strong enough to overcome negative feedback processes? Is it strong enough to perpetuate itself rather than peter out through decreasingly incremental temperature rises? Does this positive feedback interact enough with other positive feedback cycles to become irreversible?

All scientists agree that limited tipping points occur in climate change. For example, we have seen species go extinct because it got too hot, a qualitative change that qualifies as at least a small tipping point. And if a glacier melts permanently, that, too, is a tipping point, a hugely important one if the ice sheet is as big as, say, Greenland.

The most disturbing part of the revisionist climate story is that, as Hansen put it, "ominous tipping points loom."[26] This reflects, as noted earlier, that many warming feedback cycles are the type—positive, strongly amplifying, and mutually reinforcing—that can lead to consequential tipping points. In a 2007 paper, climate scientists identified nine big "tipping elements," which are anthropogenic regional warming events that could produce disruptive, dangerous, and potentially irreversible changes. They include melting of Greenland, collapse of the West Antarctic ice sheet, melting of the Arctic, collapse of the Atlantic conveyer currents, and dieback of the Amazon and boreal forests. The authors argue that "society may be lulled into a false sense of security by smooth projections of global change.... These tipping elements are candidates for surprising society by exhibiting a nearby tipping point."[27]

In a 2008 paper, Hansen and several other top climate experts identified several momentous tipping points catalyzed by small additional CO_2 concentrations. These include large sea-level rises, dramatic changes in rainfall patterns, rapid expansion of dry subtropical climate changes poleward, receding mountain glaciers that provide drinking water for "hundreds of millions of people," and dying of coral reefs that "are home for one-third of the species in the sea."[28]

Hansen does not sugarcoat the implications. In his 2008 testimony to Congress, he wrote that "the disturbing conclusion is that the safe level of atmospheric carbon dioxide is no more than 350 ppm (parts per million) and it may be less. Carbon dioxide amount is already 385 ppm and rising about 2 ppm each year."[29] In reflecting on Hansen's tipping points, environmentalist Bill McKibben blogged: "It's a tough diagnosis. It's like the doctor telling you that your cholesterol is way too high and, if you don't bring it down right away, you're going to have a stroke. So you take the pill, you swear off the cheese, and, if you're lucky, you get back into the safety zone before the coronary. It's like watching the tachometer edge into the red zone."[30] Hansen summarizes the climate's tipping point story more pithily: *"Time is running out."*[31]

Points of No Return: Mass Extinctions and Collective Death

Not all tipping points raise the scary specter of "points of no return." When I hear that phrase, I think of death; after all, all individual life has that particular point of no return that most of us recognize but do not like to think about. But the revisionist story is raising the notion that perhaps we should be thinking about collective death as well.

Collective death does not mean the extinction of all humans or a sudden cataclysm like all-out nuclear war, but it does imply something more like a drawn-out, debilitating disease afflicting the human condition in which hundreds of millions (disproportionately the global poor) might die while others survive in horrific conditions of drought, hunger, flooding, and war. By collective death, we mean the end of human civilization as we know it and the movement toward a future in which the survivors might envy the dead.

Fortunately, tipping points are not the same as points of no return, the third concept at the heart of the revisionist story. Points of no return are irreversible changes, tipping points that cross us into new realities that will never revert to the old ones—or at least not for thousands of years. By definition, tipping points always produce a qualitative change, but not necessarily an irreversible one. Woody's panic state feels to him as if it will never go away, but it represents a temporary psychological tipping point that will subside to his normal worry state. In climate, we have seen tipping points involving major changes in aerosol concentrations, but these can revert to normal levels a few weeks after the pollutants causing the spike are lowered. In contrast, the melting of the Greenland ice sheet is an example of a tipping point that not only wipes out Greenland but also has other irreversible and horrendous effects, such as raising sea levels by 23 feet.

Tipping points that are significant points of no return not only are irreversible but also carry major consequences. A disappearance of one insect species is a point of no return for those doomed insects, and it may affect their local ecosystem, but it probably does not collapse that ecosystem or have a big impact on the earth's climate and sustainability. But imagine that the West Antarctic ice shelf and all the Greenland ice sheets are melting. Together, these would represent two irreversible tipping points that raise sea levels by *200 feet*, creating hundreds of millions of refugees, massive flooding of many of the world's great cities, and huge malnutrition. Now that is a point of no return that deserves attention, particularly because both huge sheets are melting 60 to 65 percent faster than scientists could even imagine a few years ago. Marine geophysicist Robin Bell of Columbia's Earth Institute describes this irreversible catastrophe vividly: "If the West Antarctic ice sheet were to disappear, sea level would rise almost 19 feet; the ice in the Greenland ice sheet could add 24 feet to that; and the East Antarctic ice sheet could add yet another 170 feet to the level of the world's oceans: more than 213 feet in all."[32] She points out that the Statute of Liberty, 150 feet tall, could sink in a few decades.[33]

The revisionist science meets science fiction in its analysis of the ultimate points of no return. These are the ones like those we see in Hollywood films, where the world—or at least the human civilization that we cherish—is destroyed, leaving an unknown number of survivors scavenging to stay alive in gray, ashen surroundings of crumbling buildings, dead livestock, and totally parched and desolate landscapes.

Some Hollywood scenarios in the climate story are points of no return in the dark edge of the bell curve. One is a "methane burp." Scientists recognize the possibility of a sudden huge release of methane from either melting ice sheets or buried deposits on the ocean floor. In the worst case, a methane burp releases a volume of methane functioning as a doomsday machine. Scientists believe that millions of years ago volcanoes or changes in the ocean conveyor belts led to natural methane burps that abruptly heated up the climate as much as 30 degrees, resulting in total melting of polar ice, huge rises of sea levels, and extinctions of 90 percent of species.[34]

Unfortunately, there are doomsday points of no return that are not in the improbable dark edges. We know now that highly probable small additional rises in temperature create the multiple, mutually reinforcing, second-order massive tipping points that can devastate the entire earth system. This means ultimate points of no return may be perilously closer to the center of the bell curve than was envisaged in the IPCC report.

The Westminster scientists, along with Hansen and many other leading climate scientists, assert that we are already "in the early stages of a second order tipping point" that will soon become irreversible without massive reductions in greenhouse gas emissions to stabilize CO_2 at 350 or even lower, a target that many scientists believe will take the greatest human mobilization in the history of the world. "If we go beyond the point where human intervention can no longer stabilize the system," the Westminster Report observes, "then we precipitate unstoppable runaway climate change. That would set in motion a major extinction event comparable to the five other extinction crises that the earth has previously experienced."[35]

In the last chapter, we saw that getting to the IPCC 2007 target of 450 ppm is a huge challenge, requiring 90 percent reductions of current emissions in the rich nations by 2030. In the revised, unvarnished story, it will take even more, an all-out commitment to phase out coal and oil within a few decades. In later chapters, we look more closely at the revisionist policy alternatives, which may appear draconian but are less risky and spooky than the consequences of inaction spelled out by the revisionist story.

Biologist Peter Ward, a leading writer on the five earlier mass extinctions, admits the daunting challenges of 350 but says we have no real alternative, certainly not the incremental current course, which leads mercilessly toward a sixth extinction. He has painted a speculative picture of what the world would look like in 2100, when the second-order global feedback cycle has kicked in with full fury, with CO_2 concentrations at 1,100 ppm and global temperatures about 10 degrees Celsius higher than today. The great polar ice sheets are melting rapidly, and sea-level rises are so great that "all of the world's seaports are drowned." The floods, mass extinctions and human deaths, and mass migrations are overcoming any civilized order. "There is no central government in the United States," writes Ward, "in anything but name. The states have reverted to tiny nation-states, hoarding and grappling with the immigrants streaming in from other states.... Chaos is global ... as half of the world population was forced to live on minimal wheat-equivalent diet.... Half of the population was also on the move, and those moves meant war. World War III was fought over high land, food, and water, and the strongest grabbed. Tel Aviv, Tehran, and Marseilles were radioactive craters from nuclear attacks bent on settling old scores."[36]

Should You Believe This Story?

Climate science is not perfect. Nothing in climate science can be said to be as certain as death and taxes. New data keep coming in, the climate scientists differ on many details, and there is inherent uncertainty in much of the future projections.

I have become a reluctant believer in the revisionist story. No sane person would wish it to be scientific truth. But several factors persuade me. One is that leading scientists are increasingly converging on the revisionist story. These include skeptics who played an important role in forging the original IPCC consensus, including its leader, Rajendra Pachauri.

The IPCC scientific consensus and the scientific revisionists agree on many basic facts: that the earth is warming dramatically, that it is a human-induced fever driven by companies and ordinary people addicted to our fossil fuel–based global capitalism, and that dangerous feedback cycles are threatening to wreak havoc on the planet. On these basic propositions, there is rock-solid evidence based on thousands of studies—and the scientific debate is over according to virtually all of the world's climate scientists.

The revisionist story is being embraced now by more and more of the world's most distinguished climate scientists. This is not because they are Cassandras but because the newest evidence is overwhelmingly supporting it. The dates for the tipping points and points of no return remain speculative within quite broad ranges. But few scientists today reject the central role of amplified positive feedback cycles and major tipping points that are the headline of the new story.

But I need to mention one other persuasive factor for me as a writer who has always looked to history as the best way to understand uncertain futures. The history in this case is the long planetary history of climate change and mass extinctions. Scientists have established that dramatic global warmings leading to mass extinctions have happened several times before in the millions of years preceding our own era.[37] They have also shown that naturally induced spikes in CO_2, methane, and other greenhouse gases created these disastrous events. And they also have clear evidence that strong greenhouse gas feedback cycles, tipping points, and points of no return explain how it all happened. In other words, the new story today is new only in that it is human induced. In all other respects, it is spookily consistent with how the earth's climate has changed over eons.

Among the most important historical global warmings leading to mass extinctions are the late Cambrian, 490 million years ago; the late Ordovician, 450 million years ago; the Permian, about 250 million years ago; the Triassic, about 200 million years ago; the Jurassic-Cretaceous, about 150 million years ago; and the Paleocene, 55 million years ago.[38] In each of these mass extinctions, scientists tell us, volcanoes or some other natural event spiked up the CO_2 and methane in the environment in a very short period, sometimes in only a few centuries or even decades. Tipping points came quickly, with second-order whole earth system changes that scorched most of the existing species of vegetation and animals. The landscape on much of the earth was parched, desolate, hot, and dry, with at best scrubby vegetation and few animal species.[39] Although these mass extinctions varied in time and dynamics, the underlying cause was the same in all: abrupt global warming because of small increases in greenhouse gases. The consequence was the same, too: mass extinction that reflects the doomsday point of no return.

The history of the last 100,000 years can be recorded with more precision. Based on analyses of ice cores, scientists have shown that abrupt change is the name of the game. Hans Oeschger, a Swiss climate scientist, and Willi Dansgaard, a Danish geochemist, describe a series of cycles characterized by gradual cooling over hundreds of years and then abrupt cooling over just decades followed by millennia of extremely cool temperature. This was the period when glaciers formed. Then, just as suddenly, in another abrupt shift, the climate suddenly warmed up, usually for much shorter periods, to be followed by another abrupt cooling and a deep freeze.[40]

When we look at the distant history over 600 million years, and the clearer history over the last 10,000 years, what do we see? The future, at least as predicted by Hansen and other top climate scientists telling the revisionist story, is full of greenhouse gas–induced feedback cycles, major tipping points, and disastrous points of no return. That story is more persuasive to me because stories with long historical records are more credible than those never seen before.

We can see the future in our rearview mirror. When we dust it off and look closely, it is not a pretty sight. Sandwiched between long ice ages are a series of global warmings with fast and apocalyptic consequences. The future may not involve complete extinction, but it threatens cataclysmic changes in our way of life, associated with millions of deaths and massive, unacceptable tragedies for survivors on a scale impossible to imagine.

The difference between the future and the past is that for the first time humans have created and accelerated the tipping points. And for the first time we could become their victims. This gives a whole new meaning to the famous adage that those who have not studied history are bound to repeat it.

The only good news here is that the scientific truth may be spreading and leading to a tipping point in the world's social and political awareness and action. Whether that tipping point is near may be more important than anything else in the world. It is the subject of the rest of this book.

4

The New Greening of America
Truth and Truth Gaps in an Awakening Public

In 1970, a forty-two-year-old Yale law professor, Charles Reich, published a book called *The Greening of America*.[1] Reich wrote with the passion of the possessed, a pied piper of the academy who had some of the politically hallucinogenic language of Allen Ginsberg and the beatific, beatnik consciousness of Jack Kerouac. *The Greening of America* quickly became a best seller that reflected the zeitgeist of the 1960s. Reich argued that young Americans—flamboyant in their colorful bell bottom jeans, using psychedelic drugs, living in free love communes, clogging and sometimes shutting down the great cities of America with huge peace protests—were launching a personal and political revolution like none seen before: "[It] goes beyond anything in modern history. Beside it, a mere revolution, such as the French or the Russian, seems inconsequential—a shift in the base of power. Moreover, almost none of the [standard radical] views ... recognizes the crucial importance of *choosing a new lifestyle*. This has been passed over as if it were no more than an indulgent product of affluence, a more tolerant form of 'administered happiness.' But choice of a lifestyle is not peripheral, it is the heart of the new awakening. What is coming is nothing less than a new way of life and a new man."[2]

Reich believed that the cause of this new revolution in consciousness was a terminal crisis in the war state that brought us Vietnam—and in the American corporate bureaucracy that was crushing individuality and destroying the environment. The first Earth Day, which was celebrated with serious teach-ins and wild dancing on thousands of campuses and town halls, took place the same year Reich's book was published, and it signaled the new green awakening that Reich called "Consciousness III" (Consciousness I being the mind-set of the nineteenth-century self-reliant pioneer on the frontier seeking his own manifest destiny and Consciousness II being the bureaucratic conformity of the organization man, the "cheerful robot" of the 1950s depicted in the film *Pleasantville*). Without this new green consciousness,

America was destined to create perpetual wars and a "death in life," a robotic existence in a dying physical and cultural environment that could lead only to the total destruction of the life force.[3]

I remember reading the book at the time and being swept up by its utopian fervor. I was an anti-Vietnam and social justice activist, and I lived then in Waltham, Massachusetts, in a small commune, which grew some of its own vegetables, including surprisingly huge cucumbers and tasty zucchinis of which I was immensely proud. I shared Reich's view that we needed a new great transformation in our lifestyle, in our politics, and in capitalism itself. But I was uneasy with Reich's grand and sentimental focus on a cultural and lifestyle revolution that would be more transformative than all the political revolutions of history. I thought he had too much faith in the hippies and too little in the serious political activists.

The book surfed one of America's great waves of youth movements for peace, feminism, communalism, free emotional expression, socialism, and environmentalism. But the lifestyle youth revolution passed from the scene only a few years after the book's publication, with the exuberant hippie communes in Vermont and the revolutionary socialist Left in New York, Berkeley, and Madison becoming more of a sideshow curiosity than mainstream America. Both conservatives and liberals panned the book, and it is now largely forgotten.

Ironically, however, Reich's vision of a greening of America is becoming relevant again, for two reasons. The first is that the climate change crisis means that we need something like the great transformation that Reich prescribed if we are all to avoid the collective fate of the boiled frog. And the second is that a new greening of America has begun, perhaps just in the nick of time.

This new greening is another transformation in consciousness, aiming to overhaul our lifestyles as well as our economic and political systems. It sees that global warming requires something very different than business as usual, even more transformative than Reich imagined because neither he nor the rest of us knew then about climate change as a threat to survival.

The purpose of this chapter is to take a closer look at this new quieter and less visible greening of America. The question, we see, is not whether it is happening but whether it is happening fast enough to do what the old greening of America did not: sustain itself and reach within just a few years a decisive tipping point of no return.

Solutions sometimes mirror the problems they are attacking. The new greening of America is itself a series of social action feedback cycles—the mutually reinforcing actions of thousands of diverse, multi-issue, and colorful grassroots movements that are erupting in what ecologist Paul Hawken calls "blessed unrest."[4] This could lead to very rapid tipping points of green social change and blessed points of no return.

In this chapter, I focus on the changing color of consciousness, specifically the beliefs of ordinary Americans about climate change. We need to know whether they are greening, in what ways, and how fast. In later chapters, I take up the social movements and political and policy changes needed to turn greener consciousness into a cooler world. And this, we see, means not just rapidly transforming our entire energy systems along with our broader socioeconomic-political order but also creating a new lifestyle for all of us—on that score, Reich was right and his academic critics dead wrong.

Green Grass Roots?
The Color of Consciousness

The global warming crisis will be solved only if the science described in the last two chapters migrates very quickly into the brains and bellies of ordinary Americans. This is just the starting point of a much larger social and political green enlightenment and systemic "makeover"—no less is required if we are to dance with scientific truth to avoid the second-order feedback cycles that can lead to the sixth extinction. In this chapter, I look at the first step: to see if the science on warming has moved into the minds of the masses and is greening our consciousness. Then I look to see whether it is becoming gut truth, propelling us into action.

Major Survey Findings

The majority of Americans

- believe global warming is real and is caused by humans
- believe global warming is a potential danger to themselves
- believe global warming will be a serious crisis for future generations
- are making changes to reduce their personal carbon footprint
- favor strong government regulation to limit greenhouse gas emissions, especially on industry, even if doing so is costly
- do not favor gas taxes or other major personal sacrifices to reduce greenhouse gas emissions

---

Public opinion polls tell us a mixed story about the color of popular consciousness.

The greening of the popular brain starts with simple awareness. And here, we have seen a rapid tipping point that is a point of no return. In 1986, just

39 percent had even heard of global warming and the "greenhouse effect." In 1990, 74 percent had, a big spike. By 2001, 82 percent had heard about it, and by 2006, 91 percent had.[5]

This is a tipping point for which Al Gore can claim more legitimate credit than his boast to have invented the Internet. Gore published *Earth in the Balance* in 1992, a founding best-selling manifesto of the new greening of America movement.[6] The success of the book created waves of new media attention and spread awareness in tandem with the new scary scientific evidence of climate change. Gore then made his hugely popular documentary film, *An Inconvenient Truth*, which seared into our collective brain images of polar bears floating into extinction and rising sea levels that could flood or kill the 60 percent of the world's population living within 60 miles of a coast. After Gore and the IPCC jointly received the Nobel Prize for their work in 2007, a global awareness tipping point was reached, making global warming as much a part of popular vocabulary as terrorism or *American Idol*. Here is one indicator: In 2008 googling "global warming" yielded about 57 million sites or hits, whereas googling "terrorism" produced about 67 million hits, both astronomical numbers. In fact, not many terms generated more Google hits. George W. Bush, then president and hugely in the news, had about 42 million hits.

We are now at the threshold of a second critical tipping point, this one involving the percentage of the population that is personally convinced that the earth is heating up. These numbers grew gradually throughout the late 1980s and 1990s. By 2000, about 66 percent of Americans were "warming believers," but right after 9/11 the numbers dipped.[7] The ever-present images of the Twin Towers collapsing, along with the Bush administration's blatant denial of global warming, began to reverse popular belief in global warming. But a few years later, we saw another abrupt shift. In 2006 and 2007, the level and intensity of public belief about global warming spiked. Between 85 and 90 percent said they believed the earth was warming, significantly closing the gap between scientific and popular truth.[8]

The reason for this shift was a combination of factors, among them increased heat waves, western wildfires, and Category 5 hurricanes like Katrina that washed over neglected levees and created the epic tragedy of New Orleans. Media coverage reinforced the personal experience of scary and erratic weather. A student of mine from Nebraska said that the heat waves and fires out west had rattled his brain a bit and made him think about global warming. Polls showed that 70 percent of Americans felt the same thing—the weather really does affect one's mood and mind![9] But this was not a point of no return. Polls in 2008 showed a dip back to between only 70 and 80 percent who felt convinced that global warming was happening, reflecting the growing public focus on the economic crisis and the intransigent denials and antigreen measures taken by Bush's Environmental Protection Agency and other government bodies.[10] Nonetheless, the overwhelming majority of Americans now sees warming as real.[11]

Mass beliefs about the causes of global warming are also greening, but more slowly. Scientists overwhelmingly view humans as the main perpetrators, and in 2008 about 63 percent of Americans agreed.[12] An even larger majority, 73 percent, of Americans saw both natural and human causes of warming.[13]

A greening American majority now shares Pogo's view that "we have seen the enemy and he is us." And Americans increasingly understand the gravity of the crisis. By 2006, 57 percent of Americans said that if nothing is done, it will be a "very" serious problem for the world.[14] Although about 40 percent view warming as a crisis already, 80 percent see it as a very serious problem in the future.[15] A plurality of Americans sees it as the most serious environmental problem facing the United States, and a majority of the world's population in twenty-five of thirty-seven countries surveyed in 2008 saw global warming as a "very serious" problem.[16] The United States lags significantly behind other countries in polling on the belief and severity of the global warming crisis, but global warming remains a serious concern for a majority of Americans.[17] This is another important tipping point, with popular majorities in the United States now embracing the three core truths of the scientific consensus: that the world is warming, that humans bear at least some responsibility, and that the threat is grave.[18]

Does this constitute a green awakening? Yes, because we have passed some tipping points in awareness, with growing clarity about the reality, causes, and frightening danger of global warming. The speed with which Americans are coming to embrace the truth of an existential crisis they had never even heard of a few decades ago is unprecedented. New profound and threatening truths are always resisted and tend to spread slowly, but perhaps we can hold on to some hope that in the age of the Internet new truths, especially ones of apocalyptic proportions, can spread faster than we ever imagined.

But there are significant limits on the green awakening to date. The public is deeply divided about the truth of global warming. Although there are differences by gender and age, there is a significant partisan divide, which in 2008 was growing into an unbridgeable chasm. Compared to 27 percent of Republicans, 58 percent of Democrats say global warming is "mostly caused by humans." Likewise, whereas 57 percent of Democrats call global warming "very serious," only 22 percent of Republicans do. In 2006 and 2008, Republicans listed global warming as the "lowest priority" issue, dead last and way below gay marriage and flag burning.[19]

Even the majority who has accepted the truth of climate change does not tend to see it yet as the all-out emergency it is. It as if this greening majority has been singed but not yet so significantly burned that it is willing to stop and shift gears, no matter what the personal sacrifices involved. We see danger but not the dark edges of the bell curve, which may touch us more immediately and more disastrously than we are allowing ourselves to contemplate. This suggests we need to look now at how much we have allowed the truth to move from our brain to our gut.

The Belly of the Frog: Is Global Warming Becoming a Gut Truth?

In late 2008, a poll announced that 71 percent of Americans said that they were now acting to reduce their personal carbon footprint.[20] Most were doing it by trying to drive less, use less electricity, and recycle more.[21]

But is concern for saving the planet the motive? The summer of 2008 will go down in history as the first American season of $4 for a gallon of gas. When it costs $70 or even $100 to fill a tank, people drive less whatever their views on global warming, unless they are Donald Trump or Bill Gates. Economic concerns appear to trump environmental ones.

But although 25 percent say they are driving less and conserving power and water because of rising prices, 33 percent say they are doing so to help the environment and another 41 percent says they are doing so for both reasons "equally."[22] That makes almost 75 percent who are trying to reduce their carbon footprint not just to protect their self-interest but also to help sustain the planet.

This is one small sign that the scientific truth about global warming and the environmental crisis may be becoming a gut truth. Only gut truth spurs activism, and only activism can create a new greening of America. But are Americans truly feeling the global warming truth in their guts?

In 2007, 52 percent of Americans said that global warming was either "extremely" or "very" personally important to them, compared to 27 percent who had said the same thing in 1997.[23] This hints that global warming may indeed be getting to Americans as a blow in the belly, not just an abstraction in the mind. Another belly sign is the percentage who say they worry "a great deal" about global warming, which was 41 percent in 2007.[24] That is about 125 million warming worriers. And it is clear why they are worrying: 40 percent of Americans say that global warming is "extremely" or "very" dangerous to themselves and their immediate family, and another 25 percent say it is "somewhat" dangerous.[25]

This sense of personal risk is translating into support for major governmental action. By 2008, about 70 percent of Americans supported higher auto emission standards and 80 percent supported stronger regulation of industrial emissions. More than 70 percent supported tax incentives for utilities to produce wind and solar energy. Seventy-five percent favored direct government spending on renewable energies. This majoritarian support for strong government action was first seen in 2000 and has gradually grown.[26]

But there is even bigger news. In the America that journalist Thomas Friedman likes to call "free market vanilla," 75 percent say they support governmental "mandatory limits" on carbon emissions.[27] This applies especially to industry, where more than 60 percent of the public explicitly favors government caps and mandates rather than the less coercive option of tax incentives.[28] This is in line with public opinion in Europe and much of the world, but the fact that Americans are now calling for mandatory government controls ought to be rattling the brains of Washington politicians.

A majority of Americans in 2008 were calling for strong government action even if it is costly. About 33 percent of Americans supported action even if it "involves significant costs"; another 42 percent supported steps that are "lower in cost." That is a majority that also understands that controlling global warming is going to take "major changes in lifestyle" and political costs that are far from trivial.[29] And in 2008, an ABC News poll found that more than 65 percent of Americans said that the United States should act even if countries such as China and India do not.[30]

These are signs of a green consciousness that has begun to move to the gut and churn around in there. But it is also the case that people are not as pumped up about global warming as I seem to be suggesting. There is another side to the data. It shows that Americans, although greening, are far from green enough.

In the 2008 presidential elections, for example, climate change was close to the bottom of most priority lists endorsed by both Democrats and Republicans. There was a lot of talk about gas prices and some talk about the need for conservation, renewable energy, and green jobs. Barack Obama talked about promoting a new green economy and ran on a platform of an 80 percent mandatory cut in carbon emissions by 2050. But even though the public seemed receptive, at least 65 percent of the public, according to an August 2008 poll, also got behind McCain's argument to drill, drill, drill, with 63 percent supporting drilling in waters where it is not now permitted and 55 percent favoring drilling in U.S. wilderness areas where drilling is not now permitted.[31] John McCain felt that drilling was so popular that Obama joked that McCain wanted to drill beneath every campaign platform he delivered his speeches from. Drilling for oil equaled or trumped the public concern with conservation, renewables, and global warming.

Americans also tend not to support paying higher taxes themselves to prevent warming. In 2006 and 2007, when asked whether they favored taxes on electricity and gasoline to help prevent global warming, only about 20 percent favored a tax on electricity and 30 percent on gas.[32] And when it comes to creating more energy efficiency in homes and offices, the majority supported tax incentives rather than government mandates, the opposite of its preference on industrial emissions.[33] In other words, to deal with global warming, Americans want strong controls—except on themselves. This means most Americans are pale green.

Every American should ask himself or herself, "Am I pale green?" A pale shade of American green—where we worry about global warming but are unwilling to make the personal sacrifices and the rapid, major political

---

Pale Green

Pale green is the color of a consciousness that sees global warming as a scientific truth but not a gut truth moving us to act urgently to save civilization.

Pale green Americans see global warming as a real and a serious problem.

Pale green Americans favor action to save the environment and stop global warming.

Pale green Americans are not sufficiently worried to take the drastic action necessary to solve the crisis.

Pale green is the color of the majority of Americans, both leaders and ordinary citizens.

---

changes that we know are necessary—is not good enough. The simple reason is that global warming is an emergency now that should gnaw at the gut of every American. We saw in the last two chapters that getting to either the IPCC benchmark of 450 or the revisionist 350—the simplest way to measure success in the "new greening of America"—is going to require a Michael Phelps heroic effort. Now most of us are admittedly not Olympic gold medalist Phelps, whose 2008 swimming competitors called him a creature with a "wingspan from another planet." But all of us non-Phelpians are capable as ordinary mortals of becoming a brighter shade of green, which means simply accepting scientific truth and acting to save ourselves.

In the rest of Part I, I look at the critical factors that are stirring denial of the emergency and creating a crucial race between blind paralysis and enlightened action. Major personal and political forces are blurring our own consciousness, dividing the population, and constraining our personal activism and government policy about global warming. They are turning us pale green rather than the bright green of the frog that survives. In Part II, III and IV, I look at what we need to do to overcome the hurdles and get to the solutions we need urgently if we are to avoid the fate of the boiled frog.

5

The New Denial of Death
The Psychology of Pale Green

In 1988, while researching a book on the nuclear arms race, I spent a week at the Pentagon talking to the strategists who think about the unthinkable: total nuclear war.[1] I remember interviewing a man known affectionately in Pentagon circles as Dr. Doom. His job was to plan post–nuclear war scenarios after the United States and the Soviet Union had been charred to smoldering ruins in the first nuclear war.

Dr. Doom was telling me how once the United States had been hit by a nuclear attack, and Washington had been "decapitated," satellites would be able to launch their own postnuclear attack, even if nobody in the military was still alive to direct them. Computers could activate the new attacks automatically. After millions of Soviets were killed in the initial nuclear war, the computers would be able to destroy the remaining Soviets and declare victory.

We were sitting around a large circular coffee table. Dr. Doom, who had a Ph.D. in math, was an impressively rational and analytical thinker, in command of the numbers as he drank from a steaming cup of hot coffee. His mood remained calm and reasonable, as if we were talking about millions of pesky insects being exterminated rather than millions of people. Then his young son, whom he had brought in for a visit that day, ran into the room and jumped on Dr. Doom's lap. In the process, he spilled Dr. Doom's hot coffee onto the table and rug and a little on his father's slacks.

Dr. Doom suddenly lost his cool, leaping out of his chair and yelling angrily at his son. I remember how surprised I was. Here was a man who had kept perfect equanimity while talking about hundreds of millions of deaths in all-out nuclear war. But when his cup of coffee spilled, he went berserk.

This story leads me to the subject of denial. Dr. Doom clearly was in possession of some truth about nuclear war. He also understood the truth of hot spilled coffee. But he could not deny the truth of the hot coffee scalding his leg, whereas his mood suggested that he was in denial about the rather larger catastrophe of nuclear war that he had been describing so calmly.

Nuclear war, as noted earlier, is one of those horrifying threats that political scientists call "existential." Existential threats carry the potential to destroy the planet, wipe out the human species, or, at minimum, kill millions of people and wipe out whole countries or change civilization as we know it. The two most important existential threats in the world today are all-out nuclear war and climate change, but others include global influenzas, such as SARS, that could, like Europe's fourteenth-century Black Plague, wipe out millions of people in a few weeks or months.

It is no surprise that existential threats tend to produce denial. We all find it hard to process emotionally overwhelming information. The information about climate change, as with total nuclear war, is as overwhelming as anything we can imagine. We can deny in our minds, refusing to believe what the scientists are telling us about the threat. Or we can deny in our bellies, accepting the truth abstractly but rejecting it as a gut truth. Dr. Doom obviously preferred the second choice, his brain processing the cognitive information as coolly as an advanced computer. But his belly tuned out, at least until the hot coffee scalding his leg offered him perhaps some gut reminder of the deadly heat from nuclear explosions that would vaporize millions of people.

During the cold war, the fear that presidents would engage in the same gut denial as Dr. Doom led some to suggest that the code for activating a nuclear attack be embedded inside the body of one of the president's children. That way, he would have to kill one of his own progeny before he could start a nuclear war, a way of ensuring that the decision would be based to some degree on gut truth.

Climate change is creating both cognitive and gut denial. Millions of Americans still deny it as a scientific truth. But among the majority who accept the science, most are still involved in belly denial.[2] They know that our precious human civilization is at peril, but they have filed that truth in the attic and have barricaded it from their gut. It has little power to move them and is not likely to cause even an occasional sleepless night.

In this section of the book, I explore both forms of climate change denial. The cognitive denier sees climate change as a hoax or a huge scientific error. The millions of cognitive deniers are, for the most part, victims of manipulation by the denial industry. Those who see the scientific truth of climate change but deny it in their guts are a shade of pale green. They see the science and believe it. But they do not act, and thus their knowledge is pale and impotent. The boiled frog can be either a cognitive or a gut denier. In America, and in most of the world, the greatest danger is gut denial. If we do not find a way out of it, one thing is certain: We will live out our days in a shade of pale green until it is too late.

In what follows, I look at the race between denial and awareness as the world begins to absorb the threat of climate change. I begin by looking at the power of denial in coping with our own individual death. I then turn to the lessons for dealing with the "collective death" threatened by climate change, a death that does not mean a sudden cataclysmic extinction of all humans but something closer to a drawn-out debilitating disease, in which hundreds of millions could die and millions of survivors may well envy the dead.

Becker's Truth:
Denial of Death as a Way of Life

Death—and denial of death—is not a new subject. Philosophers such as Søren Kierkegaard and psychologists such as Sigmund Freud have written about it over the centuries. Today, filmmakers such as Woody Allen—who says that love and death are the only things that matter—make careers on the topic.

About forty years ago, philosopher and psychologist Ernest Becker created his own synthesis of what we have learned over the centuries in his famous book *The Denial of Death*.[3] The book won a Pulitzer Prize in 1974, and many still read it today.

Becker was not writing about climate change and the denial of mass collective death. He was writing about how we as individuals come to terms with the inevitability of our own individual death. Collective and individual death are two different things, so we cannot just extrapolate from Becker's analysis to our current predicament. But Becker's thoughts about denial of our own individual mortality shed light on our current epidemic of denial of collective death.

Denial is the lead actor in Becker's story. As he sees it, no human can escape the overwhelming reality that each of us is going to die. It is a shocking, overwhelming, merciless, and relentless fact. William James called it the "worm at the core" of our "pretensions to happiness."[4] Our own death is the biggest, most mysterious, and most frightening truth in our own life—and Becker describes his whole book as "a network of arguments on the universality of the fear of death, or terror as I prefer to call it."[5]

As a reader, I could relate to that part of Becker's story. I have always been afraid of death, a bit like Woody Allen in his own autobiographical depiction. In his films, Woody, even as a young man, obsesses that any day now he will hear that knock on the door, open up, and see Death, a figure shrouded in a white sheet, beckoning to him. "It's your time," Death will say.

Becker might have been consumed by that worry himself. In 1974, shortly after his book was published and the same year it won the Pulitzer Prize,

Becker died of cancer. We still are not sure whether he knew he had cancer while he was writing the book.

It does not really matter, however, because any reader will see the universal truth in Becker's story. Sick or well, neurotic or tranquil, young or old, we each know that death is at the center of our life stories. It unites us all and concludes each of our narratives. It is, Becker suggests, the inevitable existential reality of the human condition. Because it represents the destruction of our existence, and because life seeks to affirm itself, death is the greatest threat. It is so overwhelming a threat, says Becker, that all of life is in some way shaped by it.[6]

The main way that humans cope with such existential terror is denial. "Those who speculate that a full apprehension of man's condition would drive him insane are right," says Becker, continuing that "everything that man does in his symbolic world is an attempt to deny and overcome his grotesque fate."[7] Death is such a massively threatening and unchangeable reality that no human can truly live without some form of denial. There is cognitive denial, pushing our pending death into such a distant future that it is not on our radar screen, the denial option most often used by the young. There is also, among all of us, massive belly denial of our death, partly because letting it penetrate our emotional defenses would be too overwhelming and also because, even though we can diet, exercise, and engage in other delaying strategies, there is nothing we can do to prevent the ultimate knock on the door from the grim reaper.

Given this irreversible truth, says Becker, denial of death inevitably takes over as a central life task. For most people, and particularly those most "sensitive" or reflective on the human condition, it becomes virtually impossible to live without shutting out the truth.[8] Death, in this sense, consumes us long before we die, essentially defining how we live.

Becker reminds us that there are several denial strategies that can make life at least somewhat meaningful and tolerable. One is sublimation, Freud's view of how humans cope with overwhelmingly stressful beliefs and feelings.[9] We sublimate by plunging into actions that divert, channel, and calm the chaotic energy of our frenzied nervous system, seeking to pacify the overstimulated neurons firing away at death's looming presence. Becker argues that Freud's entire life work—the heroic creation of psychoanalysis as a master science— was an effort to sublimate his own fear of death.[10]

Becker writes extensively about "heroism" and religion.[11] By throwing ourselves into creative writing (Freud's and Becker's choice), successful business entrepreneurship, scientific discovery, caring for others in a medical capacity, or other passionate work, we seek to become heroes who distract ourselves with obsessive pursuits and can achieve a measure of social immortality. We may die, but through the heroic achievements of our careers we can live forever in the memories of the living, a way to deny and overcome the fear and reality of our physical death.[12]

Religion is the ultimate sublimation, offering people a way to deny the significance of death both cognitively and viscerally. Most religions point to an afterlife that is better than the current one. Islamic suicide bombers believe that their death means an eternity with seventy white-gowned vestal virgins. Many Christian evangelicals see death as a passage to a new life surrounded by loved ancestors, singing angels, and God, an existence far better than life on earth. Becker believes that religion, as well as virtually all human culture and pursuits, is driven by the fear of death, an ultimately pessimistic appraisal of the impossibility of living life that is not a failed attempt to deny and stave off death.[13] All human achievements become forms of death denial.

Many believe Becker exaggerates the overwhelming presence and fear of death in life. Not everyone is a death denier. I spent two years with the dying Morrie Schwartz, the subject of Mitch Albom's best seller *Tuesdays with Morrie,* which has sold millions of copies and become required reading in many of America's high schools and colleges.[14] Morrie, my best friend for twenty-five years, was dying of Lou Gehrig's disease, and his ability to handle death without denial, while maintaining his dignity and generosity of spirit to the living, made him a national figure. Millions watched him on *Nightline* speaking with Ted Koppel on three different occasions about his impending death.[15] He was open, humorous, philosophical, and lacking in any guile, self-deception, or denial.

I can personally testify that Morrie did not deny death either cognitively or somatically. I would say to him, "Morrie, maybe you'll pull out of this thing. I mean, Stephen Hawking has lived with Lou Gehrig's for twenty-five years." Morrie would hug me and say, "Charlie, I understand where you're coming from. But I've got two years at most." He insisted on having a half-birthday, because he felt he might not make it to his next birthday. And he also officiated over his own living funeral, telling us that he wanted to hear all the nice things people were going to say after he was gone.

Morrie offers hope that we can get beyond denial of death. And we can do so in a joyous, proactive way, because Morrie was never more openhearted and socially connected than in the years he was dying. But Morrie was an unusual fellow. I think Becker got the story right for millions of people who are terrified of death. They may or may not talk about it, but the prospect of death does not make them joyous. Many turn to religion or sublimate their anxiety into the "heroic" pursuits Becker describes, distracting themselves and desperately seeking denial of the fear that death could knock at the door any day now.

This obsessive fear and denial of death is bad news for our climate change story. If denial of our personal death takes over so much of our life, the energy we will put into denial of collective death from climate change seems hard to overestimate. But because personal mortality and collective death are quite different, we turn now to look at some surprising comparisons—and see if we can learn some initial lessons about how to overcome denial when it comes to climate change.

Climate Change and Collective Death: The Incredible Seductions of Denial

I have a brother-in-law who is an eminent scientist. I trust his judgments, and before I started this book, I wanted to know his own views of climate change (although he is a geneticist and not a climate scientist). As it turned out, he had just had an operation and had spent his time recuperating by reading up on the science of climate change.

Although he is not a catastrophic thinker, the story he told me was not a happy one. He had concluded from his reading that we might well be too late. Climate change was moving forward inexorably through its own points of no return, and the consequences would likely be death of millions and millions of people. In other words, climate change was real, and it would likely lead to collective death.

In speaking of collective death, let us recall that we are not talking about total extinction of the species. Hundreds of millions may die, but millions will likely survive, though in a far different and more perilous circumstance, struggling to live under conditions of forced mass migrations, hunger, drought, floods, and incessant war over scarce food, water, and other resources.[16] The collective death threatened by climate change is a death of human civilization as we know it, with many regions of the earth no longer supporting great cities, viable agriculture, developed technology, secure food and water, or any kind of permanent peace. Moreover, unlike total nuclear war, the collective death of civilization caused by climate change probably will not occur in one explosion, although that is possible through a gigantic methane burp or other dark edge of the bell curve scenarios.[17] It would more likely occur over decades or centuries, but scientists do not claim any certainty about which way the catastrophe will unfold.

I still vividly remember my response to this conversation. Even though I am not prone to depression, I felt overcome by a sense of despair. Until that moment, I had never really taken seriously, at least not in my gut, the idea that climate change could erode civilized life so drastically. When the idea hit me, it hit hard—and I share some of my personal experiences here because they shed light on the seductions of denial and how we might move beyond it.

I responded in two different ways. On the one hand, I felt that I could not keep living as I had before. One of several changes, as a teacher and author, was to spend a lot more time speaking and writing about climate change. This was the opposite of a denial response, or so it seemed to me (Becker might see it as sublimation). I wanted to act.

On the other hand, I needed to distract myself, because I did not want to keep feeling so depressed about the subject. Thinking about the possibility that climate change was eventually going to kill so many and create something like a new Katrina every week drove me to want to deny the story my brother-in-law had told me. Dealing emotionally with the prospect of mass, collective death was even more difficult than dealing with my own personal death.

One thing that has made the idea of my own death somewhat bearable is that others are going to survive—in happy circumstances. This is humanizing and comforting for anyone who loves people. I also have hope that life can get better for most people and that the ideals of social justice and community that have given my life meaning will continue to motivate new generations and make life happier for everyone.

But when I started to think about climate change and collective death, I could not fall back on this reassuring idea. Collective death means there may be no hopeful future, no future that can support the great ideals I believe in. I can no longer draw comfort from the idea that future generations will put in place the ideals I have fought for. I had thought about this before, when I thought about the prospect of nuclear war, especially during the Cuban missile crisis. But perhaps because the crisis ended quickly or because I was younger, it created less depression. Now I carry a more sustained sense of the grim possibility that future generations will be caught up in brutal struggles for survival and that it might not be better to be a survivor.

Until climate change, I had never doubted that the path to a progressive future stretches out forever and that the great struggles in which I am now engaged, for peace and justice, have centuries, even millennia, to come to fruition. Climate change is like a missile aimed directly at my hopes. It tells me that there really may be an end, soon, to that kind of history—which is an end to everything I believe in.

For me, this intensifies the psychological pressure to deny. It is just too painful to abandon the idea of a hopeful future for humanity. Religious people, particularly many evangelical or fundamentalist conservatives, may find comfort in this kind of end of history as a blessing, a second coming. But I cannot see the collective death of climate change as a rapture or any other positive development. It is just an unmitigated disaster.

It does not lead me to cognitive denial, however, because my politics make me relatively immune to the seductions of the denial industry. For many people, the first and easiest temptation is to simply disbelieve on the cognitive level. This temptation is reinforced by the power, money, and zeal of the denial industry, as I show in detail later. But as somebody who has studied the way the ideological apparatus can control and spread disinformation on many political subjects, it cannot work its magic on me, much as I would love to believe its comforting view that climate change is all a hoax. It is worth noting, however, that there can be no similar denial industry about individual death, unless we take the religious establishment into consideration. We all know we are going to die, and nobody is likely to persuade us that death will not ultimately knock on our door.

This is a fundamental difference from collective death, where a denial industry has far more promising prospects. I can see at least six major reasons that people may be seduced, either by the denial industry or their own psychological impulses, as discussed by Becker, to deny. First, scientists cannot tell us with certainty about the inevitability, scale, or timing of collective death. If we act decisively to prevent climate change now, we might avoid collective death altogether. Even if we do not act, millions of individuals will likely survive even the worst scenarios of climate change, whereas nobody has a chance of escaping individual death. This makes it possible to fudge what we mean by collective death and to argue that the species will recover from the worst of anything climate change can dish out.

Second, as discussed in Chapter 1, many Americans harbor deep suspicions about science.[18] This does not lead them to doubt the certainty of their own death, but it does enable the denial industry to persuade them that climate change is a scientific fantasy or hoax and that somehow scientists are engaged in a grand conspiracy to fool us.

Third, there is the issue of time scale. The boiled frog remains blissfully ignorant because he is warming up slowly. Collective death from climate change might take several centuries or more, a time frame that makes us highly susceptible to denial fantasies.

Fourth, for reasons already discussed, collective death is even more frightening than individual death. Paradoxically, that intensifies the incentive to deny, because fear, and especially terror, as Becker argues, is the main engine of denial.

Fifth, the costs and personal sacrifices involved in an all-out fight to stop climate change are high. This also greatly increases our disposition to deny, because having to curb our shopping at the mall that Madison Avenue and global consumer capitalism have now made a mass addiction is enough to drive us into permanent denial.

Sixth, the ideological apparatus is brilliant at getting Americans to fear the wrong things, as sociologist Barry Glassner has proved in his book *The Culture of Fear*.[19] Glassner describes the fears that are pushed front and center by special-interest groups and the mass media, diverting attention from far more serious threats. The inflated, distracting fears include airplane accidents (less likely than being hit by lightning), the dangers of cocaine (far less serious than alcohol abuse), and the fear of criminals (a distraction from the availability of guns that allows crimes to be committed). *The Culture of Fear* is a testament to how Americans are taught to deny the threats that really matter, because entrenched elites have a powerful interest in and clever ways to cultivate such denial.[20] The ideological apparatus produces gut denial of climate change by addicting people to threats that matter far less and do not threaten corporate or political interests.

All this means that the denial industry will likely flourish for years. And even if it does not, and most of us stop cognitively denying, the psychological incentives to engage in gut denial are intense. The public will turn a pale green, but we may blissfully deny climate change in our gut until we are cooked.

When Awareness Makes Sense: Why We Might Reject the Denial Fantasy

Even though one might well make money investing in the denial industry, there are reasons to think it could lose its profits. Although the denial of collective death is easier than the denial of our own individual death for the reasons just enumerated, there are a few reasons that denying climate change may become increasingly difficult. They could even make denial look increasingly crazy and immoral, moving more and more of us to see the mass death threat posed by climate change as a gut truth.

By far the most important factor is that collective death and the horrific future that climate change portends for survivors are almost certainly one of the worst possible things that can happen. As I let my brain imagine even worse disasters, I draw a blank, except for all-out nuclear war, which would likely leave no survivors at all. Is there anything worse than the mass suffering and death of hundreds of millions of the most vulnerable, leaving millions more affluent and less vulnerable struggling with pestilence, hunger, war, and endless conflict over scarce resources?

I recognize that some religious people equate such a catastrophe with the second coming. And even some secular people argue that the planet will continue just fine without any developed human civilization, as it did before humans evolved. Some will say that advanced human civilization has done so much damage to the planet and other species that it is better that we recognize our time is up. So I understand that some people can accept or even find solace in collective death.

Nonetheless, most people will surely agree that a relatively rapid conclusion to the progressive story of human civilization as we know it is horrifying. Human life and happiness are precious. If we believe in the value of life and the development of the species, to destroy the civilized order ourselves, partly by denying what we are doing, is hard to understand or justify. But the very fact that collective death by climate change may be the worst threat humans will ever face is, I realize, a two-edged sword. The more frightening a threat is, the greater is the psychological impulse to deny it. At the same time, the greater the threat is, the more irrational it is to deny, particularly if we can act to prevent it.

Perhaps the most important fact, then, in our favor—which could sink the denial industry and lead us to accept climate change as a gut truth—is that we have the power to stop or mitigate climate change. This is not an option with our individual death; even those taking up radical antiaging strategies, such as caloric restriction, know they are just postponing the ultimate day of reckoning. But the collective death that climate change could wreak upon us all is something we can prevent or mitigate if we take decisive action now.

This puts denial in a completely different light than the denial that Ernest Becker wrote about. Denial makes a certain sense if there is nothing that can be done to change the inevitable. But although denial seems rational and functional in dealing with the inevitability of personal mortality, which we cannot prevent, it becomes catastrophically irrational when dealing with a horrific future fate that we can mitigate or avoid. If we can avoid collective death, those who fail to take action now and counsel denial should be viewed as guilty of a heinous crime, for what is more criminal or immoral than undermining actions that could save the best of humanity?

At least two other factors may contribute to our rejecting denial. One is that short-term crises are increasingly tied to climate change issues. These include national security, energy independence, poverty, migration, and war. I show later that strategies to prevent the long-term effects of climate change now can contribute to solving all these current crises. This intertwining of climate change with other current burning social issues may lead to rapid tipping points toward less denial and more awareness and action to solve climate change as well as other immediate everyday problems.

Finally, even though the high short-term costs and sacrifices of acting against climate change can produce denial, there are also short-term benefits that lead toward awareness and action. It can be more fun and healthier to ride a bike than drive a car. Eating locally produced vegetables and fruit can be very tasty, making an eating strategy that reduces carbon emissions also a way to feel better and be healthier. Buying less "stuff" saves us money and can turn our attention to more meaningful pursuits. Environmentalists such as Bill McKibben have written entire treatises suggesting how "less" can be "more," arguing that we will actually be happier if we make some of the changes toward a green lifestyle that others call sacrifices.[21] To the extent that a philosophy of "less is more" holds true in human happiness, there is every hope that people might begin to deny climate change less, if only to improve their own personal health and happiness. The question of survival now rests on a race between denial and enlightened action.

6

Boomers and Millennials

Generational Truth and Denial

If timing is everything, then a person's age might prove pivotal in affecting the balance between denial and enlightenment. Older generations might deny more because they are least likely to be personally affected. The youngest generation is likely to be the brightest shade of green, because it will be hit much harder in its own lifetime.

In this chapter, I turn to how different generations see global warming. I look at three key generations: the boomers, the busters, and the budders. Many demographers label the "baby boomers" as those born between 1946 and 1962; the busters (sometimes called "Gen X") were born between 1963 and 1978; and the budders, often called the "millennial" generation and sometimes called "echo boomers" because they are children of boomers, were born between 1979 and 2000.[1] I have included what some call Gen Y within the budder, or millennial, camp because they share many of the same views. Is global warming the cause célèbre of the budders, and can we rely on them to save us and themselves? And what kind of help will they get from boomers and busters? The answers might help determine who is truly "the greatest generation."

Boomers: Is Global Warming Their Last Great Cause?

The aging baby boomers—representing almost 80 million Americans—could be a tipping point generation on climate change. As their last contribution to social change, they could help awaken the rest of the nation to the gut truth of climate change, propelling younger Americans into a new, transformational wave of green activism.

Boomers are moving toward the last phase of life, when awareness of one's own death becomes increasingly visceral. As the boomers move into retirement, their consciousness of mortality migrates from the dusty brain attic into the belly. The boomers are entering the "fourth quarter," the period of life when we all know the final buzzer is going to sound all too soon. The baby boomers are, then, a bit like the frogs who find themselves in boiling water. Death is no longer an abstraction. We boomers are swimming with the frogs in water far too hot to ignore. Gut denial of the heat is extremely difficult.

The visceral awareness of their not-too-distant personal death could make many boomers see the collective death threat of global warming less abstractly. They are feeling mortality in their bones and bellies. When they read about global warming, the message might resonate strongly in the gut, because boomers are sensitized now to the reality of death, whether personal or collective.

Other factors suggest boomers could play a sparkplug role. Boomers are the generation that cut its teeth on activism. They grew up in the heat of the struggles for civil rights and against Vietnam. They also helped found the modern environmental movement, creating the first Earth Day in 1970. Might it not be a culmination of their own life experience to marshal their activist energies to fight the greatest existential threat the world faces, a kind of cosmic personal and political struggle with death?[2]

Moreover, even though boomers are not a homogeneous generation, the sixties activism sensitized much of the generation to the operations of the ideological apparatus. Millions of boomers learned early that they could not believe official sources when it came to reporting on Vietnam or ideas about racism, capitalism, and the environment. A significant percentage of boomers in their youth saw through the myths of the official propaganda apparatus and thus might be least likely to be taken in by the lies and denial about global warming put out by the coal and oil companies.[3]

As in their student days, the boomers, as they move into retirement, will again have time to devote to social activism. Because they did not have major job responsibilities, the young boomers could devote lots of time to activism; now, in retirement, the same is true. Jimmy Carter, even though of a "senior" generation preceding the boomers, writes of a new concept of retirement that the boomers are inaugurating: one full not of golf carts and bingo but of activist and service-oriented undertakings.[4] Carter's idea is consistent with the views of developmental psychologists such as Erik Erikson that older adulthood is the life stage of "generativity," when even the most self-centered seek to nurture and give back to others.[5] *New York Times* journalist Nicholas Kristof, taking note of this social trend among boomers, calls it "geezers doing good." Citing a poll confirming that one-half of retiring boomers are looking for a new career with "positive social impact," Kristof says, "The bright-eyed idealists are peering through bi-focals."[6]

Although all these factors are encouraging, there are opposite forces. Boomers are least likely to be personally affected by global warming. In the words of one of my boomer friends, when global warming hits hard, "I'll already be dead." This turns the boiled frog metaphor on its generational head. The frogs most likely to act should be the budders, or millennials, the tadpoles whose adulthood is going to be very hot. The boomers may be the closest to their own death but for that very reason are least likely to be personally affected by global warming. The result might be that they are least likely to feel global warming at a gut level. Concerns about their personal death can crowd out fears of a collective death that would hit only later generations.

The boomers are often labeled, fairly or unfairly, as narcissistic. Because warming is unlikely to affect them personally, the more narcissistic boomers would likely ignore it. Moreover, the assaults on their own health and well-being as they age can lead self-oriented boomers to become overwhelmingly focused on themselves. Many boomers are flocking to their doctors' offices, health clubs, cosmetic surgeons, and antiaging specialists rather than to environmental groups battling global warming.

And narcissism may play into boomer tendencies to deny personal death, even as it approaches on cat's feet. Polls show that many boomers are a new breed of death deniers who are attracted to cryonics and longevity movements that promise the possibility of living forever. For these boomers, denial of death may exceed even what Ernest Becker described as life's greatest obsession.[7]

Nonetheless, there are signs that the boomers could be canaries in the global warming mine. For one thing, many leaders of the global warming movement are boomers. Al Gore is a boomer. So is James Hansen, the chief NASA climatologist who is the most outspoken public scientific voice on the urgency of the crisis. So are long-term ecological thinkers and activists such as Paul Hawken and Amory Lovins. Thomas Friedman, the influential *New York Times* columnist and a younger boomer than Gore, is now writing about global warming as the number one problem.

Polling shows that the majority of boomers are green and that many believe in action. The greening of America is not a new agenda to boomers, who have long believed in environmentalism and social transformation. Repeated major polls show that boomers share the broad public view of global warming as an extremely serious threat that humans have helped cause, and they support strong government mandates for restricting dirty fuels, toughening fuel efficiency standards, and using tax incentives to promote wind, solar, and other renewables as well as conservation.[8]

What makes boomers more distinctive, particularly for an aging group, is their dispositions toward action, imprinted for many by the activism of their youth. Studies by sociologists Richard Flacks and Jack Whalen have shown that 1960s protesters have maintained their values over their lifetimes and that many are still labor, peace, or environmental activists as they move into their own fifties and sixties.[9]

Most boomers were never wild protesters in the streets, but they had a belief in their ability to make a difference, a psychological disposition that studies have shown to be a dominant factor affecting how people respond to global warming.[10] The boomers' sense of efficacy is a vital factor in the greening of America, partly because boomers have passed it on to their millennial kids.[11]

Eighty-four percent of boomers say they believe in action on climate change and feel their activism can educate the public and have an impact.[12] Fifty-four percent have participated in an Earth Day event, and 69 percent feel those events have intensified their concern and personal action about warming and other environmental issues.[13] Ninety-two percent report "great confidence" in environmental organizations and recognize that we need major systemic economic and political solutions—rejecting faith that technological change alone can solve the problem, an attitude more often seen among younger Americans.[14]

When it comes to acting to reducing their own carbon footprint, boomers say they are making shifts in their lifestyles. Sixty-four percent of boomers say they have "reduced the amount of energy used in my home," 47 percent have "purchased more energy efficient appliances," 25 percent are "purchasing more locally grown food," and 19 percent have "stopped drinking bottled water." Only 25 percent of boomers say they are doing nothing to help prevent global warming.[15]

The boomers are approaching their own deaths in new ways, including talking about green funerals and recycling their remains to the winds and the oceans. There are reasons to hope that as the boomers age and ponder their own mortality, they will work to prevent collective death and sustain their legacy as a generation that always believed it could save the world.

Gen X: Are the Busters a Bust on Global Warming?

Gen X has gotten a bad rap. Its very name—whether "busters" or Gen X—sounds a sour note. Does Gen X have a real personality—and, if so, where is a name it can be proud of? Pundits have labeled Gen Xers "slackers," "the gap generation," "latch-key kids," and "the generation after."[16] Demographers call them "baby busters" because they are small in numbers compared to the boomers preceding them and the budders who follow: 78 million boomers and 95 to 100 million budders (millennials) dwarf the 50 to 60 million busters.[17]

Gen X is hammered for its pessimism, cynicism, distrust, and caution, all qualities that polls have tended to confirm.[18] The boomers did not want to turn over the world to a younger, less idealistic group, hoarding the good jobs that Gen Xers wanted themselves. So Gen X had to ratchet down its expectations, harboring resentment of boomers and lacking confidence.[19]

When it comes to climate change, busters are being stereotyped unfairly. They are greening along with the rest of Americans, with the majority convinced that warming is occurring and more than one-half persuaded that humans play a role. Moreover, they see global warming as a serious long-term threat and believe that people can do something about it. They are making their own lifestyle shifts to reduce their carbon footprint. Sixty-one percent are reducing home energy use, 32 percent have bought more energy efficient appliances, 23 percent are buying more locally produced food, and 23 percent have stopped drinking bottle water. Only 29 percent of busters say they are doing nothing to lighten their carbon footprint.[20]

The greening of America is thus a rising tide changing the attitudes and lifestyles of all generations. Politicians should take note: Americans of every age are getting it and want both personal and political action on warming now. Nonetheless, it is true that Gen X is moving slower than either boomers or budders to support rapid and comprehensive government intervention, especially if it involves higher taxes. This probably reflects the Xers less idealistic and more cynical approach to politics, exacerbated by Watergate, their growing up under the go-go free-market Reagan years, and their more pessimistic views about personal efficacy and positive social change.[21]

Gen X is also vulnerable to the boiled frog syndrome because its members are old enough to believe that global warming is not going to hit them hard in their own lifetimes. As with George, the frog who swims on unperturbed, global warming is not an emergency to Gen X. This is probably the most important factor differentiating the busters from the budders, who are feeling the heat and are a far brighter shade of green.

Millennials in Heat: Will the Budders Save the Planet and Themselves?

If we take the boiled frog parable seriously, we can hope that 100 million American frogs named Al are set to inherit the earth. The budders are the tadpoles who are feeling the temperature rising fast on their own tender skins. They do not have the luxury of the boomers or busters to see this as another generation's crisis. Climate change is going to hit them hard in their own lifetimes.

The millennials are the first generation in human history whose collective life and well-being will be decisively altered by global warming. The fate of the earth will rest on what the millennials do. There are reasons for hope, because we know a lot already about this generation, and it is greening more rapidly and deeply than its elders. Yet it remains an open question whether global warming truth is churning powerfully enough in their guts to catalyze the ultimate global makeover we need.

The good news is that the millennials have the progressive mind-set and can-do optimism necessary to get the job done. They are a blend of the best of the World War II generation, which Tom Brokaw dubs the "greatest generation," and of the boomers, their parents.[22] They have the altruism, optimism, pragmatism, and willingness to sacrifice of Brokaw's greatest generation. They have the progressive politics, idealism, political engagement, belief in government, and personal sense of efficacy that helped drive the social activism of their boomer parents.[23]

The millennials are the biggest generation in American history, more than 100 million people. Like the boomers, they are destined to have a major impact, if only because of their size. All the positive aspects of their outlook on life will be amplified by the sheer power of numbers. One hundred million progressive can-do politically engaged Americans can create a true greening of America.

The millennials are the most diverse and globally oriented generation in history. Almost 40 percent are minorities, with Latino/as the largest group. This is also a generation that has grown up in a globalizing economy and is evolving from American nationalism to global citizenship. The Internet, globalization, and immigration have changed the American mind-set, with millennials seeing problems and solutions as global and the world as small and interdependent.[24]

This mind-set is just what the doctor ordered for global warming, the ultimate global issue. The extensive polling on millennials, one of the most studied generations in history both by social scientists and marketers seeking to cash in on their preferences, shows that this is the "global warming" generation, swimming with the issue almost since they were placenta in their boomer moms' wombs. They see climate change as real, understand the huge threat it poses, and are already acting on it to change politics and transform America and their own lifestyles.[25]

In 2007, the respected Pew polling agency did a set of comprehensive surveys of the millennial generation. The surveys confirmed how politically engaged and progressive millennials are. Ninety-four percent disapprove of current inequality and poverty levels and support strong government intervention to level the playing field. They fiercely oppose racial and sexual discrimination, and a majority, 54 percent, support gay marriage, far more than in any other generation. They also strongly prefer diplomacy to militarism.[26] These attitudes make them more progressive than any older generation and could help bring the holistic sociopolitical revolution essential to a true greening of America. The Pew poll highlights the bright green focus of the millennials, specifically on the environment and global warming: "They take concern for global warming and the environment as a given. Millennials overwhelmingly believe that the country should do 'whatever it takes' to protect the environment, that stricter environmental laws and regulations are worth the cost and that people should be willing to pay higher prices in order to protect the environment."[27]

The willingness to sacrifice by paying higher prices to protect the environment suggests global warming truth is going to the millennial gut. Unlike older generations, which are not willing to make the same sacrifice, the budders will trade off growth and "stuff" for green ends. In a 2005 Gallop Poll, 58 percent of millennials say that the environment should be given priority "even at the risk of curbing economic growth." Only 32 percent disagree.[28] Among boomers, only 48 percent are willing to oppose more economic growth if global warming requires it, whereas 41 percent oppose it, showing that the boomers feel global warming less in their guts than do the millennials.[29]

The youngest budders, born between 1993 and 2000, show the greatest fear that they could be cooked in their own lifetimes. Eighty percent see climate change as a "very serious problem," 75 percent see it as "a threat to all life on the planet," and 67 percent agree that global warming "is a threat to my future well-being and safety" and "feel afraid of what might happen."[30] By the age of ten, these tadpoles see a horrifying personal threat, but as good millennials, they are optimistic that their generation can lead the political and personal change that will keep everyone from getting boiled.[31]

Mike Farrell, an executive at Youthography, a polling outfit focusing on attitudes of young Americans, says that "younger generations have grown up with recycling and the notion of being green, and they're experiencing the most dramatic effects of global warming we've seen."[32] But, says Farrell, government denial and inaction have left them both angry and motivated to act. Their fear, "coupled with the fact that they feel the government has not taken a leadership role on the environment has left them with a feeling of 'we need to do this, it's our future at stake.'"[33]

About 60 percent of young female millennials and 53 percent of young millennial males say that "taking care of the environment" is the most important issue their generation faces.[34] Their frustration at government paralysis, Farrell adds, "has brought many of them together, and they are starting to show some momentum as a powerful force." But, he also adds, "these attitudes have not reached a mainstream tipping point in terms of real effects on their actual behavior—yet."[35]

Farrell puts his finger on the key point: Scientists tell us we need to take emergency action now, but even the millennials, the generation with the most to lose, have not yet reached the tipping point for emergency action. The budders may be a brighter green than any other generation, but they have yet to show either in their politics or their lifestyle choices the urgency required. Studies show that a gap remains between the changes they believe are necessary and those who actually are changing behavior, whether it comes to lifestyle changes, such as recycling and saving energy at home and in driving, or wholesale economic and political transformation.[36] This gap reflects not only the failure of the emergency to churn strongly enough in their guts but also the absence of any mainstream party that is treating the issue as the existential crisis that it is.

Another problem among millennials is that they may be *too* optimistic, at least when it comes to technology. A majority believes that technology can save us, a higher percent than elder generations.[37] This is a classic American misconception, and it is dangerous because it inhibits the political and economic changes we need.

And despite the broad concern about global warming, young people are not at the critical mass we need, by any stretch of the imagination. At my own university, Boston College, I see many signs of hope. Dedicated students leading sustainability campaigns on campus won top undergraduate prizes for their achievements. They helped build a college sustainability Web site, greened the dining services, have begun to create a garden where students can grow their own food, are encouraging greener buildings on campus, and are politically engaged in national campaigns for politicians who support green agendas. Yet when I went to an end-of-the-year celebration and teach-in on this new green campus movement, a disappointing crowd of less than 100 students showed. Most were out getting a better tan or playing volleyball.

The youth of America give us hope that we might yet stave off the worst. But we need to light a hotter fire under them and under ourselves. This will require, as discussed in the next chapter, taking dead aim at the denial industry that, in the service of short-term profit, is laying the groundwork for long-term disaster.

7

The Denial Regime

Exxon, the GOP, and the Official Doubting Thomases

In 2008 testimony to Congress, NASA's top climate scientist, James Hansen, made a statement that should be debated in every classroom in America: The CEOs of fossil fuel companies *"should be tried for high crimes against humanity and nature."*[1] I was startled when I read this testimony. Had Hansen, an eminent climate scientist, gone bonkers by meditating too much on the dark side of the bell curve? Or was he a pioneer in explaining the new meaning of genocide in the age of global warming?

The truth is that it is hard to exaggerate the immorality of what I call in this chapter "the denial regime." Hansen was telling us that the CEOs making billions of dollars off potentially "runaway global warming" are orchestrating the world's most important disinformation campaign:

> Special interests have blocked transition to our renewable energy future. Instead of moving heavily into renewable energies, fossil companies choose to spread doubt about global warming, as tobacco companies discredited the smoking-cancer link. Methods are sophisticated, including disguised funding to shape school textbook discussions.
>
> CEOs of fossil energy companies know what they are doing and are aware of long-term consequences of continued business as usual. In my opinion, these CEOs should be tried for high crimes against humanity and nature. If their campaigns continue and "succeed" in confusing the public, I anticipate testifying against relevant CEOs in future public trials.[2]

Hansen said that anybody deliberately seeking to deceive the public and prevent action to save human civilization is complicit in global genocide. He was right that the denial narrative is one of the most dangerous propaganda campaigns in the modern world. *Time* magazine's environmental editor, Charles Alexander, agrees that "this will go down as the greatest act of mass denial in history."[3]

The denial regime adds a new twist to the boiled frog syndrome. George, the boiled frog, denies not just because it is so pleasantly and gradually warming but also because the highest officials in frogland have told him everything is fine. In response to Al, the frog who survives by feeling the heat and raising the alarm, George responds, "Chill out, not to worry. I've got it on the highest authority."

What Hansen made clear is that denial—the first and greatest obstacle to solving the global warming crisis—is a matter not just of psychology and timing, as discussed in the last two chapters, but also of a story about how a new political regime has succeeded in reprogramming the truth we believe. Hansen exposed impolitic truth about the pin-striped plutocrats who bankroll denial from the high perches of Exxon-Mobil and other big oil and coal companies.[4] When I first read Hansen's testimony, an image flashed through my mind of the moment when the shamed CEOs of Phillip Morris and the other big tobacco companies were paraded in front of Congress to admit their documented lies about tobacco that had led to the deaths of millions. Suddenly, a group of the most affluent and respected corporate executives, honored speakers at hundreds of the nation's business schools and at official national economic summits, looked like a lineup of gangsters and murderers from *The Sopranos* or *The Godfather.*

The denial regime is actually a triangle of three intertwined groups. The first group contains the big oil, gas, coal, and other mega–fossil fuel companies, led by Exxon-Mobil, that gush multi-billion-dollar quarterly profits—in Exxon's case adding up to $40 billion in 2008, the largest bounty in corporate history—by keeping the public cool about global warming. The second group comprises their political allies in Washington, centered in the Republican Party, who run their own disinformation campaign to justify do-nothing policies. The third group is the intelligentsia of doubting Thomases: the think tanks, policy institutes, and media outlets that offer a scientific patina of respectability for denial. Largely funded by the oil and coal companies, this is the ideological apparatus of the denial regime: the wonks, policy advisers, consultants, lobbyists, and pundits who pedal disinformation from the marbled halls of Congress to the malls of Main Street.

Excellent muckraking journalists have exposed the denial regime, the most important of these muckrakers being Ross Gelbspan, who has written definitive exposés of what I call stage 1 denial.[5] Benefiting from Gelbspan's work, I describe here the more recent evolution toward stage 2 denial—and its aims and current strategies. For the last twenty-five years, the regime has been in stage 1 denial, roughly spanning the era from 1988 to 2008. As I write today, in 2009, it is evolving toward stage 2. This stage appears to represent a very dramatic change, because stage 2 initially involves an acceptance of the reality of global warming and a commitment to act. But a closer examination shows that stage 2 is something quite different from what it appears.

Stage 1: Don't Worry; Be Happy

The Denial Regime: Stage 1

Leaders of regime: big oil and coal companies and the Republican Party
Dates of regime: 1970–2007
Message: Global warming is a hoax perpetrated by liberals, and scientists are deeply divided about whether it exists and whether it is caused by humans.
Motto: Drill, Baby, Drill!

Stage 1 could be called a story of "the two Freds." I feel a personal tie to one of them, Frederick Seitz, the most distinguished scientist in the denial industry, who chaired the National Academy of Sciences from 1962 to 1968 and later became president of Rockefeller University. He was a professor of physics at the University of Illinois from 1949 to 1968, almost exactly the period when my father was a professor of economics and labor relations at the same school. I met Professor Seitz at university events.

I was thus more than startled to learn that Seitz was one of the denier regime's most important scientific leaders. By the early 1990s, Seitz was part of an outlier group of about a dozen scientists who saw global warming as a hoax. Seitz became the head of the George C. Marshall Institute, one of the leading climate think tanks during the last two decades churning out reports and press releases criticizing the IPCC global warming reports as "exaggerating risk—solely, we suspect, to satisfy an ideological objective of excessively constraining the use of energy."[6] Seitz, in fact, like all his denier colleagues, turned out to be an ideologue with a fanatical commitment to allowing market forces to burn unregulated, as I show shortly. But the story begins with Seitz's mantra of stage 1 denial: that there is no scientific consensus and that "therefore it is presumptuous and quite out of order for the IPCC to claim such a consensus when all of the evidence points the other way."[7]

In 1998, Seitz wrote the astonishing and widely cited "Oregon Petition," claiming that "there is no convincing scientific evidence that human release of carbon dioxide, methane, or other greenhouse gasses is causing or will, in the future, cause catastrophic heating of the Earth's Atmosphere." Seitz then went beyond denial. He argued that pumping out more greenhouse gases was actually good for the world: "There is substantial scientific evidence that increases in atmospheric carbon dioxide produce many beneficial effects in the natural plant and animal environments of the Earth."[8] In a later widely circulated letter, misleadingly using the same format and print style of the National Academy of Sciences that Seitz had once led, close Seitz associate and Christian fundamentalist Arthur Robinson waxed exuberantly about the blessings of carbon pollution:[9] "As coal, oil and natural gas are used to feed and lift from poverty mass numbers of people, vast numbers of people cross the globe, more carbon dioxide will be released into the atmosphere. This will help to maintain and improve the health, longevity, prosperity and productivity of all people.... We are living in an increasingly lush environment of plants and animals as a result of the carbon dioxide increase.... This [carbon emissions and global warming] is a wonderful and unexpected gift from the Industrial Revolution."[10]

Like most Americans, I love happy stories with happy endings. But we should be *grateful* for global warming? Having grown up with such respect for Seitz, I did a double take after reading his work and reading about his collaboration with Robinson. Who was this man I thought I knew? It did not take much research to find out. In 1979, Seitz became a paid consultant to huge tobacco giant R. J. Reynolds and worked to "refute the criticism against cigarettes."[11] Seitz headed a tobacco coalition allocating millions of dollars for research that raised doubt about the dangers of smoking and for work with Congress to convince its members not to regulate cigarettes. Seitz personally earned $575,000 in total from Reynolds, a tidy sum even for a university president.[12]

In the early 1990s, Seitz became the head of the Marshall Institute, the think tank that Exxon funded to the tune of at least $715,000 in total from 1995 to 2005.[13] The Marshall Institute asserts that there is no scientific consensus about global warming and that changes in the sun, not greenhouse gases, might be creating warming. Its reports are widely circulated in Washington and became the gospel for the Republican leadership intent on preventing any regulation of oil and coal.[14]

Seitz's well-heeled connection to both the tobacco and oil industry is an important part of the history of stage 1 denial. This connection is also shared by Fred Singer (the second Fred), a climate scientist for many years at the University of Virginia who joined Seitz as a leader in the denial industry and had especially close funding ties to Exxon.[15] Singer told a 2007 conference at the Heartland Institute, a leading denial organization, that "the science is settled in the sense that we have evidence that most of the climate change taking place today is caused by natural forces and not by human activity."[16] This flat denial of the scientific consensus—and Singer's argument that global warming is part of a natural cycle—undercuts any grounds for action.

Singer was the most widely cited and politically active climate scientist in stage 1, and he made no bones about the corporate ideological leaning of the denial regime. Early on, in the 1980s, he openly threw in his lot with tobacco and chemical companies, denying they had complicity in smoking deaths or in depletion of the ozone layer.[17] He founded his own institute, the Competitive Enterprise Institute (a name brazenly advertising Singer's political ideology), funded lavishly by nearly all the oil giants—Exxon, Shell, ARCO, Unocal, and Sun Oil, as well as by bizarre fringe groups such as the Reverend Sun Myung Moon.[18] Singer joined forces with Seitz's Marshall Institute to launch a $5 million disinformation campaign funded by Exxon. In a memo leaked to the press, the campaign aimed "to convince the public that the science of global warming is riddled with controversy and uncertainty." The goal was "raising questions about and undercutting the prevailing scientific wisdom."[19] The plan, hatched by Seitz, Singer, and Exxon at the headquarters of the American Petroleum Institute, had to be scratched because the leaked memo was so damaging, but Singer continued as the most publicized stage 1 denier, targeting IPCC reports as nonsense and quoted widely by laypeople who even today believe there is no global warming problem.[20]

Just as important, Singer, along with Seitz and a third highly credentialed and influential denier, Richard Lindzen, an MIT climate scientist, worked closely with the Republican Party congressional leadership seeking to discredit and defund global warming science and policy initiatives. The GOP leaders included Representatives Tom Delay, Newt Gingrich, and Dana Rohrbacher and the arch-denier, oil-rich Oklahoma's senior senator, James Inhofe, who in 2006 called global warming "the greatest hoax perpetrated on the American people."[21] Rohrbacher, for his part, is famous for his propensity to confuse hydrocarbons and carbohydrates, and both he and Inhofe dismiss the IPCC reports as the kind of nonsense and "bad ideas" to be expected from world government loonies. Rohrbacher and Inhofe have given Seitz, Singer, Lindzen, and the "dirty dozen" or so outlier scientists a national platform for helping them discredit the truth of human-induced global warming.[22] The two Freds, along with Delay, Gingrich, Rohrbacher, and Inhofe, led Congress to denounce the Kyoto agreement, undo funding for climate research, and prevent any limits, regulations, or taxes on oil and coal during the twenty-five years of the stage 1 denial regime, the period critical to human hopes to stave off future disaster.[23]

The stage 1 denial regime reached its final and apocalyptic stage during the George W. Bush administration, when a new president and vice president, both former CEOs of oil companies, were the regime's greatest political allies. The Bush administration was determined to make America the denial nation, the superpower that stood down the rest of the world and repudiated the scientific truth in the name, as Bush spokesperson Ari Fleischer put it, of protecting the American way of life: "The American way of life is a blessed one."[24]

God was on America's side on global warming, as on Iraq and the war on terrorism. Bush's first Environmental Protection Agency (EPA) director, former New Jersey governor Christine Todd Whitman, thought she had Bush's ear, being told in 2001 by Secretary of State Condoleezza Rice and Chief of Staff Andy Card that Bush was ready to regulate greenhouse gases, but from day one Dick Cheney ran the administration's energy and global warming policy. Cheney had made his own classic denial views clear early on, in 2001, when he said that global warming was now just "a big debate" among scientists and that there was not nearly enough evidence "to just sort of run out and try to slap together some policy that's going to 'solve' the problem."[25]

In 2001, as Cheney convened a secret energy summit with big oil and coal to shape the Bush administration's energy policy, the public was already learning that Cheney, a former CEO of Halliburton and still receiving millions from the company in deferred compensation, would be dictating the administration's global environmental and global warming policy. That policy was so radically "denialist" that, according to the *London Observer* on October 31, 2004, it evoked "a rare intervention in world politics" by Queen Elizabeth, who summoned Prime Minister Tony Blair to tell him of "her grave concerns over the White House's stance on global warming."[26]

Cheney, the most important political figure in the stage 1 denial regime, made an end run around Whitman's EPA by deciding that policy about climate change would be made by the White House Council on Environmental Quality (CEQ); that policy would be "enforced" by Karl Rove. The body was so obscure that Bush, when confronted by Whitman about Cheney's and Rove's move, looked blankly and said, "What's CEQ?"[27]

Bush deferred to Cheney, Whitman resigned, and stage 1 denial became the policy of the Bush years, with the administration's complicity so tragic and consequential that Hansen should certainly have included Bush and Cheney, along with oil and coal executives, as regime leaders who should be tried at the Hague for "crimes against humanity." Cheney installed as the head of the CEQ James Connaughton, a former lobbyist for chemical and oil polluters; acting on direct demands from Exxon's chief lobbyist, Randy Randol, Cheney got Connaughton to fire scientists such as Robert Watson, who had chaired the IPCC. This was the beginning of a wholesale purge of government scientists who researched global warming, as well as of a suppression of their reports and a release of official denial statements that legitimated the administration's refusal to sign the Kyoto Accord, failure to endorse any limits or taxes on greenhouse gases, or unwillingness to regulate big oil and coal.[28]

The great chronicler of stage 1 is Ross Gelbspan, a *Boston Globe* and *Washington Post* journalist whose books *The Heat Is On* and *Boiling Point* are required reading on the denial regime.[29] I have met Gelbspan, who lives near Boston College. Before most of us were thinking about global warming, Gelbspan was explaining why most of us were acting just like the boiled frogs the denial regime aimed to produce. Gelbspan concludes that the denial regime won exactly what it wanted. "The goal," Gelbspan says, "was simply to keep the debate going. When the public hears the media report that some scientists believe warming is real but others don't, its reaction is 'Come back and tell us when you're really sure.' So no political action is taken."[30] And no action was.

Stage 2: Drill, Blow, and Shine

> ### Denial Regime: Stage 2
>
> Leaders of regime: big oil and coal companies and the Republican Party
> Dates of regime: 2007–present
> Message: Human-caused global warming exists, but must be solved gradually; we can safely use oil and coal for decades while we phase in renewables.
> Motto: Drill, Blow, and Shine!

On June 19, 2007, Kenneth Cohen, the top global spokesperson for Exxon, announced that the corporation had "evolved" in its understanding of climate change. "We're very much not a denier," Cohen announced. Anticipating new global and American initiatives on global warming, he said, Exxon is now "very much at the table with our sleeves rolled up."[31] We can call this the symbolic date of the denial regime's shift from stage 1 to stage 2.

It seemed quite a change from 2006, when Exxon CEO, Rex Tillerson, had repeated the soothing stage 1 mantra on global warming: "At a minimum there's an enormous amount of uncertainty around this whole question."[32] Yet a year later, the firm claimed that "it never doubted the risk of climate change," an assertion that was probably true but would provide even stronger grounds for the legal case of crimes against humanity against the company, the lead underwriter of the denial regime for the last two decades.

The shift from stage 1 to stage 2 is a transition still in process, and it signals a basic change in the ideology and tactics of the denial regime, though not in its ultimate goals. An important transitional step took place in May 2008 when Exxon announced that "in 2008, we will discontinue contributions to several public policy research groups whose position on climate change could divert attention from the important discussion on how the world will secure the energy required for economic growth in an environmentally responsible manner."[33] The pronouncement that Exxon was now embracing a green identity and a socially responsible posture on global warming, repudiating the denier scientific groups, was a headliner of the new stage 2 regime.

Exxon reported that it would no longer fund the Marshall Institute as well as nine other research and policy groups that had been part of the stage 1 denial regime. The head of Greenpeace, Kent Davies, said, "The organizations eliminated in this latest round of cuts could be called the engine room of the climate skeptic industry."[34] But in a sign of the contradictory colors of stage 2, Exxon continued to fund, according to Greenpeace, "two dozen other organizations who question the science of global warming or attack policies to solve the crisis."[35]

Nonetheless, it is important to recognize the regime change to stage 2, as Exxon begins cutting off funding to denial groups such as the Marshall Institute and officially acknowledges the reality of human-induced climate change. Exxon's shift came only after embarrassing global public pressure. In 2004, as noted, no less a symbol of conservative aristocracy than the queen of England had sounded the alarm about the American denial regime, a sure sign that the stage 1 regime was in trouble and had to change.[36] And the global pressures continued to mount, as the scientific evidence offered by the IPCC kept rolling in and more scientific groups in America and around the world called the debate over.

In 2006, a year before Exxon made the regime change official, the Royal Society, the United Kingdom's most prestigious scientific academy, took the unprecedented step of demanding that Exxon stop funding the Marshall Institute and similar groups that "misrepresented the science of climate change by outright denial of the evidence." The society said that in 2005 Exxon had distributed $2.9 million to denial groups and that "if Rex Tillerson is serious about his company shaking off this shameful legacy, he needs to make a wider sweep."[37]

But even if all of the current "doubting Thomas" groups are defunded by big oil and big coal, the engine room of stage 2 denial will not be eliminated. For one thing, oil and coal companies can turn to more shadowy sources of support, whether private billionaires, antiregulatory free-market zealots, or religious fringe leaders such as Reverend Moon. More importantly, Exxon and other big fossil fuel companies, as well as their GOP allies in Washington, are going to be going ahead full steam with stage 2 denial, even when they are decked out in their bright green corporate social responsibility initiatives and sporting their new watered-down cap-and-trade, market-based climate change policies, likely to be approved with applause in Congress and the White House.

The stage 2 denial regime is made up of the same players as stage 1—spanning big oil and coal, GOP (and many Democratic) political allies in Washington, and a more nuanced cast of scientists, ideologues, wonks, and pundits belching out corporate green clouds of denial. The new denial regime has the same basic goals as well: Keep the short-term profits flowing to the fossil fuel companies while preventing the revolutionary long-term greening of America that would radically transform American capitalism and the "blessed American lifestyle" as we know it.

The ideology and tactics of stage 2, however, are profoundly different from those in stage 1—and potentially can have life-saving unanticipated consequences. For one thing, stage 2 denial acknowledges the truth of human-induced warming. It is still the case that the Web has hundreds of dyed-in-the-wool bloggers-in-denial ranting against the scientific establishment, each offering his or her own interpretation of science or the Bible to show that global warming is not happening or is natural and is even a blessing, a sign that stage 1 is not going to disappear. But as Exxon and the rest of big oil and big coal—and new Republican leadership—move toward stage 2, the world is going to pay less attention to the stage 1 deniers, consigning them to the fate of those who still argue that smoking cannot hurt a smoker.

The official rejection of denial forces the denial regime into a tricky position, as it seeks to prevent the radical changes in our politics and lifestyle necessary to deal with core elements of scientific truth that it now acknowledges. Much of the public continues to languish in stage 1 denial; recall that between 40 and 50 percent of Americans still do not believe that climate change is caused mainly by humans, something that stage 2 deniers now accept. But the persistence of stage 1 in the general public greases the skids of the emerging stage 2 denial regime, giving stage 2 players time to work out the contradictions between acknowledging certain terrifying truths and denying the full consequences that follow upon them.

The secret to stage 2 is to propose lines of action that appear to be credible responses to the truth now officially acknowledged but do not run the risk of hurting big oil and coal companies or toppling the entire capitalist applecart. Among corporate players such as Exxon, the key is to join the pioneering stage 2 big oil companies, many of them European based, such as British Petroleum and Shell, as well as some of the largest U.S. coal companies and electricity utilities, such as GE and Duke Energy, which moved more quickly than Exxon into stage 2 and showed that they might have the key to solving the denial regime's new problems.

British Petroleum was the earliest stage 2 corporate pioneer, moving in the late 1990s toward a different regime. In October 19, 1997, at Stanford, CEO John Browne made a major speech on the dangers of climate change and his firm's response. Drawing on early IPPC reports, Browne said, "There is now an effective consensus among the world's scientists ... that there is a discernible human influence on the climate, and a link between the concentration of carbon dioxide and the increase in temperature."[38] In 1997, that was revolutionary talk, especially from the head of one of the world's biggest oil companies. And Browne said it was time to act: "It would be unwise and dangerous for us to ignore the mounting concern"; the answer was to embark on "a journey taken in partnership by all those involved."[39]

Instead of denial and inaction, British Petroleum called for truth and a green partnership in action. Browne distinguished the right and wrong form of the stage 2 journey. The wrong form, Browne said, "would be drastic ... actions which sought, at a stroke, drastically to restrict carbon emissions or even to ban the use of fossil fuels." The right action would be "a step by step process to develop solutions and continuing research." It would involve "investment to make existing facilities more energy efficient" and "partnerships" to "get the right technology strategy," figuring out the right mix of oil and alternative fuels.[40]

There are three emphases here helping to define stage 2: solutions to climate change through greater efficiency, new technology, and incremental change. But the most revealing development was British Petroleum's decision to change its name to BP, branding itself as "Beyond Petroleum." BP would become the symbol of the greening of the oil industry, a leader in the search for alternative energy. BP's rebranding is corporate "greenwashing," a key strategy by stage 2 energy *and* nonenergy companies in all sectors. An environmental group, Friends of the Earth, defines greenwashing in this humorous vein: "Green*wash: (gren-wôsh) -washers, -washing, -washed 1) The phenomenon of socially and environmentally destructive corporations attempting to preserve and expand their markets by posing as friends of the environment and leaders in the struggle to eradicate poverty. 2) Environmental whitewash. 3) Hogwash."[41]

Friends of the Earth even gives greenwashing Oscars to the worst offenders. The corporate greenwashers—including a majority of global corporations today—proclaim in their mission statements their commitment to fight global warming and show colorful charts in annual reports measuring environmental performance and highlighting a reduced carbon footprint. Green accounting measures, created and monitored by environmental groups and investors, can serve an important function, but in a stage 2 corporate culture, the benefits are outweighed by the propagandistic and deeply misleading conclusions that corporations are our new green saviors. McDonalds and Exxon both sponsor Earth Day and boast of bold green corporate responsibility initiatives, some of which are real. But McDonalds is a leading destroyer of the rainforests to make way for cows and Chickens that will end up as Big Macs and Chicken McNuggets in millions of petroleum-based plastic containers.[42]

The Poland Spring ecoshape bottle says, "A little natural goes a long way," but 80 percent of beverage containers go to landfill. A more nuanced greenwashing is corporations specializing in "ecotourism," which may reduce the carbon footprint of traditional tourism but promotes transoceanic flights that are the most carbon intensive of all human activities, now undertaken by tourists who feel they have absolved themselves and companies that get awards for saving the planet.[43]

Environmental marketing firm Terrachoice did a study that "found that more than 99% of 1,018 common consumer products randomly surveyed for the study were guilty of greenwashing. A total of 1,753 environmental claims made, with some products having more than one, and out of the 1,018 studied only one was found not guilty of making a false or misleading green marketing claim."[44] The most common of six "greenwashing sins" was "the hidden trade-off," a sin found, for example, in "energy-efficient" electronics that contain hazardous materials; 998 products and 57 percent of all environmental claims committed this one.[45]

But let us return now to the core of the energy companies' own deceptive claims of beyond petroleum. Although Browne's speech was a brilliant PR move, and a sneak preview of stage 2 "nondenial denial," BP, in fact, was determined from the first to remain an oil company. Browne made no bones about this in his 1997 talk. After going through his sustainability initiatives, Browne made clear that, despite the rise of renewables, "the oil industry is going to remain the world's predominant supplier of energy.... Alternatives will take a greater share of the energy market as we go into the next century. *But let me be clear. That is not instead of oil and gas. It is additional.*"[46] In other worlds, oil was not going the way of the dinosaur. As long as there was oil anywhere, BP would pump it. Stage 2 means shine, yes, but drill, too. The new message is this: We want to go solar but keep gushing oil profits. The new denial, cleverly concealed in the beyond petroleum brand, asserts that there is no need to drastically cut back on oil now.

BP's Greenwashing became painfully apparent on July 7, 2009, when BP shut down its Alternative Energy Business and confirmed it would focus on oil. BP's new CEO, Tony Hayward, pronounced that "oil and gas are in the company's DNA." He said that when he took over "too many people were trying to save the world.... " BP would follow its DNA and make money for its shareholders from oil and gas. As *Financial Times* journalist, Ed Crooks, wrote, "Yet having led the charge, BP is now leading the retreat. When the world does move beyond fossil fuels, neither BP nor any other big oil company is likely to be in the vanguard."[47]

Its nondenial denial colors all the stage 2 oil and gas giants. In 2007, General Electric and Duke Energy, both leading electricity producers, brought together a group of oil and coal giants in the U.S. Climate Action Partnership, a corporate umbrella lobbying group leading the stage 2 charge. These partners embrace the new message of Shell's president, John Hofmeister: "From Shell's point of view, the debate is over. When 98% of scientists agree, who is Shell to say 'Let's debate the science'?"[48]

Let nobody doubt that this is regime change—and a mind-bending change, especially when combined with big oil and coal's new coordinated advocacy of national carbon regulation and a low-carbon future. The devil, however, is always in the details. Duke CEO James Rogers, a leader in the stage 2 regime shift, gave a major speech at MIT in 2008 headlined "Coal not going away."[49] Rogers argued for new cap-and-trade policies to move us toward a low-carbon world. But Duke produces 90 percent of its electricity by burning coal and nuclear, and Rogers boldly claimed that "coal is not a four letter word."[50] Duke would support efficiencies, market-based regulations, and a heavy new emphasis on technology, including sequestration to capture and store coal-burning carbon emissions. "I think the technology can do it," said Rogers, emphasizing the need for a cautious transition blending traditional and new energies.[51]

Rogers highlighted here the stage 2 headlines: The debate is over; global warming is real; we need a low-carbon world; we support national market-based regulation; we need efficiencies; technology will get us there. And the punch line is this: Drill, blow, and shine. We will support wind and solar, but let us get real; those can come online only slowly and cannot do the job on their own. As long as there is coal, it will be a big part of the low-carbon future (and of Duke Energy's profits).

Here, CEO Rogers sounds like Mr. Rogers, the legendary star of happy television programming for kids. Big coal and the kids of the future will live harmoniously together in a healthy green world, with clean coal and windmills firing up the energy grids of the future. The nondenial denial: We do not need to cut back drastically on coal or oil now. This Mr. Rogers approach is what Van Jones, a prominent environmental activist, Obama advisor, and author, calls "Dirty Green"—talking green but walking the other way, keeping one's eye focused on the prize (oil and coal profits now).

In 2008, the CEO of ConocoPhillips, Jim Mulva, gave the same stage 2 dirty green pitch at a big gathering of environmental and energy leaders. Mulva made a forceful argument for confronting the truth of global warming, for developing new energy sources, and for instituting cap-and-trade market regulation. But Mulva also emphasized that "we need to realistically educate the public on a simple fact—that it will take years to develop alternative sources at the scale required for sustainable economics." Big oil is here to stay—so says Conoco, a leader in the stage 2 nondenial denial of the need for immediate and drastic cutbacks of production and use of oil and coal.[52]

At the heart of stage 2 denial is rejection of the truth of a crisis requiring immediate and drastic change. We can define stage 2 as accepting the scientific consensus on a cognitive level, but denying the gut truth that will propel the all-out action we need now.

Meanwhile, the political allies of oil and coal were beginning to embrace the new official stage 2 nondenial denial. In 2006, as GE and Duke Energy were launching with great fanfare their new Climate Action Partnership, pressing for regulatory hearings in which their own voices would be heard and their own interests duly protected, Republican leaders in Washington had to take note. These were the guys who paid their campaign bills.

The Republicans, long wedded to a vehement stage 1 denial and even more zealous than the fossil fuel companies in their antiscience and antiregulation ideologies, are in the earliest stages of transition to stage 2. As GE, Duke, and Exxon officially pronounced that human-induced global warming is the real thing, a few leading Republican senators, including Lindsay Graham of South Carolina, Mike DeWine of Ohio, and Pete Domenici of New Mexico, began to talk about the reality of global warming and the need for clean energy. Although generally espousing voluntary greenhouse cutbacks, along with support for greater efficiency and technological innovation, a few supported mandates, usually of the cap-and-trade market-driven variety favored by the energy companies. John McCain, the most important congressional convert to stage 2, joined with Democrats to sponsor legislation to limit carbon emissions and, in the face of Republican opposition, said that he would "make the Senate keep on voting and voting and voting"—and "in time we will win."[53]

But John McCain kept flip-flopping, especially in the several years leading to the 2008 election, revealing the unstable, still evolving, and still distressing story line of stage 2 Republicans. McCain's initial acceptance of global warming was the political equivalent for Republicans of Exxon's conversion for corporations—an important, regime-changing break from the denial regime of the past twenty-five years. Most of his fellow Republicans still languished in stage 1—and many still do today. In this respect, McCain's claim of "maverick" could initially pass more than the laugh test; it was a shot at the heart of Republican orthodoxy.

But as he moved into high gear for the presidential race, the shaky status and weaknesses of stage 2 became clear, even for the self-proclaimed maverick. His campaign Web site continued to include discussion of global warming and the need for a new energy approach. Most importantly, he continued to support rhetorically the need for clean energy and for mandatory cap-and-trade regulations on carbon emissions, supporting a 60 percent reduction in carbon emissions by 2050 (a huge break from Bush but well short of the 80–90 percent reductions needed by 2030 according to IPCC projections).

In the heat of a campaign year, however, McCain slid drastically back toward stage 1, keeping only visuals of wind turbines and claims of a Teddy Roosevelt reverence for conservation. In 2008, he voted against important tax credits for renewables, including wind and solar, and opposed tougher auto efficiency standards. As the campaign heated up, along with the Gulf storms lashing New Orleans and South Florida, McCain did not go back and start drinking the Kool-Aid of stage 1 denial. He continued on paper to acknowledge the reality and dangers of global warming. But in his speeches, which were increasingly filled with talk about energy and oil, as prices at the pump shot up to more than $4 a gallon, there was little evidence that this was a man worried about climate change. The campaign slipped between stages 1 and 2, proclaiming the need for a post-Bush clean energy and conservation approach while supporting policies that only a shareholder in Exxon could love.[54]

McCain proclaimed that he believed in energy independence using all sources of energy—oil and coal, wind, and solar. His campaign wrapped itself in the stage 2 corporate green mantra: Drill, blow, and shine. This was, of course, the classic stage 2 nondenial denial of global warming: Global warming is real, but, heck, there is no danger in burning lots more oil and coal now.

McCain then slid back further. He chose a vice president nominee, Sarah Palin, who did not believe in human-induced global warming, an overt stage 1 denier. And at the GOP convention at St. Paul in September 2008, McCain's main theme—beyond his war hero biography show—was drilling to lower gas prices and secure energy independence. It was red meat for the delegates, bringing these rabid conservatives to their feet. They shouted in unison for several minutes, "Drill, Baby, Drill; Drill, Baby, Drill; Drill, Baby Drill."

Drill, Baby, Drill is back to stage 1 denial, where most conservatives still live. Sarah Palin rises as a leading new face in the Republican Party, making clear that the elephant will be, for some time, very pale green. We should welcome the many Republicans who join the green revolution but must fight against and overcome the blind deniers in the Palin crowd, who are likely to resist to the bitter end.

But stage 2 now reigns. If the new denial succeeds, civilization will be destroyed in the name of green incremental reform.

PART II

How to Green America

8

Good Timing

Economic Meltdown and Regime Change at Home

This chapter is coauthored with Yale Magrass

There are two complementary paths for mobilizing our short-term society to address our long-term climate crisis. One—a frontal attack—is to mobilize and join the Americans who have short-term worries but still are long-term thinkers. They may be a minority, but because global warming is the biggest challenge humans have ever faced, millions of visionaries are already acting to stop it now. It is striking how much has been done so quickly. Global warming has become a core concern of millions of ordinary people,[1] activists, and policy leaders in the United States at the local and state as well as national levels and around the world. Their actions will continue to grow rapidly and rattle the fossil fuel regime. If there is a future, generations to come may look back and burn incense in gratitude to these green visionaries who helped save the world.

But because of the short-term thinking of the majority, the frontal long-term attack is insufficient in itself as a path for mobilization. It must be accompanied by a second path—a "time-tricking" strategy that seeks to solve the long-term crisis by hitching a ride on the back of short-term issues now churning the guts of the majority of Americans. The time-tricking strategy is based on solutions to global warming that not only ward off the long-term catastrophe but also help solve today's most burning crises: economic deep recession, vanishing jobs, unstable oil prices, energy dependence, Middle East wars, rotten education, deteriorating public infrastructure, poverty, and financial insecurity (all discussed in Chapter 12). Time-tricking redefines time by eliminating the pathological ways in which we think about it short and long term. Fortunately, the time-tricking strategy can have a dramatic effect because many things we should do now to deal with global warming long term—both on the personal and political levels—are just the medicine that a smart doctor would prescribe for today's crises, offering hope for dealing with long-term climate change in a nearsighted society.

This strategy is not just a theoretical possibility. With the perfect storm of the economic meltdown and the election of Barack Obama as president, we are already seeing the initial framing of a multi-issue time-tricking change model in the United States. Although this book is being written in the earliest stage of Obama's presidency, he has already defined the wave of change he plans to promote as a politics linking responses to the meltdown and other short- to mid-term problems, such as energy dependency and U.S. global economic competitiveness, with shifts toward a long-term green society.[2]

Now there are many slips between cup and lip. Obama could renege on his promises or be blocked in implementing them. Enormous structural obstacles lock America into a purely short-term model, and hugely powerful interests will resist a shift from a fossil fuel order. Moreover, Obama's politics does not go far or fast enough to save us. In the chapters that follow, I look at the time-tricking green vision and strategy and the contending forces that will likely shape the outcome of Obama's presidency and the prospects for a new greening of America.

The key to and measure of success are a regime change at home from our current fossil fuel corporate order to what I call a "green regime." The rest of this chapter discusses what is meant by a U.S. "regime" and why the United States may be ripe for a regime shift from greed to green.[3] It will require great change in our capitalist system, leading toward a sustainable order with many market aspects but qualitatively different from capitalism as we know it today. The next two chapters look at what that new economy and regime will look like, and following chapters look at Obama and his prospects for slaying the dragons blocking the gates of regime change as well as the grassroots social movements that can help him do so. In the end, all will come down to what we do to transform our own society and lifestyles.

Regimes: A Brief History of Corporate Systems and the Unsustainable Life

Two things are propelling us toward a possible green regime change at home. One is the weakening of the existing U.S. fossil fuel corporate regime, which sometimes seems to be melting down faster than the Arctic icecaps. The second is the need to save humanity from global warming, one of the biggest moral obligations any generation has ever faced. Together, they are giving rise for the first time to a green change strategy that intertwines short-term and long-term solutions in a green DNA chain and tricks time.

Regimes are the architecture of our political house. They involve the ownership and governance of our dominant institutions, our social contract, and guiding ideology or way of thinking. When they change, as in 1932 with the election of Franklin Roosevelt and in 1980 with the election of Ronald Reagan, they are like earthquakes shifting the ground under our feet and creating a new future. They can create change for better or for worse.

Recall the Russian dolls, or *matryoshkas,* discussed in the Introduction. Each regime can be seen as a large societal doll with a different shape or structure. By creating rules and boundaries about how and where each of us live, get to work, pursue our dreams, and meet our daily needs, these structures dictate much of what we small individual dolls do. Corporate regimes during the last century have shaped the carbon-intensive system of highways, gas-guzzling cars, suburban sprawl, and big energy-inefficient homes, office buildings, and shopping malls that, while offering us creature comforts, narrow down our lifestyle choices and lead us toward ecological disaster.

Throughout much of U.S. history, our country has been governed by various corporate regimes, all ruled by giant corporations allied with corporate-funded presidents. Since the end of the Civil War, we have had five U.S. regimes (and thus four regime changes at home).

American Regimes

1865–1900: the first corporate regime
1901–1921: the progressive regime
1921–1933: the second corporate regime
1933–1980: the New Deal regime
1981–present: the third corporate regime

We live today in the third corporate regime. It follows the 1890s Gilded Age first corporate regime and the 1920s Hooverist second corporate regime. Industrialism unleashed a new dirty fuel economic system several centuries ago, and today's corporate regime brought that system to its extreme conclusion: turbocharged and lethal doses of fossil fuel energy and fossil fuel politics. Fossil fuel power in both senses is the Achilles heel of the system, as the energy base becomes too expensive and environmentally dangerous, big oil and big coal too influential, and the entire system addicted to the militarism needed to ensure access to Middle East oil.[4] Each successive regime has deepened the population's dependency on carbon-intensive, gas-guzzling automobiles; suburbia; and the malls.

Corporate regimes over time have enhanced our sense of freedom and created certain forms of environmental protection, even while creating an unsustainable American life. In the Gilded Age first corporate regime, life was short, brutal, and coal-black. The regime was built on government policy after the Civil War that granted large tracts of land to the railroads.[5] The government and railroad companies removed Indians and buffalo and encouraged restless Americans to hop the rails and settle in unsustainable mining towns. When the mines failed, settlers got on the rails again and moved westward, leaving scarred ghost towns. The railroads made money but left a despoiled landscape.

The frontier mentality at the heart of the first corporate regime was anything but green. The railroad barons, along with a rising Wall Street, helped finance the dream of the yeoman farmer taming the wilderness. Americans could settle on their own free land, and if they used up the water or topsoil, they could get back on the rails, settle more land, or prospect for gold. The idea of infinite land that we could use up and then move on became part of a culture of conquest and disposal, ultimately creating unsustainable development in the western United States marked by extinct species, eroded soil, giant dust bowls, and, now, vast water shortages. In the East, while the railroads were building westward, John D. Rockefeller, Andrew Carnegie, and J. P. Morgan were inventing the modern industrial corporation and financial system, based on oil, steel, and fast money.[6] The robber barons exploited immigrant workers in dirty and disposable jobs while offering the nation a shimmering model of fast wealth and a glimmer of the new twentieth-century consumerist dream.

The seductive but unsustainable culture of consumerism took a giant step forward in the short but spectacularly flamboyant second corporate regime of the 1920s. Corporations began to take a scientific approach to structuring the consumer society, honing their skills as commercial propagandists and Madison Avenue salesmen. Led by propaganda experts such as Edward Bernays,[7] the father of "public relations," who succeeded in selling bacon by paying physicians to testify about its health benefits, advertisers created a fevered desire for corporate-produced goods once made at home. Advertising evolved as an industry to create desire for things not needed. Rural folk looked forward to the Sears and Montgomery Ward catalogs for the "latest fashions," and new credit and installment plans encouraged people to buy cars, radios, and refrigerators they could not afford.[8]

The second corporate regime's financial system created our now familiar easy credit, fast profits, and leveraged debt. The madcap consumer life of the "roaring twenties" was fueled not only by Madison Avenue's growing sophistication but also by the stock market's irrational exuberance and easy credit, speeding up the frenzied pace of life enjoyed by returning soldiers ready to spend on themselves and their newly liberated dancing partners— wearing lipstick, smoking, wearing short skirts, and doing the swing and the Charleston.[9] Meanwhile, Henry Ford was hiring and paying workers $5 a day so they could buy creature comforts and speed around in the fast new world of the automobile.[10] Cheaper goods and easy credit all drove the nation toward economic and environmental excess. The second corporate regime shifted America definitively from self-reliance and toward a seductive corporate dependency and an unsustainable carbon-intensive consumerism, all in the name of freedom to move, buy, get rich, and be happy. As I show in the next chapter, the 1920s shift toward a "coerced" consumer culture driven by advertising and fueled by unsustainable debt reflected contradictions in capitalism that have now brought us toward the edge of intertwined economic and environmental disaster.

Life in the Roaring Twenties was good, but the stock market crash showed that life was economically unsustainable (the growing environmental unsustainability remained largely invisible). There was nothing lucky or pretty about the 1929 crash and subsequent Great Depression, but the silver lining was that they made possible the best regime in U.S. history. The New Deal was a new regime emerging with FDR's election in 1932. This regime provided jobs for millions of unemployed workers; built infrastructure of trains, roads, and dams; created new regulation of Wall Street that prevented excess speculation; offered relief to homeowners threatened by foreclosure; and created a public energy complex, such as the Tennessee Valley Authority (TVA), that could deliver affordable electricity. The Civilian Conservation Corps (CCC) and the TVA were the greenest and most popular parts of the New Deal, with the former planting 3 billion new trees and the latter providing renewable hydropower for the long term while also immediately stimulating job growth and economic development for a huge impoverished region of the country.[11]

While working on the short-term crises, the New Deal regime put in place long-term new rules of the road. They restrained the huge power of corporations, gave rise to labor unions, and created new regulations and ownership that would transform America and secure the middle class for the next fifty years.[12] The Depression created deep changes in the American mind-set, as the corporate greed of the 1920s gave way in the 1930s to greater worker and neighborhood solidarity (where neighbors got together to block sheriffs from evicting their neighbors) and populist anger rooted in shared suffering and need. Regime change thinking and activism arose from the most basic need: survival. But the New Deal had many political and environmental contradictions, because it sought to save capitalism from itself by encouraging wealth distribution and economic recovery through state investment and mass consumption. The New Deal demonstrated that short-term and long-term solutions can be married together, but it is also a cautionary tale about the power of corporate resistance and the environmental dangers of Keynesian liberalism.

The New Deal embraced a new role for governments and new limits on corporations. Following the theories of the great British economist John Maynard Keynes,[13] who showed that massive government spending and investment could pump up the economy and make up for the collapse of consumer spending, Franklin Roosevelt was ready to spend billions. But the New Deal era, which lasted from 1933 to Ronald Reagan's election in 1980, although helping workers and building a middle class, also saved corporations and helped enshrine the fossil fuel lifestyle they had begun to shape.

New Deal planners had no idea about the climate crisis to come and promoted policies that, tragically, would help lock into place an environmentally unsustainable American life. The New Deal moved through an evolution from pure "butter" Keynesianism (1933–1939) to "guns and butter" Keynesianism (1939–1970s).[14] Ironically, New Deal spending, especially in the latter stage, catapulted America decisively into the carbon-intensive world of highways, cars, and suburbs.

In the butter phase, when the government spent about $40 billion, it invested in the greenish TVA and CCC but also in not-so-green "highways to provide construction jobs for the unemployed and to stimulate the economy by increasing demands for automobiles."[15] But the real shift toward America's unsustainable life came in the guns and butter approach adopted by FDR with the onset of World War II (government spending was $259 billion between 1939 and 1945).[16] This huge pump-priming rebooted the economy with a bang. But when President Harry Truman and then President Dwight Eisenhower took over after World War II, their version of guns and butter—massive state spending justified for fighting the cold war—became a huge and decisive step in creating the unsustainable American life.

The most important environmental policy was Eisenhower's massive funding of the interstate highway system begun in the mid-1950s[17] that put the United States literally on the road to disastrous unsustainability. Ike promoted the highway system as part of a defense project, but it was a backdoor strategy of military Keynesianism for boosting the domestic economy and the profits of the construction and auto giants. Eisenhower's defense secretary, Charles Wilson, had been CEO of General Motors, famously claiming that "what's good for General Motors is good for the country."[18]

In the early butter stage, FDR promoted the earliest phases of the suburbanization of America, building "bedroom suburbs" such as Greenbelt, Maryland, and in 1934 creating the Federal Housing Administration, which financed housing only with "suburban densities."[19] This paved the way for the Levittown suburban boom of the 1950s,[20] which was financed by the Eisenhower administration as the lynchpin of the American Dream for veterans and the postwar middle class. The 1950s guns and butter model drove America at top speed into the fossil fuel world of highways, cars, and suburbs.

This result represents the ironic and tragically contradictory dimension of the New Deal. It created jobs, labor unions, and a social security and welfare system protecting ordinary Americans, but it also promoted corporate profits in Detroit, Texas, and Wall Street, laying down the infrastructure of the unsustainable American life. Here we see a serious environmental problem inherent in Keynesian liberalism: It promoted not only the freeway/suburban complex but also a broader corporate-sponsored "gospel of consumerism." And this liberalism promoted a model of work—today it has become extreme and often forces overwork—that restricts people's abilities to share work or to work shorter hours and to opt out of a vicious spiral of work more, consume more, enjoy less.

I discuss the crucial issue of work hours more in Chapter 11, but I want to note here that in the early 1930s unions fought for a thirty-hour workweek and that on April 6, 1933, the Senate passed the Black-Connery bill to make the workweek thirty hours; the bill was supported strongly by William Green, head of the American Federation of Labor, as a way to help reduce unemployment. But corporations fought back, arguing that rather than reducing work hours, the better way to fight unemployment was to induce more consumer spending. FDR compromised by standardizing a forty-hour workweek,[21] with benefits and government jobs tied to fixed, longer hours than unions had demanded. FDR created millions of essential jobs—a major victory for workers and the public interest—but in rejecting labor demands for reduced hours and for benefits for part-time work, he unwittingly laid the foundation for a future American work more–consume more treadmill corrosive of human happiness and the environment.[22]

The New Deal ended in 1980 with the election of Ronald Reagan, who ushered in the third corporate regime. The new regime dismantled the best features of the New Deal while intensifying the worst. It dismantled the regulations and social welfare system protecting the public and broke up the unions protecting workers and their jobs, which were now being outsourced and downsized.[23] Workers who kept jobs were forced either into overwork and compensatory excess consumption or into degraded part-time jobs with low pay, no job security, and no benefits. Corporations themselves, new global giants, took new decisive control of Washington as the World Trade Organization and International Monetary Fund shaped globalization in a corporate mold.

At the same time, the third corporate regime took the auto-suburban-highway life to new extremes. Autos became bigger gas-guzzlers, with two- or three-car garages in four-bedroom houses made to store ever more "stuff" zoned for 1 acre lots or larger. Highways became horribly congested freeways, with government policies starving public transportation and subsidizing even more highways as the only way to get people to work and home.

Sprawl created exurbs, which meant longer daily commutes on bigger and more congested freeways, with cars burning more carbon. The exurb became the latest manifestation of an unsustainable frontier mentality.

The third corporate regime also turned increasingly to a more heavily guns-oriented military Keynesianism. The butter to people in the form of social welfare was reduced, although government policies to subsidize the freeway exurban frontier proceeded apace and Reagan deregulated Wall Street again and unleashed the junk bonds and speculative finance that led to both economic and environmental unsustainability. Reagan also increased butter to the corporations, increasing corporate welfare to hundreds of billions of dollars a year.

Military Keynesianism became the signature of the Reagan Revolution and the hegemonic third corporate regime. Reagan spent billions to bankrupt the Soviet Union and to fight wars on the ground and from the sky that were deadly *and* acutely carbon intensive. Journalist Tom Friedman writes of a new "green military,"[24] with the Pentagon touting its carbon-reducing technologies and clean high-tech weapons. But even with new greener high-tech wars, contemporary warfare—built on the wings of Boeing—burns more carbon than most other publicly subsidized corporate enterprises. Militarism is the great destroyer of people and the environment.

The world's military forces are responsible for the release of more than two-thirds of the CFC-113 into the ozone layer. During the cold war, the U.S. and Soviet armed forces produced enormous amounts of hazardous wastes. As a result of naval accidents, there are at least fifty nuclear warheads and eleven nuclear reactors littering the ocean floor. There are more nuclear reactors at sea than on land. The Pentagon generates five times more toxins than the five major U.S. chemical companies combined. The U.S. military is the largest single source of U.S. environmental pollution.[25]

Green Regime Change:
The Good Timing of Very Bad News?

Death by global warming is the ultimate fate of the system should we continue to try propping up the third corporate regime, but a variety of near-term problems may sink it sooner. These short-term problems are weakening the regime and could rapidly bring it down, sparing it from the cosmic tribulation that unmitigated climate change would unleash.

The regime has been declining for at least a decade for many reasons: overexpansion in the pursuit of Middle East oil; ever-greater reliance on more costly oil to support the auto-highway-suburban-exurban life; rampant financial speculation on Wall Street; loose credit and debt in government and households; a failed war in Iraq; a hollowing out of U.S. bridges, sewer systems, roads, and other infrastructure; a slow bleeding of the middle class as jobs outsource, wages fall, and pensions and health care erode; and a corruption of a corporate elite focused on its own short-term benefits at the expense of its own long-term interests and survival. A major regime disruption came in September 2008, when Wall Street seized up in the worst financial crisis since the Great Depression. On September 28, 2008, the Dow crashed, losing 777 points and spelling doom for the current regime.[26] As the Wall Street firms became an endangered species, the disappearance of the capitalist elite that had once looked after the long-term interests of the system became obvious. Every CEO tried to jump ship with a golden parachute.

The number 777 signals the disastrous loss of $1.2 trillion in a single day but also symbolizes the possible good timing of some very bad news. The very bad news: For Wall Street and millions of people on Main Street, September 28 was one of the worst days ever, wiping out retirement nest eggs, freezing credit for daily living and investment, threatening millions of Americans with foreclosure of their mortgages, and portending to bring down the entire economy. Pundits speculated this was 1929 all over again.[27] The possible good timing: The economic meltdown in 2008 may mean a green shift in our power system and way of thinking that will cure current ailments while giving us a fighting chance to save ourselves from climate change. As with the Great Depression, the new meltdown has created a collapse of trust in the ruling authorities and an openness to new thinking and politics that historically propels regime change. With green regime change, the unsustainable life could be reversed by the same policies required to save the economy.

Of course, the meltdown is going to create problems as well as opportunities for a green agenda. People may regard climate change as one of many distractions and put it way down on the national to-do list. Ordinary citizens are the first to recognize the economic meltdown as a tragedy, as it has depleted their own savings and 401(k)s (now jokingly called 201[k]s, worth half as much as the 401[k]s), a stomach-churning source of anxiety.

As the meltdown developed, green thinkers realistically worried that green initiatives would be put on the back burner. Plans to fund clean energy, retrofit houses and offices, and subsidize electric cars are now too expensive, say many politicians, both in the United States and Europe. Congress began to scale back green clean energy subsidies and cap-and-trade schemes as too costly, and deniers such as Senator James Inhofe rejoiced this was not the time to go on green goose chases. The financial meltdown could create terrifying setbacks in timing, because the public is pale green and not sufficiently worried about global warming to force leaders to carry out a green bailout right now.

Even in Europe, where the public feels much more strongly about climate change, there is no guarantee the bailout will be green. In late 2008, Italian, German, and Polish leaders said it might be too expensive to introduce climate change initiatives during Europe's own financial crisis. This led European Commission president José Manuel Barroso to express alarm that the financial crisis "could be the end of the global [warming] effort. This is not a luxury," Barroso argued, "we now have to forgo. Saving the planet is not an after-dinner drink, a 'digestif' that you take or leave. Climate change does not disappear because of the financial crisis."[28]

Barroso is right. We should be very worried that the crisis may not turn the United States or Europe green—or green enough. The optimistic strategy outlined here and in following chapters is far from a done deal. The financial meltdown could help melt the icecaps faster rather than help save them.

But there is also reason for optimism. The green agenda and a great green bailout are, despite some short-term costs, the best strategy for dealing with the economic crisis and will become a crucial part of a sustainable economic recovery program—if we the people fight our hearts out for it. If regime change is blocked for some time at the national level, it can ripple up from innovative players at the local, state, and regional levels who have already broken from some corporate regime policies and are moving us toward a new era. History may record our economic meltdown as a tragedy and as a disguised blessing. If we are lucky, it will be viewed as the meltdown that helped to save future generations.

Green Greek Theater: The Chorus in the Money Pit

Even without complete regime change, it is more probable than not that we will be moving toward a greener society over time. This movement must go beyond what Thomas Friedman calls our current "green party,"[29] all the little green logos, mission statements, and recycling bins that cause us to feel good but are doing little to save us from global warming. Green regime change—what we really need—is a rare systemic power shift, and like most regime changes, it will feel turbulent and disruptive, not celebratory. It will not feel good much of the time, and it will bring costs and dangers. But it has the virtue of tricking time by marrying short- and long-term initiatives to help solve one of our greatest problems.

At the heart of a green regime change is a shift in systemic power, both in energy and in politics. This shift is becoming possible now because the "greed is good" regime is creating such severe problems for ordinary Americans. A regime change struggle will have to go on at every level, from local to national to global. We will have to answer three questions: What does a green regime look like? How will it come into being? Can we build it fast enough? I answer these questions in the next few chapters, and one way to begin is to imagine a "green Greek theater."

In ancient Greek theater, dramas helped publics explore and struggle with impending tragedies. There was always a chorus in the drama and often an oracle, as well as other characters. The oracle foresaw the future and warned of tragedies the gods could visit on the people if they did not act, often against corrupt rulers. The chorus reflected all the anxieties and desires of a public faced with moral and political challenges of cosmic import.

An updated American version would illustrate the epic struggle the American public faces as scientists and activists speak of the need to confront global warming and the current corrupt regime. The story would show the ways in which short- and long-term crises are blending to help move an agitated, angry, and struggling public on its first tentative steps toward green regime change.

The Characters and Setting

Greed Rulers: the CEOs of our current corporate regime and their political allies in Washington
Oracle: the climate change scientist who foretells the future of our species in a world of unmitigated global warming
Green Activists: the members of social movements (including labor, peace, and environmental groups) seeking to educate and lead the public to stop global warming, end social injustice, and create a new green regime
Chorus: the American public beset by short- and long-term crises
American House: the current American corporate regime
Green House: the green regime
Date: 2009 in America during the Great Recession and an age of warming

The Play

GREED RULERS: Thank the gods for our great American house. It is the best house ever built on the planet—and the best that ever will be built.

CHORUS: Yes, we love our great American house. We love our houses in the suburbs and exurbs. And we have trusted you, our rulers, for years. But now you have gambled our money away and we are paying the bill. We can't even pay for our heating bill this winter to heat our own house, and we can't afford to fill up the tank on our SUV.

GREED RULERS: Things will settle down—America has the energy and grit we need to fix these problems. We have always had problems—and our national house and great free market always fix them. That makes our country great.

CHORUS: We are losing faith. We can't pay our mortgage. We have no health care. We are afraid of losing our houses and our jobs, and it's too expensive at the pump.

ORACLE: Hear me! Your problems are great, but they are just the beginning. Throw the Greed Rulers out, and trade in your exurban house and SUV fast. I see a future Hell of drought, floods, fire, and storms—all bred by global warming and short-term unfettered corporate greed and your own suburban lifestyle—destroying your children and your children's children.

CHORUS: Enough with your global warming fears. We have more immediate worries. But we are beginning to hate our Greed Rulers. We love our children. But, Oracle, we can't keep our heads above water today, so how can we think about the floods tomorrow?

GREED RULERS: Drill, baby, drill,[30] and we'll get you those cheaper pump prices and better jobs today that will keep paying for those wonderful big suburban homes.

CHORUS: That sounds good to us. We can't afford the price at the pump, and we can't afford to lose our jobs or homes; that's certain.

GREEN ACTIVISTS: Watch what the Greed Rulers are doing, not what they are saying. Their oil and coal will become more superexpensive as they deplete it. They will outsource your jobs and shutter more failing companies. They will be laughing all the way to the bank with the sky high prices and subsidies their friends in Washington are giving them.

GREED RULERS: The greenies are scaring you. We will get you back on the road in your SUV or your hybrid and home safe to your exurb on even faster freeways. You choose. And the economy will recover.

CHORUS: That sounds good, Greed Rulers. But our national house is a money pit. Our bridges are falling down. Our jobs are going overseas. Our mortgages are going up. Our wages are going down. Our commutes are getting longer. We keep borrowing more to get less.

GREED RULERS: Yes, because government is stealing your taxes and sapping our economy. We will invest to fix the national house if you'll take the government off our back and trust in us and in our free enterprise system again.

CHORUS: You ran up your own debts by gambling on and leveraging our mortgages, mutual funds, and pensions, and now you're asking for bailouts from us, your victims. We don't trust you anymore. We are mad as Zeus and won't take it anymore.

GREEN ACTIVISTS: Now you're waking up. How can you listen to big oil and big coal? They are on big-time corporate welfare, socialism for the rich. You're being left to fend for yourselves.

CHORUS: We do want them to pay for their crimes, but we need the gas. We want to drill, because we just want to go back to our big houses and big cars and Wal-mart stores and wonderful malls that have made us free and great.

GREED RULERS: Give us the tax breaks and subsidies, and we will innovate and create clean coal, cheaper oil, and renewables, too. We will bring you back to your American Dream.

CHORUS: We want that, Greed Rulers. We want that. But we truly feel like Tom Hanks and Shelley Long in America's new money pit.[31] Every day, another room or appliance or wiring in our national house gets flooded, breaks down, or burns up. We are running out of money, and we can't pay the plumber or the mortgage or our health insurance.

ORACLE: Hear me! You cannot go back to the old house or patch it. It is burning up—and inflaming the whole world. Change your ways. Change your ways, or all will perish across America and the planet.

CHORUS: But we love our old American house. We are not ready to rebuild it from the ground up, and we still aren't sure we believe your wild-eyed prophecies.

ORACLE: Time is running out, you foolish people. You must act now if you love life and want humanity itself to survive.

GREEN ACTIVISTS: The Oracle is right. Yes, there is much to love in America's house, but it is becoming the money pit from hell—and there is little time to patch it. But we have a new way if you will only reject the Greed Rulers and help us build a green house.

GREED RULERS: Their green house will destroy America. It will make you pay more taxes, stop driving, pull down the malls, and wipe out our greatest asset: freedom. The freedom of our free market. The freedom of our small government. The freedom to live as we want.

GREEN ACTIVISTS: Do you feel free in your money pit? Do you feel free to pay $200 to fill up your gas tank? To pay $1,000 to heat your house in winter? To borrow more to pay the mortgage on a house falling apart?

CHORUS: Yes, we feel chained to our money pit. We feel less free and less safe. But we love our big house and big lawn and big car. We can't give them up.

GREED RULERS: Bail us out and you will bail yourselves out and save this great house of yours.

GREEN ACTIVISTS: Our green house may be smaller, with less lawn and a smaller car. But it won't be an endless and hotter inferno of a money pit. It will free you from debt, save your job, keep your house, keep your family healthier and you more educated. It will connect you with your neighbor and make you feel less alone. And it will preserve our environment and just might save humanity.

GREED RULERS: Have you heard of Europe? European socialism?[32] That is their green house.

CHORUS: We will not tear down our house to live in a European house. It's a nice place to visit, but it's not us.

ORACLE: Be careful in your contempt of Europe, for the footprint of its house on the earth is far lighter than the overstuffed American mansion. The earth will not long hold the heaviness of the American house. And, remember, our democratic heritage began in Athens.[33]

GREEN ACTIVISTS: Our green house will not be Europe, but it will be lighter on the earth. And it will take you out of the money pit the Greed Rulers have designed for you. Our new American house will have smaller but cleaner rooms, it will be well heated and cooled, it will be built on a new solid foundation, and it will run on a energy system that can last forever, sheltering your children and their children.

CHORUS: We need to know more about the green house and whether it will be a green prison robbing us and our children of our freedom.

GREEN ACTIVISTS: You will have more freedom, not less, coming with a thriving and more competitive green economy, more secure jobs, better social benefits, and a safer and more peaceful environment—all by throwing out the Greed Rulers and using the wealth we create for us, for our new green house, not for them.

ORACLE: The green house is not just for you but for your children and your children's children. Building the green house will be your eternal legacy for all future generations.

CHORUS: We need to know more about the green house before we buy into it. We need more time to think. We are angry at the Greed Rulers, but we are attached to our old ways.

ORACLE: Time is running out, humans. Time is running out.

Like any good Greek theater, this scene foretells a potential tragedy. The oracle is shouting its warnings of collective death by warming. But most of the people are too overwhelmed by their current problems, too seduced by their rulers, and too addicted to current suburban houses, SUVs, and mall-crawling lifestyles to listen.

But the green activists add a new voice—one that links the oracle's warnings to the crises of the moment. Their green house will shelter the people in the current storm—and thus speaks to the immediate worries of the people—but also wards off the long-term great storm. The voices of the oracle and the activists work together, helping to draw people from the greed rulers while bringing solutions to both the present and future tragedies.

Without the crisis of the moment, the oracle might never be heard. The public is trying just to survive, but it has also lost faith in the rulers and is in such pain and confusion that it is ready to hear new voices and ideas and is already being forced to consider lifestyle changes more consistent with a green regime. With the collapse of faith in the current regime, the activists and the oracle together have a chance.

That chance has materialized in the deep disenchantment with the politics of the third corporate regime. President Obama is the fruit of thirty years of growing disillusionment with the values of the greed rulers and the painful outcomes of their policies. His call for change could resonate as widely and deeply as it did only because the third corporate regime has melted down and failed the people—and because we have had oracles such as Al Gore and a dazzling array of new green and antiregime movements bubbling up in resistance to regime extremism under President George W. Bush.[34] The 2008 meltdown—the most unexpected "October surprise" in U.S. presidential history—confirmed the crack-up of not just the financial markets but also the economic and social system swept in by the Reagan Revolution. The people voted for change, despite the ambivalence about how deep that change could be and the fear that it could undermine the creature comforts to which we have all become addicted.

It is still just a chance that the call for change will help the president and the people converge in a green regime change politics. We will meet with lots of resistance from a corporate regime far from ready to yield its power. Many in the Obama administration have decided this is not the time to listen to the oracle. But the receptivity of ordinary people and governments—at local and state as well as the national and global levels—to bold green new visions is the unexpected gift that the Great Recession of 2008 may have brought.

9

Blind Markets

How Capitalism Creates Climate Change

Solving global warming requires a revolution in our capitalist markets, politics, and culture. This solution goes beyond the energy-sector focus in much of the environmental movement itself and remains scarily outside the mainstream of public debate and Washington politics. For the sake of future generations, the public conversation must change quickly to address the causal relation between capitalism and climate change, as the window of opportunity closes.

In this chapter, I look at how capitalism, especially the U.S. model, creates climate change. In the next two chapters, I examine the systemic changes in capitalism required to solve the climate crisis, describing what a new sustainable politics and economic system, as well as a green American Dream, look like. I focus on the president's and the public's responsibilities in bringing these changes quickly to fruition.

Proposing big system changes seems very daunting when time is short. How can we be optimistic about change that must be both radical and fast? To use a football metaphor, it is a little like rooting for a home team that is down by three touchdowns in the fourth quarter. Boston College's Doug Flutie threw a "Hail Mary" pass to win in the last second of the Orange Bowl against Miami. But it seems as if I am proposing four Hail Mary passes to solve climate change.

Nonetheless, there is reason for hope. At this writing, we live in the deepest crisis since the Great Depression and we have elected a president with a mandate for change. The economic crisis is so serious that it opens Americans—out of necessity—to big new ideas and programs. The president has shown signs of a transformative green vision and policy, and he has deep public support. He is already making proposals to renew and remake the economy by greening America. We cannot expect miracles, but there are practical reasons to believe that this is an extraordinary moment—a perfect storm making possible much of the change we need.

From Blind to Green Markets

In February 2009, the *Boston Globe* editorialized that "coal is the cheapest source of electricity. One major reason is that mining companies and coal-burning utilities have managed to pass many of its health and environmental costs—from the dust miners breathe to greenhouse gases—onto society at large."[1] This editorial points to an urgent and systemic problem with our current capitalist system: It creates markets that ignore and are blind to the costs of environmental pollution as well as of social "pollution," such as wages keeping people in poverty. Corporations are indifferent to such costs because they do not have to put them on their books but can just let society or other individuals pick up the tab (what economists call "externalizing" the cost).[2] If a company spews untreated sewage into a river or carbon dioxide into the air, people will get sick, but the patient or a medical insurance company, not the corporation, will pay for the cost of that illness. An "externality" is a cost that a company or producer does not have to pay itself; it can "pass the buck" on to the rest of us. It is a real cost to society, but it never has to appear on the company's books—this externality does not exist in the minds of company accountants. The cost is socialized, absorbed by the public or government; the benefit is privatized, enjoyed by the corporation.

The underlying assumption is that self-interest, or even greed, can work to better society. There is an "invisible hand" premise here, an ideological dictum integral to capitalism according to which each company and individual pursuing a selfish interest will create the best society. The assumption is that if each individual follows his or her own private individual selfish interests, the competition among conflicting needs will balance itself out and the net result will be the best for everyone. The "commons"—that is, the air, the water, the earth itself, and all the natural and social resources that the human community needs for survival and well-being—will take care of itself as long as each individual pursues his or her own goal.

This view produces a tragedy of the commons.[3] If people look out only for themselves and pay no penalty for the consequences, then nobody has to look out for the common good and it will be neglected. This is, in fact, the deepest ideological and structural reason for the unsustainability of capitalism: It cannot protect the commons. If it could, we would not have a global warming problem—the ultimate crisis of the commons, a tragedy built on modern, distorted interpretations of economist Adam Smith, the creator of the invisible hand ideology.[4] The common good requires a steward and cannot take care of itself.[5] In U.S. capitalism, there is no obligatory steward, the government abandons that responsibility, and sustainability depends on the goodwill of voluntary corporate stewards that have abdicated that role.

In *For the Common Good,* a pioneering book on environmental economics, Herman Daly and John Cobb wrote: "All conclusions in economic theory about the social efficiency of pure competition and the free market are explicitly premised on the absence of externalities. The undeniable importance of externalities in today's world is therefore a serious challenge" to our whole economic way of thinking.[6] Many did not listen then, but it has become impossible to ignore Daly and Cobb in the age of global warming. Externalities have moved from being a distraction to being a doomsday machine. CO_2 pollution is the most dangerous externality of all time, and it should lead the entire world toward green markets rather than toward our idealized capitalist "free markets."

We must cap carbon emissions and tax them in some form to ensure they reflect their real costs to humanity. There are two fundamental mechanisms: a direct carbon tax and a cap-and-trade system. The two can be melded, but both can work. Barack Obama has already endorsed a cap-and-trade system for the United States to reduce CO_2 emissions 80 percent by 2050 from 1990 levels, and in 2009 members of Congress introduced cap-and-trade legislation. Producers in this initial plan, which has been modified in the House cap-and-trade bill passed in June 2009, would have to pay the government for CO_2 emissions they spew out; this system would essentially tax carbon emissions but allow flexibility by permitting one company to sell its permits to others if it burns less carbon than allowed by its permits. The aim is to create a national (and ultimately global) cap that will be reduced over time. Scientific analysis tells us the ultimate cap must reduce global CO_2 atmospheric concentrations to less than the critical 350 parts per million (ppm) threshold. This cap is the anchor and touchstone of a sustainable America and world.

When properly designed—in a model often called cap-and-dividend that would return money raised by the program to ordinary citizens—capping carbon emissions could win majority public support, given the high stakes and the short-term economic gains it offers. As carbon analyst Peter Barnes argues, returning the money raised by the program to the population will make "the carbon cap (with monthly dividends) the most popular federal program since Social Security."[7]

Carbon taxes, including gas taxes, are simpler than cap-and-trade systems. There is no selling of permits to pollute, no complex trading of the right to emit,[8] just the taxing of people directly for polluting the atmosphere with carbon emissions. We know this system works—when gas prices spike up, people drive less and buy greener cars. If the political will is present, carbon taxes could be the best approach. To create the political will, a carbon tax would have to be progressive—with the rich paying more—and made palatable to a tax-resistant public. The tax would also have to be high enough to cap carbon consumption at the 350 ppm limits. Some combination of the cap-and-trade and tax may be necessary, depending on global negotiations described in Chapter 14.

There is nothing utopian about capping emissions using a carbon tax. Costa Rica has been doing it since 1997, when it put a 3.5 percent tax on carbon emissions and invested the proceeds in a fund for indigenous people to protect their forests. The Costa Rican environmental minister, who is also the minister for energy, mines, and water, has directed heavy investment in renewables as a cheap alternative to fossil fuels, whose true costs are now known. What has been the result? Costa Rica operates with 95 percent renewable energy. It has oil, but it has decided to ban drilling for it. Costa Rica has seen large economic payoffs: Tourists flock to the country's pristine waters and forests, and the full-cost accounting has led to much lower poverty rates among Costa Rica's poor.[9]

An ambitious U.S. cap is the core around which a U.S. green regime must be built. It requires people to attend to the atmospheric commons and pay when they damage it. It means requiring greenhouse gas polluters to pay the true cost of their production or consumption. But to truly solve global warming—and to make the cap into a political reality that works rather than a Hail Mary fantasy—we need to create the broader political and economic transformation of our society.

Cause and Consequence: Corporate Capitalism and Climate Change

Regime change is a systemic shift in power. The third corporate regime, developed in the period from Presidents Ronald Reagan to George W. Bush, has been run by a small oligarchy of capitalist and political elites, all devoted to ensuring maximum short-term profits for the nation's largest corporations.[10] This regime must be changed because it is incompatible with essential long-term solutions to warming. To achieve success, the new green regime must be democratized, moving us from our current capitalist economy and the corporate stranglehold over politics to the popular sovereignty our leaders always talk about.

As noted in the Introduction, solving climate change is impossible within our current system of corporate capitalism. But communist and other economic systems have not created solutions either. We must thus move rapidly to innovate the best blend of different economic models, including elements in the United States, Europe, and many other nations, to create a green economy. The systemic change I describe in this and later chapters requires deep changes in the U.S. economic model and mind-set, including the shifting of our current system of corporate-managed markets and government to a more democratic system in which business serves the public rather than the opposite. Businesses, of course, will survive, but more will be smaller and local. The large corporations that survive will be restructured and subject to greater public accountability.

Many environmentalists and climate change thinkers, as well as President Obama and many congressional leaders, say they want big change, but they have been unable to spell out the scale and nature of the systemic economic and political transformation that is at the heart of the matter. Their focus has been on a technological revolution and major new government subsidies, incentives, and regulations for clean energy. But this leaves out what will make all the other changes possible and is at the core of the green regime itself: ending corporate control of society, creating a new sustainable economy based on full-cost accounting and protection of the commons, and building a long-term culture of sustainability. We need an internal regime change that involves a fundamental shift in the power structure and short-term mentality of our corporatized capitalist society and a shift toward a new model of a social and green economy that many will view as social democracy or brand as socialist. Such change does involve a shift from capitalism as we know it but actually combines freer markets with smarter government.

Before describing the new regime, I need to raise a simple question: Why do we need regime change—indeed, basic change in the capitalist system—rather than reforms within the current order? The answer is this: The fundamental values and core institutions of a globalized U.S. capitalism—and the scale and urgency of the climate crisis—make incremental reform a recipe for disaster.[11] Climate change is a symptom of systemic capitalist problems that have intensified during several centuries.

As discussed in this and the next two chapters, solving climate change in the United States requires changes in the short-term profit engine and speculative financial system, the corporate-driven political system, and the debt-driven consumerism that are deeply embedded in the U.S. capitalist system itself.[12] We need to remake the larger economy rather than create recovery for our current capitalism, a recovery that would prove neither economically nor environmentally sustainable.

The underlying problem—both in the economy and in the environment—goes beyond the greed of a few "bad apples," of the top executives on Wall Street, or of Wall Street itself. It is systemic and rooted in the intertwining of big government and big companies at the expense of public needs—all characteristic of capitalist systems in late stages of crisis. Corporations have harnessed the state as an instrument of unsustainable short-term capital accumulation tied to unsustainable consumerism that eats away at the commons and destroys it.[13]

At least since the Civil War, the corporate rich have used the government to serve them, and the history of capitalism reeks with corporate schemes to take control of the government to repress labor and other countervailing class forces that would interfere with corporations' intention to "get rich quick." As early as the 1600s, the Dutch economy imploded after speculators paid ten times the average craftsman's annual wage for tulip bulbs. In the late 1800s, American railroad barons managed to have banks and the government finance the railroads for more than they were worth. Post–World War I credit and stock speculation for quick wealth ended in the Great Depression.[14]

Today's sped-up and crisis-ridden capitalist model is thus not new, but it operates globally and electronically at a pace never seen before and produces environmental destruction at an unprecedented level. Our present economy is an extreme form of monopolistic and financialized capitalism. In a financialized economy, unregulated financial speculation replaces industrial productivity when too much capital flows to the financial sector, which absorbs excess profits and starves nonfinancial sectors. Short-term yield overrides long-term security, and speculative debt and credit instruments proliferate on Wall Street. Meanwhile, stagnation in manufacturing and other nonfinancial sectors creates a long-term double-whammy crisis for the economy and the environment.

Double Whammy: How U.S. Capitalism in Crisis Creates Climate Change

Kevin Philips, a best-selling political analyst and historian, argues forcefully that the current economic crisis is rooted in the financialization of U.S. capitalism as the United States enters its stage of hegemonic decline.[15] The history of capitalist empires—from the Dutch to the British—shows that as they mature, the hard work of creating long-term profits from selling real goods succumbs to the lure of short-term speculative bonanzas. Capital in the entire economy migrates rapidly, in our case to Wall Street, which has transformed itself into a high-tech, sci-fi, mathematically modeled, unregulated system of derivatives, futures, swap defaults, hedge funds, and commodity trading. Trillions of dollars are exchanged across computer screens on a daily basis; the whole financial system becomes a supercharged, superleveraged day trader. The state, meanwhile, acts to remove regulations and restraints, putting politics at the service of speculative finance.

This is a Wall Street operating on an extreme, toxic, invisible hand model. Each bank chases its own short-term interests with no concern for the effects on the larger system. There is no need for stewardship because the financial commons will take care of itself. The consequences of this reasoning are now obvious.

Phillips observes that financialization is unsustainable economically, creating bubbles, such as in the housing market, doomed to burst. But looking just at the housing bubble, we see that such speculative finance also locks consumers into their own turbocharged and unsustainable personal lifestyles, racking up credit debt and leveraged money on their inflated house values to buy second homes, cars, and other big-ticket items neither they nor the environment can afford. Speculative and excess consumerism follows inevitably on the heels of speculative finance (before the crash). As we all used easy credit and balloon, variable-rate mortgages, we were burdening the earth with an ever-heavier personal, national, and global carbon footprint.[16]

Phillips's argument is that the United States is following a well-trodden path in which Wall Street becomes the model and center of gravity for the entire economy. As Wall Street accelerates speed, shrinks time focus, and accelerates debt-induced consumption, the larger economy is unable to respond to a longer time scale. The real economy accelerates toward the unsustainable pace of Wall Street.

Sociologist John Bellamy Foster, a pioneer in linking environmental sociology and social theory, offers a related but deeper systemic analysis of the roots of financialization—and of the larger economic and environmental crises.[17] Foster shows that financialization is caused by an enduring stagnation in the nonfinancial sectors that is endemic to capitalism as it develops during decades and centuries. Stagnation is the unhappy but unavoidable result of many factors: a maturation of industries, growing monopolization, globalization, and increasing inequalities, with the biggest firms soaking up greater profits and paying U.S. workers low wages in a globalized labor market. As corporations seek to lower labor costs, thereby creating greater profit for individual firms, they create a collective problem plaguing all corporations: a systemic crisis of insufficient consumer demand as wages fall and workers cannot afford to buy. In U.S. capitalism, neither government spending nor corporate investment can solve this "demand-side" problem, although governments ratchet up military spending (military Keynesianism) to try to prime the economic pump, or restart the economy, through demand for planes, guns, and other military goods and services.[18] Corporate investment in the United States itself, however, declines with the expectation of lower profitability as worker consumer power declines. Ultimately, the only solution is to financialize the system and introduce easy credit and debt, encouraging U.S. workers to spend well beyond the means of their diminishing wages. Business invests in the financial sector itself as the one last, great opportunity for huge quick profits. This works for a while but leads to bubbles and unsustainable debt in households, banks, and the government, which in the current case led to the 2008 Wall Street crash.

At least six core reasons explain why U.S. capitalism creates climate change and why the current crisis exacerbates these structural causes.

How U.S. Capitalism Causes Climate Change

1. Blind markets externalize environmental and social costs.
2. Wall Street grows like a cancer, creates "financialized capitalism," and promotes extreme short-termism.
3. Low wages, driven down by the core capitalist drive to maximize profits, create a manic work-and-spend cycle that is unsustainable.
4. The ideological apparatus creates a religion of unlimited growth and unsustainable consumerism; Madison Avenue makes us all believers.
5. Big corporations intertwine with political elites and dominate Washington, with both parties promoting profits over people and the environment.
6. American consumer capitalism becomes entrenched in a fossil-fuel-intensive lifestyle based on cars, highways, malls, suburbs, and exurbs all rooted in hyper-individualistic values.
7. In the name of property rights, the commons are privatized and destroyed.

Mainstream economists largely ignore this analysis of inherent capitalist contradictions and the system's built-in environmental unsustainability, which are greatly exacerbated in the current crisis and in the global economy. Global U.S. firms push down wages far more easily through outsourcing and exploiting billions of impoverished workers in Asia, Latin American, and Africa. Global sweatshops and pollution created by transnational companies in poor nations strip naked for all to see the crises of the global economy and the environment as intertwined systemic capitalist time bombs. Capitalist conflicts between labor and capital—and the squeeze on U.S. workers facing competition in a globalized labor markets—create declining consumer demand, growing inequality, slack productive investment, financialization, speculation, and accelerated financial transactions, credit, and debt. The aim is to speed up short-term consumption in order to buttress a stagnating real economy and feed the financial services industry that produces the easy credit and loose debt as well as the last great profit opportunities for big business. The debt system and the short-term mentality of easy credit fuel madcap environmentally unsustainable consumption, which leads toward even more debt that is economically unsustainable and brings the economy to its knees. At the same time, workers are induced into the short-term thinking of the consumer culture that redefines excess (bigger carbon-intensive houses and cars, more "stuff") as happiness while burning up the planet. This all might be called "capitalism's bonfire," a real-world variant of what novelist Tom Wolfe called "the Bonfire of the Vanities."[19]

Sociologist David Harvey argues that the globalization of financialized capitalism in the electronic age transforms culture itself, creating "time-space compression" that locks workers and consumers into the frenzied short-term frame of the capitalism controlling them.[20] The whole history of capitalism, says Harvey, "has been characterized by speed-up in the pace of life."[21] But the current time-space compression is so extreme that it engulfs and over-whelms all of life. Disposable workers embrace a fast-paced lifestyle, which is consistent with the sped-up pace of the work that they need to pay for their sped-up consumption and compensate for their own rapid skill obsolescence. The experience is "challenging, exciting, stressful, and sometime deeply troubling," but the end result is that our own personal psychology reinforces an unsustainable economic order that is victimizing us.[22] The personal and egoistic clock of each of us—and debt-financed, turbocharged consumerism—reinforces the financial order (now disorder) on Wall Street that keeps this new hyperaccelerated systemic clock and global warming time bomb ticking until the bomb blows up, as in our current crisis.

In short, the current corporate order is structurally incompatible with the long-term thinking, moderated consumerism, and social and environmental conditions essential for democracy and for survival of not just the planet but also the economy itself. The systemic incentives, driven by the threat of long-term stagnation, are all for short-term profits rooted in unsustainable debt and consumption. Corporations are (1) tightly wired into the short-term financial-ized model inspired by Wall Street, (2) addicted to fossil fuel global production to ensure short-term profitability while underinvesting in the real economy and overinvesting in the financial sector, (3) wedded to the fevered systemic advertising sales pitch that induces workers into unsustainable debt and con-sumption ravaging the planet, and (4) so gigantic that they have the power to impose their own policy agendas on the state, on the regulatory agencies presumed to regulate them, and on our own personal consumerism. If we are to create economic and environmental sustainability, we need to move rapidly away from a financial system organized by Wall Street, from corporate control of America, and from the current U.S. model of global corporate capitalism itself. Some corporations with a green business vision and long-term investors (such as church and labor pension funds) can play a constructive green role, but they lack the vision and power to get the systemic change we need.

The Disappearance of Capitalist Stewards and What to Do about It

Although Wall Street has always been built on a flawed model of finance, in earlier eras such as the New Deal core capitalist elites sustained a view of their responsibility to preserve the capitalist system over the long term. These "capitalist stewards" have historically been in finance. Wall Street leaders are located at the center of the capitalist economy and have the greatest interests in ensuring that the entire system is viable. Many Depression-era financial leaders looked out for the long-term interests of the capitalist system, as had earlier financiers who believed that great power brings great responsibility.[23] In the progressive era, J. P. Morgan helped coordinate Wall Street efforts in concert with Teddy Roosevelt to save the country and capitalism from the runaway financial panics and speculation at the turn of the twentieth century. Morgan supported the creation of the Federal Reserve and the beginning of national regulation. The capitalist stewards in the New Deal, including Nelson Aldridge, CEO of Chase National, and Henry Morganthau, secretary of the Treasury under FDR, went further, supporting social welfare systems and major government regulation, intervention, and stimulus to create jobs and infrastructure.[24] Both earlier regime changes had a very pale green tint, as discussed in later chapters, and were far from radical enough to deal with the current crisis. The stewards sought to deal with the stagnation tendencies at the heart of the problem through Keynesian measures of greater government spending and regulation—offering relief in the short and medium term—but were never prepared to carry out the deeper systemic changes necessary to solve the problem for the long term.

The extreme short-term time frame of U.S. capitalism in decline reflects the deepening of structural stagnation and the disappearance of capitalist stewards, although there are financiers like Warren Buffet and George Soros who try to play that role. In the third corporate regime, finance intensified its focus on the short term because of new irresistible and superprofitable opportunities created by globalization and the Reagan Revolution.[25] Reagan's deregulation and free-trade policies made possible the rise of totally unregulated global speculative instruments involving hedge funds, complex derivatives, mortgage securitization (bundling of mortgage loans into "collateralized debt obligations" for resale), and related "toxic assets," all of which escalated into a madcap speculative Wall Street house of cards, built on unsustainable leverage and debt, that had no long-term viability. Had the capitalist stewards survived and played their earlier role, the current crisis might have been deferred, but that would not have resolved the longer-term structural crisis of stagnation, short-term profit maximization, accelerated debt, and unfettered consumerism. To save business and finance, as well as the environment, we will need new economic and political stewards, not just in business but also in civil society and the larger political system, working to help build the larger green long-term economic system.

The implications are unequivocal. At the very moment when we most need a long-term sustainable vision, capitalism itself no longer breeds the sustainable conditions or stewardship ethos—not to mention the political movements and politicians seeking deeper and essential systemic change—to sustain both prosperity and the environment. The Wall Street implosion and the astonishing irresponsibility of Wall Street leaders looking out only for their own bonuses—doling out to themselves an eye-popping $32.6 billion in nine huge bailed-out banks—make this clear. The government (at federal, state, and local levels), along with democratic movements in the larger civil society, has to step in and assume the stewardship role that financial leaders have abandoned. Government, led by the president and driven by accountable empowered citizen movements, is the only institution with the constitutional authority and political power to take on the stewardship role and rapidly create the change in political and economic institutions necessary to get the job done.

The economy cannot function without business or credit; even a perfectly green economy will require both small and large businesses. The effort, rather, is to restructure the economy systemically to operate in a democratic manner with long-term vision and full and true cost-accounting. Inefficient and costly overinvestment in Wall Street will be replaced by investment in sustainable nonfinancial sectors and in local community banks. This will require major public investment and transformations of the corporate structure itself, as we see in the next chapter, to overcome stagnation in the real economy by means that are not based on hyperconsumerism.

To summarize, we need systemic changes in capitalism toward a green economy that include the following shifts:

- from short-term profit maximization to sustainable long-term enterprise
- from externalizing environmental and social costs to internalizing them
- from monopoly corporations to smaller and midsize businesses
- from financialized Wall Street capitalism to a sustainable Main Street economy
- from corporate-controlled government to popular sovereignty
- from shareholder-owned businesses to stakeholder, labor, and community businesses
- from the invisible hand to the preservation of the commons
- from poverty and low worker wages to living wages for all
- from consumerism to quality of life
- from growth to sufficiency

10

The 90 Percent Solution

How to Change Wall Street, Energy Firms, and the Corporate System

Given the urgency of the climate crisis, and the very short time we have to act, the human future requires decisive action by the president. Constitutionally, the president is charged with the obligation to secure the safety and well-being of the public. In the age of global warming, with science telling us that the window of survivability is now closing, we need new emergency actions led by the president. These will require drastic changes in both the federal government and our system of corporate capitalism.

The president must assume the role less of chief executive or commander-in-chief than of chief steward, although two of these roles converge in the age of warming. Beyond nuclear war, the gravest threat to long-term security is climate change—and it requires immediate action. The president can discharge these responsibilities only by invoking judicious executive powers to restructure the priorities of the federal government. These powers must be used in partnership with Congress, civil society, grassroots movements, and the larger public to create the national conversation and regime change shift we need. In this chapter, I argue that President Barack Obama, and future presidents, must lead the nation toward what I call the 90 percent solution, one major piece of the overall international solution discussed in later chapters.

The Constitution wisely endows the president with limited emergency powers, because the Founders were aptly fearful of making the president a king. Since President Abraham Lincoln's time, presidential emergency and executive powers have been expanded by congressional statutes and executive orders to meet both wartime and domestic economic needs.[1] Even though the recent expansion of wartime executive powers—taken to new levels under President George W. Bush after 9/11—is extremely dangerous and subverts the Constitution,[2] the president needs to invoke the judicious and limited

---

The 90 Percent Solution

1. Citing his constitutional powers, the president orders each federal department to create an emergency plan to cut greenhouse gas emissions in its sector by 90 percent by 2050.
2. The president orders regulation, public ownership, and "trust-busting" on Wall Street and in the entire financial sector to create a green financial system.
3. The president orders regulation, public ownership, and financial incentives in the energy sector to create an extremely rapid shift from oil and coal to a new clean energy foundation of the economy.
4. The president proposes immediate rewriting of corporate charters to help ensure a sustainable, full-employment system of green production.
5. Using his constitutional authority, the president takes these initiatives now and keeps Congress in session until it passes legislation enabling these changes.

---

powers invested by the Founders for extraordinary peacetime challenges as a strategy to help create a new national and global partnership to steer the ship of state in a new direction.

The entire section of the Constitution (Article 2) dealing with presidential powers is brief and restrictive, reflecting the Founders' fear of creating a monarch. But the Founders did vest the president in Article 2, Section 3, on unspecified "extraordinary occasions" with the powers to "convene both houses or either of them" and "may adjourn them to such Time as he shall think proper." They linked this with the need to inform Congress and the public about vital knowledge regarding the state of the union and to pass vital legislation. These very restrictive constitutional emergency powers—which are levers by which the president can help catalyze congressional and public focus on an extraordinary collective challenge without exercising dangerous unilateralist powers—are precisely what is required now.

We need to recognize that there are other executive powers presidents now can invoke, but they are dangerous instruments subversive of the Constitution and unlikely to create the public partnership and consensus we need. The president is authorized by statute—the 1976 U.S. International Emergency Economic Powers Act—to declare a "national emergency" arising from both global and domestic economic crises posing "any unusual and extraordinary threat."[3] This law allows the president, among other measures, to "investigate, regulate, or prohibit—(i) any transactions in foreign exchange, (ii) transfers of credit or payments between, by, through, or to any banking institution, . . . (iii) the importing or exporting of currency or securities."[4] Another and even more dangerous source of presidential emergency power is a series of presidential executive orders issued during the last thirty years empowering the president to order government control of everything from "all modes of transportation" to "the communication media" to "all electrical power, gas, petroleum, fuels and minerals" to "all food resources and farms."[5]

These approaches could facilitate some of the changes I propose in the following pages, but they imply a constitutional suspension and potential authoritarian regime that are so dangerous that even the climate change crisis does not justify them. Many of these powers threaten constitutional democracy and should be rescinded. Moreover, they establish a unilateral-ist presidential approach contrary to the societal partnership that a climate change solution requires.

But the president should invoke the judicious and highly restrictive powers framed by the Founders to summon the nation to a new set of core missions that spell out our collective responsibility to current and future generations. These begin with a restructuring of the government itself to ensure long-term survivability. The president should draft a national address describing the "extraordinary" existential crisis that climate change creates—with a call to Congress and the public for cooperation in coming together to frame both short- and long-term solutions. Practically speaking, this might best be done in concert with explanations of the ambitious cap-and-trade program that the president has embraced to drastically restrict greenhouse gas emissions, the first giant step toward a solution and aptly timed for the 2009 global climate change talks in Copenhagen. This should be the first of a series of "fireside chats," like those developed by President Franklin Roosevelt but now delivered on Facebook and YouTube as well as radio, to create a new public conversation about the climate change crisis and how to deal with it. If Congress has not passed a strong cap-and-trade measure or carbon tax before the Copenhagen meetings, Obama should invoke his Article 2 powers to convene a special session of Congress to ensure that carbon cap and tax legislation is taken up, debated, and passed in the strongest form.

Based on the vision and public concern integral to his fireside chats, the president should instruct every federal agency to create a road map for a 90 percent reduction from 1990 greenhouse emissions in its sector—whether it be housing, transportation, defense, or health. Every department needs to produce a short-term and a long-term proposal showing how it will achieve phased drastic and sustainable greenhouse gas reductions by 2050. The president must mandate every federal department and agency to consider how much nationalization is required, how to restore true market competition in non-nationalized sectors, and how to design the appropriate social reinven-tions and green policies in crucial areas such as transportation, suburbia and urban living space, homes, and office buildings. This requires coordination among different departments—a transportation plan will intersect with a housing plan—and Obama's climate czar, Carol Browner, must help coordinate different department proposals, while offering flexibility on the target, with 90 percent too great for some and too little for others. All plans must be developed in intensive consultation with a large number of public stakeholders (discussed in this chapter).

The president must charge the Transportation Department with the responsibility to create a new vision of public and private transportation consistent with creating a 90 percent carbon reduction, a proposal that will involve major investments in public transit, light rail, and electric cars, shifting the infrastructure from highways to public transit. Likewise, the president must task the Department of Housing and Urban Development to come up with major social innovation in our suburban/exurban social sprawl system, with a comprehensive plan developed in close coordination with local governments. This plan will be based on new zoning rules, Federal Housing Authority regulations, and financial incentives for limiting the size of lots and homes; urban redesign ensuring walkable neighborhoods and permitting pedestrian or bicycle access to local food markets and other community businesses; location of houses near public transportation stations; and housing and building codes to meet the 90 percent reduction target in all homes and offices, which in America are far more carbon consuming than in Europe. Even though these goals are extremely ambitious, there are promising models already in place; Europe has moved rapidly to accomplish such carbon reduction in its own highly developed public transportation and urban planning, with low-carbon houses and offices becoming the norm. Europe's success—with European per capital carbon footprints less than one-half that of America's—shows that social and political redesign can make a developed economy and high standard of living environmentally sustainable.

Environmental thinkers such as British policy analyst George Monbiot and U.S. political theorist Charles Siegel have already fleshed out detailed policy proposals for drastic greenhouse gas reductions in transportation, housing, and other sectors that can be a foundation for each department's work.[6] All the stakeholders—government, labor, scientists, communities and local governments, state governments, activists, and the general public who can be actively mobilized by the president's fireside chats—should be consulted in order to meet the stringent deadlines the president must demand.

Carol Browner is the first government official in American history charged with coordinating all the federal government's policies related to global warming. As noted previously, she has a central role in coordinating plans from different sectors of society and compiling a vision and a legislative package, which would emerge from these various cabinet department proposals.

Major congressional leaders would be consulted, as would industrial, labor, and environmental authorities along with other public stakeholders, including state governors working on their own state plans. The president would deliver monthly fireside chat updates to promote even more public participation. When the plans are developed, the president should use Article 2, Section 3 powers, if necessary, to convene special sessions of Congress to consider and pass legislation based on these proposals encompassing the entire economy.

Even though all departments of the government must participate, Treasury and the financial sector have a special place because they are at the heart of both the economic meltdown and global warming crises. I look first at a revolutionary design for the financial system. I then describe essential transformations in the energy sector. I conclude this chapter by spelling out essential green changes in the larger corporate system.

Regime Change on Wall Street

As discussed earlier, much of the climate crisis arises from the financial sector's abandonment of capitalist stewardship. The government must step in to restore long-term vision and invent a new financial system for a sustainable economy. The president should issue a series of proclamations on the need for a sustainable financial order. He should show how the intertwined economic and environmental crises reflect Wall Street's inherent systemic flaws and explain its current suicidal shift toward short-term speculative finance and the disappearance of a culture of stewardship. He must show that the U.S. government needs to step in to steward the entire economy after Wall Street's failure. The government must restructure Wall Street and the financial system itself to prioritize new systems of credit and financial incentives for businesses to remake themselves to help ensure a sustainable future, making clear that the stakes for humanity have never been higher.

Part of the president's responsibility is to open an honest discussion with the American people about the nationalization of gigantic Wall Street firms. Nationalization scares business and most Americans. But it is the only way to transform the financial system fast enough to help solve the climate change crisis.

We need nationalization not only to save the environment and civilization, but also to remake the economy and prevent a cycle of ever deepening Great Recessions. The alternative is to keep shoveling money to the bankers and the very system that have catastrophically failed us by financing fossil fuel development, creating the easy credit–easy debt system that has fostered runaway consumerism, and moving the entire economy to short-term profit at the expense of the long-term sustainable development needed to preserve the planet and the economy itself.

In both temporary and permanent versions, nationalization has a long place in U.S. history. Today, nationalization already exists de facto with the huge infusion of public funds in the banks after Lehman Brothers collapsed and other huge financial firms, such as AIG, deemed too big to fail, teetered on the edge. On March 3, 2009, the *New York Times* used its lead editorial to call explicitly for nationalization of the biggest Wall Street banks that are requiring extensive government bailouts; this would achieve a "comprehensive solution: a government-run restructuring, or nationalization."[7] Even Alan Greenspan, former Federal Reserve chair and champion of free markets, told the *Financial Times* in early 2009 that nationalization on Wall Street may now be inevitable: "It may be necessary to temporarily nationalize some banks" to save capitalism itself.[8]

Few people want one big politicized bureaucracy running the economy, and nationalization is only one of several major ways to "green" the financial system. Others include breaking up the biggest banks and returning many mid-sized and small banks to community ownership, imposing strict new regulations on reserve requirements to curtail unsustainable debt and credit, and creating incentives for banks to issue loans for green job creation and renewable energy projects. For those concerned about bureaucratization and big government power, there are new models of nationalization—based on public/private partnerships and stakeholder/citizen participation—that will actually decentralize power in local and regional bodies as well as green the financial system. Many government controls should be administered by localities and monitored by public interest and stakeholder groups independent of government. Many insolvent banks will be liquidated, and others will be returned to community ownership, which can become a finance system more prudent than Wall Street and more oriented toward sustainable community development and a new low-carbon economy.[9]

Nationalization in any form, however, will create huge corporate resistance and a political firestorm, and Obama's own economic team has close ties to many Wall Street bankers who donate heavily to the Democratic Party and will fight to the end. But Americans may be willing to consider nationalization of the largest banks when they see that (1) their own tax funds already finance the banks and they deserve control like any investor; (2) we already live in a highly statist economy, bulging with corporate welfare masked in the language of laissez-faire; (3) nationalization of very large publicly subsidized or financed banks on Wall Street is actually not "more" state intervention but different, smarter, and faster government action essential to solve the emergency in both the economy and the environment; (4) Wall Street works as a failed monopoly, propped up only by taxpayer money, whose functions can be transferred either to the government or to local banks, creating more public accountability; and (5) radical change in our financial system—with government stepping in to assume the economic and environmental steward-ship role abandoned by the lords of finance—is necessary to save both the long-term economy and the planet within the narrow time frame dictated by nature. Nationalization of the largest banks, properly designed, is the one potential corrective to the larger capitalist flawed commandment: There shalt be no *mandatory* stewardship because the invisible hand will ensure the common good and the market knows best.

Earlier lords of finance—such as Andrew Carnegie in his espousal of the "gospel of wealth"—*voluntarily* embraced the idea that their power carried responsibilities beyond the invisible hand.[10] Carnegie's version was that if a businessman proved his virtue by winning in the market, he had the respon-sibility to help those less capable. When current Wall Street leaders abdicated these responsibilities and embraced the invisible hand premise once again, Wall Street dropped off a cliff. Nationalization is the government stepping into the stewardship role.

The current Wall Street implosion led to bailouts by the Bush admin-istration that represented corrupted partial nationalization. It temporarily saved the biggest, greediest, and insolvent financial institutions, including Citigroup, AIG, and Bank of America, at the expense of the public, which was understandably furious. Nonetheless, the public's anger at bailing out the bankers whose greed and fraud had caused the meltdown suggests why a very different kind of Wall Street nationalization—one truly serving Main Street's interest—could meet with public approval in the current crisis.

At this writing, President Obama has backed away from explicit talk about nationalization, but dire circumstances led him to take over one-third of the common stock of Citigroup and 79 percent of AIG. On April 19, 2009, Treasury officials announced that they plan to convert many of their earlier cash infusions into the biggest banks into common equity, essentially mak-ing the government a controlling owner.[11] Much more will be required and likely implemented—and Republicans are already calling Obama a "social-ist." To get the public's backing, the president must use some fireside chats to explain the myths and realities of our current economic system. The first step is to show that widespread de facto nationalization has long existed in the capitalist order—and now especially on Wall Street. As Nobel econo-mist Paul Krugman has written: "Wall Street is no longer, in any real sense, part of the private sector. It's a ward of the state, every bit as dependent on government as recipients of Temporary Assistance for Needy Families, a k a 'welfare.'"[12] Krugman is referring to all the credits extended to the banks by the Federal Reserve as well as the huge bailouts and other subsidies to Wall Street, but this is part of a far more general system of "corporate welfare," or chronic government life support for big business across the board.[13] Obama should expand on this in his fireside chat number 1: "the myth of the free market"!

Here is what the president should say:

My Fellow Americans:

I understand the anger you feel as you watch your own hard-earned money used to bail out the giant banks that got us into this mess. They made bad loans and invented super-risky and often fraudulent securitized instruments, such as derivatives, that my friend Warren Buffet calls "financial weapons of mass destruction."[14] The bankers passed the bad risk onto others and have already spent billions of your bailout money on their own bonuses, private jets, and luxury vacations.

I am as outraged as you are, and I will stop these abusive CEO practices and ask Congress to launch an investigation into the huge and systemic speculation and fraud leading to the crisis. Wall Street's transformation into a gambling casino is an enormous threat right now to the economy and to your jobs, pensions, and homes. But as I will show in several speeches, it creates an even greater risk to future generations, threatening the environmental conditions necessary for civilized life. Money is at the root of both our economic and environmental crises, with casino capitalism a root cause of both the economic meltdown and global warming. Remaking Wall Street to protect your economic well-being will also help to protect the possibility of a civilized life for your children and children's children, who face a climate crisis driven by fast money and short-term thinking.

Neither the economy nor the species itself can survive with the broken financial system that we now have. It runs on short-term profit and undermines the capacity of business to pursue long-term strategies that are both economically and environmentally sustainable.

Because the economic and environmental crises are so urgent, my responsibility is to make immediate change that offers hope for the future, the theme I promised in my campaign. You may wonder, then, why I am infusing trillions into the Wall Street system at the heart of much of our problems. The hard truth is that the banks that we are funding, such as Citigroup and Bank of America, are too big to fail. They are what Treasury secretary Tim Geithner calls "systemically critical"—if we let them fail, we will lose the credit that allows the entire economy to function and not completely collapse. We are helping the banks only because it is necessary right now to save you. But I am planning to change the entire financial system so that it will serve you, rather than the banks, while also saving the environment and preserving life for your children.

I am very unhappy about the bailouts myself. When you, the little guy, go under, perhaps because of bad decisions or risk-taking, nobody comes in and bails you out. But when the big banks take bad risks, you, the public, forks over billions to pay their bad debts and save them.

There's a truth here about our "free-market" economy you need to understand as we right these wrongs. This is the truth that most presidents have not had the courage to tell you. These public bailouts of the big banks are just an extreme version of something that goes on all the time in our economy. Each year, hundreds of billions of dollars of subsidies, research grants, tax write-offs, and other aid from the government go to giant banks and other big corporations. Since the beginning of our country, the government has played a huge role in financing our free-market economy and the banking system—and that role is now central. Every year, the government plows millions of dollars into corn and cotton subsidies for agribusiness, research and licensing grants to pharmaceuticals, millions to help export California wines, and millions in tax breaks for oil companies. Former labor secretary Robert Reich has called it a system of "corporate welfare."[15]

According to the conservative and respected Cato Institute, corporate welfare amounts to several hundred billion dollars a year. This is your money going to rich businesses and banks. You pay even when your wages decline. Much of this corporate welfare is unacceptable and should be eliminated, but some of it is now necessary to keep our financial system solvent.

So the truth that you have not been told—and I have promised to always tell you the truth—is that our system has never been a truly free-market system. The government intervenes in a thousand ways to keep Wall Street and business afloat. Corporate welfare involves "socializing the costs" of production, and the bank bailouts are "socializing the risks." But the profits keep being privatized, going just to the guys at the top.

Some people call this system "state capitalism." In state capitalism, your taxpayer money always keeps the banks and corporations afloat and bails them out when they are in trouble. Economist Paul Krugman has called the bailouts "lemon socialism," which is one way of talking about the worst excesses of our state capitalism.[16] The taxpayer massively finances business and cushions its risks but doesn't get the rewards. It's socialism for the rich, and "you're on your own" for the rest of us. That is what our free-market economy really amounts to.

If that sounds unfair to you, it is. And I am going to propose big changes. State capitalism is a marriage among banks, corporations (including big energy companies), and government—a marriage that hurts you and is also becoming unsustainable for the environment as well as the economy. It makes the government a handmaiden of the banks instead of a servant to you, the people.

Thank you for listening. I will soon share with you my proposals for how to solve these problems.

When the president has offered this rarely told truth to the public, he will lay the groundwork for the reforms that he should propose. He will have made clear that the state is already creating a kind of de facto nationalization of Wall Street and big business. It has enabled the banks to pursue short-term, risky, and superleveraged financial practices—as well as short-term profits that are dangerous to the economy and the environment. Surely, we can have a green form of nationalization that is better than this corrupted and unsustainable one we already have. By the time this book is published, the president may already have begun this new approach.

The president should propose a series of reforms, building on changes already begun at the biggest at-risk financial firms, including AIG, Citigroup, Bank of America, Fannie Mae, and Freddie Mac. They have received so much government cash and oversight that they are already essentially nationalized. He could use these and other financial institutions getting the biggest bailouts as a test case of green nationalization that would begin as temporary and then have to meet certain key tests before being considered as permanent. He must also propose other systemic reforms and regulations:

My Fellow Americans:

I am happy to talk to you again about our economic crisis and the intertwined environmental and energy crisis. And today I have several specific proposals. I call for a temporary nationalization of the biggest Wall Street financial institutions that are systemically critical and require government aid to survive. Nationalization means the government will buy ownership of a majority of common voting shares in these firms. Most other financial companies will remain in the private sector and will compete with the public ones. The aim of nationalization will be to stabilize the economy and prevent depression while moving rapidly toward a new sustainable and clean energy foundation that can help not just our economy but also the survival prospects of the entire human species.

Let us not forget what is at stake, for in the age of climate change human civilization itself is in peril. This requires me, as your president, to break completely new ground. Nationalization on this scale is new in America, but it is a modest reform when matched against the threat we face. I will ask Congress to consider whether to extend nationalization or return the banks to private control (1) when they can survive on their own and (2) if the public banks are competing less efficiently and with less economically and environmentally sound credit financing than the privately held banks. But if they are competing better on both economic and environmental criteria than privately held banks, I will propose continuation of public ownership for further future review.

When it comes to the largest at-risk Wall Street banks, government must take ownership not only to ensure economic stability but also to help ensure the broad and extremely rapid shifts in green credit allocation and lending and financing priorities to meet the deadlines imposed by nature in the age of global warming. The government will ensure that vast new credit flows very quickly to reboot the economy with a new foundation and sustain the planet through new green investments. I will also shut down the speculative finance that is driving our short-term profiteering and unsustainable consumerism.

We will close some major Wall Street failed banks. Government will take over some of their functions and transfer others to local banks. And even though we will nationalize the biggest system-critical banks, some will be broken up, as President Teddy Roosevelt would have proposed, to limit the power and lobbying influence of Wall Street.

I will also be proposing other major regulatory reforms to stop the systemic gambling endangering your jobs and pensions and putting at risk your children's very prospects for a civilized future. You must never forget that in the age of global warming, we all need to embrace a long-term vision and stewardship mentality that casino capitalism makes impossible. I will regulate the shadowy unregulated world of hedge funds, derivatives, and other speculative instruments; impose new reserve requirements on banks, hedge funds, and other financial institutions; and once again separate out the commercial, investment, credit rating, and accounting functions that have become corrupted in a huge systemic conflict of interest and undermine any possibility of long-term thinking in the climate change era. I will also streamline the more than 200 fragmented financial regulatory agencies that compete for funds—believe it or not—from the companies that they regulate, creating a classic race to the bottom. That race to the bottom in the molding of our casino capitalism—now threatening the survival of both the economy and the planet—is over.

Nobel economist Joseph Stiglitz says this: "It is very clear that the banks have failed. American citizens have become majority owners in a very large number of the major banks. But they have no control. Any system where there is a separation of ownership and control is a recipe for disaster." Stiglitz has proposed that "nationalization is the only answer."[17]

I agree that we can no longer separate ownership and control. But I am proposing nationalization of the biggest critical banks as a pragmatic experiment in remaking the economy and saving the environment. I have indicated the criteria for success or failure both in the economy and in the environment. Our next steps will depend on where we see successes and where we see failures. I have promised you a solution based on truth and flexible new ideas—and now I am delivering what I promised. Stay tuned.

Transforming the Energy Sector

The president and population must make the shift from fossil fuel to a renewable energy system our new national mission. Even with comprehensive green regime change, we cannot convert 100 percent from fossil fuels in the next decade or two, so in addition to shifting toward renewables, we need to radically conserve and reduce our total energy use, maximize energy efficiency, and minimize the amount of energy we will continue to use even as our national population and economy grow.

Emergency Change in the Energy Sector

1. Structural change involving a public ownership option offers the best chance to save our species.
2. It is the best way to provide jobs to all, including minorities and blue-collar workers.
3. It creates jobs that are impossible to outsource.
4. It is essential in order to keep the United States economically competitive.
5. It will revive communities and unite them in a common mission.
6. It is the most direct and fastest way that government can build a new sustainable foundation for society and the planet.

A hyperaccelerated shift toward more efficient and clean energy is the best way to get out of our current economic crisis, making it one of the most favorable opportunities for President Obama to achieve a "two-fer": solving climate change by remaking the economy. Creating a green efficient energy system requires massive investment in exactly what we most need now: jobs. These will be green jobs for building and retrofitting green houses and office buildings, installing solar panels and smart power grids, and building public transit. These are construction jobs for the unskilled and poor, engineering and planning jobs for the highly educated, service jobs for the greening service employees and for millions of other workers laid off in the current downturn. They are mainly jobs that cannot be outsourced or made technologically obsolete, and the majority will pay a living wage. They will keep the economy and jobs growing even after we get through the current downturn. They are the foundation of a full-employment economy in a world where jobs are vanishing. They combine the hope of short-term stimulus with long-term salvation.[18]

Solar, wind, and the entire green energy sector are far more labor intensive than the capital-intensive fossil fuel sector, promising to create many millions of new jobs globally. As big oil and coal make billions of dollars, they are shedding workers fast. In contrast, the relatively tiny U.S. clean energy sector already had 500,00 employees in 2006, with the numbers growing rapidly. In Europe, even more rapid growth of green energy workers has occurred because the European Union and central government policy has stimulated rapid growth of solar, wind, and other renewables. In 2006, Germany, a country one-fourth the size of the United States, there were 259,000 workers in green energy; that number is expected to double by 2020. Mushrooming numbers of green energy sector jobs are being seen in Spain, Denmark, and the United Kingdom, where governments, as in Germany, strongly promote renewables to deal both with global warming and job creation. The same is taking place in China and India.[19]

The United States will likely move toward clean energy and more efficient conservation, but getting there fast enough to achieve quick economy recovery and save humanity is another story. Doing so will require wholesale changes in our mind-set and our politics. Beyond multi-billion-dollar subsidies and tax credits to stimulate the renewable energy sector (with the money taken from the disgracefully enormous $4 billion a year subsidies to big oil and big coal), we will need a regime change in our socioeconomic concepts, much as occurred in the New Deal but far more ambitious.[20]

Let us start with ideas about vast public investment. We simply cannot get to an efficient green energy system fast enough without massive public investment on a scale never seen before. Our corporate regime calls this "socialism." In fact, it is common sense, partially tested during the progressive and New Deal eras and consistent with the massive government spending in our state capitalist system supported by Republicans such as Ronald Reagan and George W. Bush and Democrats such as Lyndon Johnson.

Fortunately, the economic meltdown makes an unprecedented big green stimulus, which would be almost impossible to achieve in other circumstances, simply sensible medicine for today's economic crisis. This stimulus will also save future generations, a time-tricking cure that President Obama has enunciated as a top priority. Obama proposed to create 500,000 new green jobs in his first stimulus plan, a small down payment on the far more massive investment in green jobs during his presidency and beyond.[21] The rationale, economically and environmentally, short and long term, is unassailable. The U.S. Apollo Institute, a coalition of firms and environmental groups seeking to stem climate change and create jobs, says we can create 3 million new jobs with a $500 billion green public investment over ten years.[22] Without such a massive economic stimulus, the United States could easily fall into a new great depression. A green public investment system, built around public and public/private green enterprises, is our best short-term weapon against depression and the best long-term hope for planetary survival.

Such vast public investment will spike the deficit. But staring at a looming depression, most mainstream economists, including Nobel laureates Joseph Stiglitz and Paul Krugman, believe that vastly increased public investments—ones that raise the deficit in the short term—are essential to recovery and long-term debt reduction. Krugman has argued that creating a truly bold stimulus, much bigger than Obama's first stimulus plan passed in 2009, even ultimately as much as $5 trillion, is far more economically and fiscally prudent than being too timid, risking a slip into a depression.[23]

The president must act decisively to ensure that energy companies are in his sights as he moves to solve the climate threat and economic crises together. As on Wall Street, the president must address the public and introduce legislation that structurally transforms the energy sector. Because we are dealing with both short-term and long-term crises, we cannot rely on a voluntary shift "beyond petroleum" by big oil and big coal, or by the Big Three in Detroit, which remain in stage 2 denial and, in the case of the big auto companies, have already been forced into bankruptcy and restructuring around production of small fuel-efficient cars. The big oil and coal and car companies have become hugely dysfunctional and addicted to fossil fuel, focused on short-term profits that they are wringing out of their entrenched fossil fuel investments when the getting is good, while taking themselves and the country down an unsustainable course.

The president must announce that a form of public ownership of big oil and coal may be necessary, along with the massive government intervention in the car industry that has already taken place with the bailouts and restructurings of GM and other U.S. carmakers. This does not mean nationalization of the entire energy sector, because innovation on a massive scale will require a less monopolistic market among many competing public and private small energy companies. It is the very largest companies—which currently restrict such competition and that are actively perpetuating stage 2 denial with more than 1,000 lobbyists in Washington fighting against climate change legislation—that need a new publicly guided green business strategy. President Obama should propose an experimental and temporary approach to public ownership to green immediately the largest oil and coal companies. Here is what he should say:

My Fellow Americans:

I have already proposed some very big reforms on Wall Street. Now I want to talk to you about the energy companies. Moving these companies immediately toward a green business strategy is necessary to preserve national security against the greatest existential threat faced by humanity today: global warming. This is not a discretionary political choice; it is my constitutional obligation. I am required to protect the U.S. public and future generations, and unless we take drastic steps immediately to revolutionize our energy system, I will fail in that mission.

My secretary of energy, Nobel physicist Steven Chu, has already told me that we may be too late to get carbon emissions below even 450 parts per million, even though some scientists believe 350 ppm is the safe limit. The scientific consensus is clear on this, and I have no choice but to align my policy with scientific truth on questions of the survival of civilization.

There are also strong economic rationales for drastic restructuring of the energy sector. Fossil fuel will become more and more costly. Our global competitiveness depends on extremely rapid shifts toward alternative energy as oil becomes scarcer and more costly. Fossil fuel dependence is the Achilles heel of our current economic order.

Rapid transformation requires temporary nationalization of the biggest energy firms, such as ExxonMobil. I have explained that we do not really have a free-market economy and that your taxpayer dollars have always subsidized big banks and other big companies. That is especially true in the energy sector, where big oil and big coal receive billions in tax breaks, loopholes, and other subsidies each year. But they are using your money to pad their own CEO bonuses and hike up your own heating and gas costs. They have failed to act to preserve the world for future generations.

Today, I am proposing that we temporarily take 51 percent ownership of these giant, dysfunctional oil and coal companies. As I have said before, I am not a fan of government ownership, far from it. But today's crises of the economy and of global warming make this a necessary step. Big oil and big coal have had their chance to help us, and they have done the opposite. We can do better, and we will.

Temporary nationalization is smarter government intervention—not more government intervention. The supersubsidized energy sector is already essentially a ward of the state both nationally and globally. My plan simply makes the government serve you rather than the CEOs of big oil and coal.

My plan also increases market competition. The temporarily nationalized companies will compete with all the other privately held energy companies. We may return them to private ownership when they demonstrate that they have moved beyond denial of climate change and are truly transforming themselves into clean and efficient renewable energy companies.

We have long had public utilities and public energy companies. Here is why we need to consider big oil and coal as public utilities today, in the age of warming:

- First, the fossil fuel energy giants, such as Exxon, are making so much money from oil and coal they have become addicted. Oil and coal are their crack cocaine. We need transformed companies accountable to the public to break this suicidal addiction.
- Second, they are already on the public dole. You finance these huge companies—ExxonMobil alone makes $300 billion a year in revenues—by paying for the wars we fight for them, the public lands and water we allow them to lease for nominal fees, the research and development grants we give them, and all the depreciation write-offs we allow them. They take huge profits—in 2008, Exxon made $45 billion in profits; Chevron, 24 billion; ConocoPhillips, $16 billion—through massive tax subsidies from your checkbook.
- Third, the history of the giant energy companies and current developments globally show a shift to energy nationalization. As private sector companies, they cannot compete with the public sector government-owned firms, lacking both the financing, access to oil fields, and deal-making capacities of the government firms in the Middle East and elsewhere.
- Fourth, the giant energy companies have helped lock you into sprawl and a carbon-intensive lifestyle. It is expensive for you, extremely dangerous

for the planet, and very profitable for them. It is permanently embedded in their business strategy and the mind-set of their executives.

- Fifth, the Chinese, our biggest competitors in the twenty-first century, will soon surpass us in solar and wind power by strategic use of their own state-owned energy companies. State-owned Chinese companies have doubled their wind power capacity in each year between 2005 and 2008 and in 2009 are building the six largest—truly immense—wind power projects in the world. Their nationalized energy companies are also furiously competing among each other in a race to create vast leaps in solar production financed by state-owned banks, even as the central government bans three of its five biggest nationalized coal producers from building new plants because of failure to comply with environmental regulation. China, which will invest more in wind and solar and nuclear than in coal and oil-fired electricity, is becoming what the *New York Times* calls "a green energy superpower."[24] The United States cannot afford, either economically or morally, to fall behind China in this most important of all endeavors; we should and must be the world's leader in producing clean energy and helping save the planet.
- Sixth, big oil and coal are destroying the environment, and the public has lost faith in them. Their long history of denial and greenwashing, along with their intense use of lobbyists to stop the climate change laws we need, undermines their legitimacy as business enterprises. The faith and confidence of the public are especially important in energy, with the future of the planet at stake.

I am committed to a new world of clean energy. Our economy will rise or fall depending on our willingness to break new ground and try new approaches. The survival of future generations is at stake. That is why I am proposing these bold new initiatives in the energy sector itself, the most important single part of the twenty-first-century economy and the one that will ultimately determine our economic and human survival. I have already indicated that the oil and coal companies will return to private ownership if the temporarily nationalized companies are inefficient and do not move rapidly toward a postcarbon world. But if they are more efficient and move more quickly toward clean energy production than the private sector companies they compete with, I will propose continued public ownership for future review.

The blowback from the companies and conservatives will be ferocious. Conservatives and energy executives called FDR a "traitor to his class" and "Comrade Roosevelt" when he created public energy companies such as the TVA in the New Deal.[25] They are already calling Obama a socialist or—God forbid—a European.

Obama can overcome this blowback. The public did not buy it in the 2008 elections when Republicans called Obama a socialist and said he "palled around with terrorists."[26] The situation is too serious for this name-calling. Obama needs to show that temporary nationalization is one of several new pragmatic approaches to solving our economic and energy crises—and that it will not only quickly make the biggest energy companies more efficient and greener but also create freer markets in new small renewable energy start-ups and in the larger energy sector.

Obama's stimulus plan and budget will help support many existing clean energy private firms, and the stimulus plan will create many more of them. Temporary nationalization of the biggest firms and the breaking up of firms "too big to fail" go with greater market competition. Obama should show that the trick will be to maintain the best market-inspired innovation we can achieve in garages, basements, small shops, and university labs and public control of the big giants that have been trying to suppress real competition and have tried to prevent smaller start-ups from stealing business.

The Corporation in the Green Regime

The president cannot stop with an overhaul of the financial system, energy sector, and federal departments. The DNA of the modern corporation in every sector—created over the last three corporate regimes—clones that of the banks. Everything is wired for short-term profits and long-term environmental collapse. The climate crisis cannot be solved without rapid regime changes in corporate missions, charters, and governance systems.

The president's fireside chats will have to create immediately a new public conversation about the "corporate sovereignty" that threatens democracy and the prospect of its long-term survival. The public already understands and dislikes the power of big business, seeing it as bad for democracy and citizen well-being. But the president will have to propose a rapid and radical solution that reconstructs the corporation in the spirit of democracy and sustainability.

That can begin with a history lesson. The president should let the public in on the "secret history" of the U.S. corporation.[27] Before the Civil War, Americans worried about the concentrated financial and economic power of big companies and created charters very different from today's. The early corporate charters defined corporations as a public entity created by the government to serve the public interest. In the late nineteenth century, the Gilded Age Supreme Court redefined the corporation as a purely private entity, indeed a "corporate person" with constitutional protections of speech and privacy.[28] Corporate personhood vastly increased corporate power over government itself, giving corporations the right to exercise "speech" through political donations and dictate the unsustainable path of our current corporate system. The public interest in survival is so urgent that the president has no choice but to use his powers to initiate change, resurfacing the spirit and letter of a corporation built to serve the public interest, as in America's earliest era.

Here are some of the most important policies the president should propose immediately to create a green and sustainable business entity and a more democratized polity to ensure long-term public survival:

1. *A new democratic wall.* Democracy and sustainability require that corporate control over the state be ended. The president must act not just to create lobbying limitations but also to build a new systemic firewall protecting the government against overweening corporate power. Both require that the president propose total public financing of elections, drastic limitation of corporate ownership of mass media and schools, reversal of the trend to permit commercial speech as protected under the First Amendment, criminalization of threats of corporations to influence the vote of employees, and rescinding of "investor rights" clauses that allow corporations to sue governments for passing laws protecting labor and the environment.[29]

2. *An end to corporate personhood.* Corporate personhood offers corporations constitutional protections to political speech, privacy, and other individual rights that give them the biggest political megaphone and a political citizenship that drowns out the citizenship of the rest of us.[30] To end the corporate regime so that the government can truly serve the public interest in survival, the president should propose judicial review of the corporate personhood doctrine, based on cases arising from communities that have already begun to challenge the constitutional right of toxic corporations spewing out lethal pollution to do local business. Corporate personhood protects all advertising as free speech, and we need a new constitutional model permitting limits on advertising as a threat to public well-being and survival. Similarly, corporate personhood offers constitutional privacy protections to firms against unannounced inspections that are essential to end illegal pollution.

3. *Protection of the commons.* The president must act to stop and reverse the trend toward corporate privatization of water, forests, wildlife preserves, and other areas of the commons. These are direct assaults on the sustainability of the planet. Forests, along with oceans, are the greatest carbon sink on the planet, soaking up carbon emissions in the atmosphere. But forests and oceans are now threatened by the corporate clear-cutting of the great rainforests and by the changing ocean currents linked to corporate carbon emissions. Privatization of water as the planet warms and creates mass droughts will leave millions of the poorest people at home and abroad at risk of no access to clean water. The president, with other world leaders, must sign global agreements, starting at the 2009 Copenhagen meetings, protecting the commons as essential to solving global warming.[31]

4. *Federalization of corporate charters.* The president should introduce legislation to federalize corporate charters so as to redefine the large business enterprise as a public trust licensed by the government for the common benefit, human survival being the most important. The new charters should be based on the legal and philosophical principles of the pre–Civil War charters that defined corporations as public entities serving the public and accountable to it. The overwhelming public interest in sustainability today should be written into the new charters as mandates to protect the environment by moving rapidly away from carbon burning. At the same time, stakeholders, including workers, should be mandated with new and expansive rights to control executive compensation and to help ensure labor organization, essential to coping with the inherent stagnation crisis and growing inequality.[32]

5. *Democratization of corporate governance.* The president should introduce legislation to move toward stakeholder models of governance in which representatives of shareholders, workers, consumers, communities, government, and the public sit on the board. There should also be special environmental corporate directors to speak for the environment; they will articulate and oversee the environmental interests that stakeholders (as against just shareholders) carry because their own health and well-being are at stake. Stakeholder boards will have longer-term and greener business visions than shareholder ones, mitigating short-term profit blindness.[33]

6. *Rebalancing of equity-to-debt financing.* We are choking on debt, but there is a strong case to be made for incentives to rebalance the equity-debt financing of corporations toward debt.[34] The equity markets, even when restructured, have a tendency to push toward short-term returns. Long-term debt financing gives scope to the long-term stewardship and business strategy we need. The president should call for a commission to study this issue.

7. *A trading in of the big for the small.* The president should be a trust-buster. When a business is too big to fail, it is too big. Breaking up big monopolistic business is good for democracy, competition, efficiency, and the planet. A voluminous literature shows that community-based businesses are often less carbon offensive, although not all businesses can be localized or reduced in size.[35] A new ecopolitical principle is that production and decisionmaking in government and private enterprise are best and greenest at the lowest, most local level possible. This principle has become integral to saving the planet.

11

The Green American Dream
Living More with Less

Each regime has its own moral values, prevailing ideas, and common sense.[1] To achieve the drastic changes described in the previous chapter, we need a swift change in the basic values inculcated by corporate regimes throughout American history. This requires changes in our system of corporate capitalism, which has created an American Dream that is unsustainable. It is a dream of "more," of what a popular video has called "the story of stuff."[2] Our corporate capitalism cannot survive without it. To ensure that Americans live by the corporate story of stuff, the current regime creates what I describe in this chapter as "coerced consumption" and "forced overwork." Many Americans live in a dream world—believing that they make their own choices about their lifestyles based on their own values. This is, to a surprising degree, false. But let us consider first the values themselves.

The ideological apparatus (discussed in earlier chapters) shapes the ideas and morality specific to each regime. In recent corporate regimes, we have had a corporate mentality—churned out in recent decades by Ronald Reagan and George W. Bush, advertising, conservative think tanks, right-wing evangelical leaders, Fox News, and right-wing talk and cable shows—based on individualism, greed, and consumerism.[3] These values build on a historic American dream based on each man (or woman) in his own private castle, with his own land and property, and his happiness tied to more land and more property.[4] Until we change these ruling ideas of accumulating endless property and wealth—all tied to capitalism's invisible hand ideology of each pursuing self-interest to ensure the common good—we have no chance of stopping global warming. We will burn ourselves up in the heat of our passions for private space, big houses, and endless stuff.

The deep history of this dream makes green cultural change daunting. We can see continuities in American values, extending from the search for one's own land on the frontier in the nineteenth century, to the rush to the suburban frontier and the white-picket-fenced house in the 1950s, to the escape to the sprawled farthest tier of suburbs with the gated estates, giant lawns, and golf courses in our current exurban frontier. The American Dream seems inexorably connected to more land, more roads, bigger cars and houses, and more stuff—all part of extreme consumerism and an increasingly carbon-intensive lifestyle.[5]

These values arose from socially imposed corporate moral codes and government policies—indeed are rooted in the systemic requirements of Western capitalism itself—but they found resonance in the founding myths of the United States even in its earliest agrarian stages.[6] Early American settlers saw themselves as fleeing congested and "degenerate" European cities to create their Manifest Destiny of "new frontiers" of personal freedom.[7] Many Americans, including not only Evangelical conservatives but also some "back to the land" environmentalists, still see cities as sinful hellholes.[8]

Hostility toward the city—its spatial limits and cultural degradation—gets expressed in the flight to the suburbs.[9] Cities have been seen as places unfit to raise children, full of greedy commerce and self-interest, crime, vice, and bizarre lifestyles.[10] This is an old medieval European image, and immigrants were induced to cross the Atlantic in search of rural purity, free land, and freedom itself. In the twentieth century, antiurban values morphed into suburban consumerism, with distance from the city equated with freedom, family values, prosperity, and the pleasures of unchecked mall-crawling. Even many environmentalists have bought into this demonization of cities. But the American way of life reflects coerced choices as much as a single and unchangeable system of U.S. values.

Coerced Consumerism: How Corporations Have Shaped Our Dreams

Corporations played a decisive role in shaping each new phase of the unsustainable American Dream and lifestyle.[11] The railroads in the late nineteenth century helped create the yeoman farmer on his own land pursuing the dream of Manifest Destiny. To make the railroads profitable, railroad barons needed mass migration westward, promoting an image of the rural self-reliant virtuous frontiersman reclaiming and civilizing the wilderness. The automobile, housing, real estate, and construction industries promoted the 1950s suburban frontier boom, financed heavily with state highway and housing subsidies, because these new corporate sectors could make extravagant profits by creating the new suburban dream.[12] Likewise, the same industries, aligned with far-suburb and exurban developers focused on the current exurban boom, have helped shape the government policies moving us toward a last frontier tied to sprawl; giant houses; multiacre, chemically green-lawned plots; and endless possessions purchased at the new American mall shrines.[13]

To create these "coerced" new dreams and lifestyles, corporations had to seize the state and craft policies making it impossible for Americans to live in more sustainable ways. During the twentieth century, state policymakers did their appointed corporate job. They invested massively in highways and cut funds for trains and public transit; they required states to go through endless bureaucratic federal reviews to build public transit while state highway projects needed no federal approval; the Federal Housing Authority (FHA) financed "suburban density" houses at one-quarter acre or larger, in contrast to the one-tenth acre lots of the old "streetcar suburbs"; state governments used more flexible FHA funding for 95 percent highway spending and 5 percent public transit spending; the federal government provided large tax deductions for people taking on large mortgages in supersized houses, even as Wall Street loosened credit and encouraged all consumers to spend on mortgages and credit cards way beyond their means, making their carbon footprints ever heavier.[14]

The ideology of free consumer choice—equated today with freedom itself—has masked the truth of coerced consumption patterns. Recall that GM bought up the trolley system of Los Angeles and other California cities to ensure its market for cars. When GM dismantled, track by track and trolley car by trolley car, the existing system, it, along with other auto, banking, energy, and transit companies, forced future generations into dependency on the freeway system and the automobile, a classic model of how our coerced consumption system operates.[15]

In the 1950s, Americans migrated en masse to the suburbs because FHA loans made homes there cheaper. Surveys carried out by sociologist Herbert Gans suggest that the new Levittowners cared less about the larger plots (they found watering big lawns tedious) or suburban community than about the subsidized housing.[16] Zoning policies put in place by planners and local developers—along with the suburban incentives created by federal housing loans—led Americans into sprawl essentially imposed by the government, developers, and city planners.

Charles Siegel, following in the tradition of Jane Jacobs, a great theorist of cities and critic of U.S. urban planners, shows that the urban planning profession, often aligned with developers, played its own huge role.[17] In the name of expertise, planners drastically limited the role of "untutored" citizens in planning their own neighborhoods and cities. The planners' evolving design theories—from functionalism to the new urbanism—generally moved the population toward suburbia and cars but sometimes moved people back in the other direction toward a more urban life. But always the planners contributed to the removal of ordinary citizens from designing the cities, neighborhoods, and transportation systems that shaped their lifestyles. Siegel shows that local citizen movements to control community design, transport, and zoning—and to change rules and policies now requiring low-density auto-dependent suburbs—could move America toward a more pedestrian-friendly model of both urban and suburban neighborhoods. If local and state governments banned cars in some areas, restricted their speed in others, and rezoned housing density, we could create the less sprawled, more environmentally friendly, streetcar suburbs or urban neighborhoods that polls show most Americans now desire.[18]

We urgently need a new politics that challenges the priorities of the developers and the expert claims of the planners.[19] Cities that lower their carbon footprint should be rewarded with federal credits and special aid to pour back into their communities, helping create a new American culture of sustainable urban values. Americans have surrendered their lifestyle choices to technical and political elites and must make cities a new populist political focus, both to enhance their own lifestyles and to help save the planet. This is beginning to happen, with cities such as Portland, Oregon, taking direction from mobilized citizens. They are creating inner cities teeming with pedestrians, bicyclists, and public transit passengers. People live and work on short walkable blocks that integrate residences with shops and banks and churches.[20]

Work and Spend: How to End Overwork and Create a Sustainable Life

Forced labor—usually in the form of involuntary overwork—is another tragedy of today's coerced lifestyle. Overwork might sound like a wonderful luxury in the current recession. But the truth is that overwork is actually contributing to a shortage of jobs and to excess consumerism. It is another way in which corporations, bureaucrats, and technocratic planners dictate our lifestyles and are degrading both the environment and our own well-being.[21]

Economist Juliet Schor, who wrote *The Overworked American* in 1993, showed that Americans in recent decades have been working longer hours every year even though millions want more leisure. Corporations prefer to hire a smaller number of workers and require them to work overtime rather than hire more workers at shorter hours. They can squeeze out more profits this way, because they often do not have to pay salaried workers overtime and the overwork strategy reduces the costs of supporting more workers.[22]

To increase profit, reduce employment, and create involuntary overwork, U.S. companies do not typically pay part-time workers the same hourly wages or adequate benefits and job security. Many workers prefer working less but cannot afford to lose the benefits of full-time work. So whatever the workers' values, the realistic choice is overwork or no work.[23]

The overworked American has historically compensated for lack of leisure by spending more. Forced overwork induces excess consumption, often on credit, with people buying more stuff in a system of competitive consumerism to prove their status and success. They lack the leisure time to find more rewarding alternatives than fast splurges at the mall. Schor describes a treadmill of "work and spend" that feeds on itself, even though it exhausts the worker and degrades the environment.[24]

Government works in tandem with corporations. American law does not require corporations to offer shorter hours to workers who would prefer more leisure. Washington allows companies to refuse to pay the same hourly wage, offer benefits, or provide any job security for part-time work. This is in sharp contrast with policy in Germany and the Netherlands, where the law requires employers to accommodate worker requests for shorter hours without reducing benefits or hourly pay (except in unusual circumstances of hardship for the employer). These policies have worked successfully, and the United States should pass its own choice of work time law.[25]

Europeans have succeeded partly because unions have helped create higher wage levels than in the United States. America's relatively low wages—ranking below almost all western European countries in wage rates—make shorter hours difficult for many workers even if they are guaranteed equal hourly pay and benefits as full-time workers. Moreover, the current economic crisis makes it extremely difficult for U.S. workers to give up any wages for more leisure as their job security and wages keep plummeting.

So a choice of work time law must be combined with vigorous efforts to promote a higher wage level, particularly in a severe economic downturn, something only likely to be achieved with government stimulus tied to economic recovery and quick growth in unions. Barack Obama's first budget, passed as the economy was in free fall, provides incentives for corporations to hire U.S. workers and new tax codes that will increase the after-tax pay of most U.S. workers. He initially backed the critically important employee Free Choice Act, which will make it easier to form unions. He should guarantee the "social wage" to workers of universal health care and free higher education, all part of his current budget plans to revive a sinking economy.

An option for shorter hours is, on balance, good for business as well as workers, in periods of depression and in periods of prosperity. Studies show that productivity tends to increase when hours are reduced. During the Great Depression, Kellogg's created a thirty-hour workweek that lasted fifty years and was highly popular with executives as well as workers. Productivity reached forty-hour levels within two years of the creation of the thirty-hour week. Eighty-five percent of workers liked the thirty-hour plan, despite the lower pay.[26] In today's hard-pressed economy, many businesses and cities, such as Atlanta, are offering furloughs and four-day workweeks that are saving costs in transport and reducing sick days while increasing productivity.[27]

If government took over health care costs, far more companies would probably follow Kellogg's example. Hiring more workers would not increase the company's health care burden. A choice of shorter hours would improve workers' free time, job satisfaction, and morale, a recipe for increased productivity.

A choice of work time law has so many virtues that it is hard to oppose. In the current downturn, it offers a way to share jobs and create full employment. The benefit to workers and the economy of this policy cannot be overstated, explaining why labor has so often supported job sharing and shorter hours. Such a law gives workers the choice of more leisure and allows all workers to choose their own lifestyles. Those workers who love their jobs and want to work long hours (people like myself) could choose to do so. The majority of workers who want more leisure could choose shorter hours. This provides more free choice for all workers.[28]

A choice of work time law has enormous societal and environmental benefits. It provides a way to create full employment while sustaining limits to growth. The shorter hours option is, in fact, the only sure way to provide full employment and limit growth. It is a stunning way to provide all people jobs and improve quality of life while limiting growth and reducing greenhouse gas pollution. Economists David Rosnick and Mark Weisbrot have shown that if all Americans worked the same hours as western Europeans, it would reduce our greenhouse gas emissions by 20 percent.[29] Choice of work time legislation also breaks the link between forced labor and coerced consumption, both of which are not only coercive but also environmentally dangerous.

Shorter work time also breaks the crucial link between increasing productivity and more coerced consumption. Because productivity increases over time, constant or greater work hours lead to more and more products and services that the economy produces and must be consumed, whether the population wants to or not.[30] Shorter work time, even with growth in population, could sustain full employment that does not create even more products and more forced consumption. Since World War II, the idea that we need to consume more has justified the idea that we need to grow fast to ensure both full employment and more consumption. Based on the corporate regime's need to sell and make more profit, the nation as a whole has been induced into a level of debt not seen since 1929—$13 trillion in private household debt equaling the entire size of the gross domestic product. This debt is a potent indicator that escalating consumerism—induced by advertising, the corporate profit impulse, and the government's growth religion—has become unsustainable both economically and environmentally.[31]

We should create sustainable limits to growth to save the economy and the planet. People might choose to consume less for the benefits of more leisure, as long as they still have viable, well-paid, but shorter-hour jobs, which most American prefer. The involuntary downshifting that many Americans are experiencing is part of a national debt shedding necessity for households, the economy, and the planet. But a choice of work hours will cushion the blow both by ensuring jobs to all who want them and by opening the opportunity for more fulfilling leisure than mall-crawling.[32]

Shorter hour options offer Americans more true lifestyle freedom and leisure—a way to express their deep values—compatible with a green society. It would slow down the pace of life, creating less stress, better health, and lower health care costs for business and government. Short hours would lower consumption over time, as leisure opened up more varied and rewarding options of spending time with family and friends, exercising, self-expression in the arts and crafts—in short, living the classical idea of the good life.[33] A more leisurely society would gradually create a very different culture of time, thus moving us toward the longer-term mind-set and stewardship economy essential to solving climate change. Because most Americans want more free time, the option for viable shorter work hours is a lynchpin of a new Green American Dream that is based on personal fulfillment and community rather than coerced work-and-spend.

Greening the Dream: Regime Change, Consumerism, and American Values

Regime change can create surprisingly rapid shifts in values and ideologies.[34] The New Deal created within a few years a partial but notable shift from 1920s greed and consumerist hedonism toward a new morality of solidarity and community.[35] Such rapid changes are triggered by earthquakes like the Depression, but they are possible because all nations have an enduring rich diversity of moral stories and values, some becoming more dominant in a particular regime and other, long-enduring subordinated stories arising in successor regimes. This alternation of stories and values in turn reflects the fact that values and lifestyles always reflect the choices made available to the population by the ruling regimes.

The Reagan Revolution ushered in an orgy of extreme self-interest and materialism. In 1980, President Reagan announced the first commandment of a new corporate regime in his inaugural address when he said that his goal was for everyone to "get rich"—in a hurry.[36] The White House became a billboard for greed, with the president using his first official words to celebrate greed for all. Of course, Reagan designed policies to ensure that only a few would get rich. But that was disguised by his clever and amiable perversion of Adam Smith's invisible hand, assuring us that greed by each individual created a common good.

Excess and the pursuit of "more" took over Reagan's 1980s Wall Street, led by capitalists such as Michael Milken, the junk bond king, and fictionalized by Michael Douglas's notorious character in the film *Wall Street,* Gordon Gekko, who famously pronounced that "greed is good." This modern variant of the invisible hand as the common good became the mantra of our current corporate regime, and Reagan and two Bushes, along with some help from Bill Clinton, carried out the radical deregulation, privatization, and corporate welfare policies necessary to turn both corporations and consumers into Gekko clones.[37] The consequences have proved disastrous for the economy, the environment, and our own souls.

As Reagan ushered in the third corporate regime, he also helped create the time sensibility at the heart of our crisis. The moral aim was not just to get rich but to get rich quickly. Gordon Gekko symbolized fast money, and it became the national creed. Meanwhile, Reagan deregulated and showered with subsidies the financial and fossil fuel markets and companies that worked at hyperspeed.[38] At the same time, electronic revolutions in communications and the Internet helped entrench very-short-term thinking at the heart of the economy and daily life. Earlier capitalist stewards on Wall Street became Gekkos.

In late 2008, CNN created a list of the "Ten Most Wanted Culprits of the Collapse"—exemplars of the greed that had brought Wall Street to its knees. These included wilders such as Richard Fuld, the CEO of Lehman Brothers who took away $480 million as he ran his famous company into a ditch.[39] Lehman was giving three other top executives golden parachutes of $20 million even as they were pleading for a bailout from Wall Street.[40] These new antiheroes, with their faces splashed on cable television and visible in congressional hearings, are doing more than giving Wall Street a bad name. They are disgracing the morality at the heart of the current regime, and they reflect the disappearance of Wall Street as a center for capitalist stewardship.

We may be on the threshold of a new moral story.[41] The reigning myths of greed, individualism, and free markets are being newly challenged. The financial meltdown made clear that personal greed—abetted by the government throwing away all restraining regulations and oversight—is a recipe for disaster. But the meltdown also shows that the markets are not "free," because they are always dependent on the public till, public subsidies, and public bailouts.[42] As the interrelated myths of the invisible hand and free markets implode, our current corporate regime's moral story has begun to crack.

The greed rulers cannot survive the end of belief in greed itself. Moreover, because greed is just the far side of individualism and self-interest, the larger moral story of every individual for himself or herself—the invisible hand morality at the heart of capitalism itself—may be eroding. If we take away greed, the basis of our consumer society is itself threatened. The corporate regime lives by instilling insatiable hunger for more stuff. In fact, all U.S. regimes have been organized around the need for greater consumption because profits—and the survival of capitalism itself—require ever higher consumption.[43]

Our consumer culture has always been systemically coerced. If workers will not or cannot buy more stuff, business cannot sell and make profits. During the competitive phase of nineteenth-century capitalism, competition created low prices that could induce more consumption. The urge to buy increasingly was promoted and coerced through the massive sales pitch, the rise of advertising that began in the 1920s as the most important industry in capitalism.[44] We now swim in a 24/7 world of the electronic sales pitch that creates the most powerful advertising and sales propaganda system ever created and lures the majority into compulsive shopping.[45]

In the current phase of "monopoly capitalism," prices rise and the intensity of the sales pitch correspondingly rises to create more and more consumer demand and reduce the inherent tendency toward stagnation discussed in Chapter 9.[46] The fundamental capitalist dilemma is that each corporation wants to reduce its labor costs but the system as a whole requires workers having enough money to keep buying more to overcome systemic stagnation and boost profits. Modern capitalism resolves this by (a) intensifying the sales pitch even further and (b) inventing the modern system of loose credit and debt that keeps consumer demand high.[47] But the debt was unsustainable and led to the current crisis. Capitalism's fundamental dilemma forced it into the twin unsustainable practices of extreme advertising and extreme credit, which led to debt levels that would ultimately crash the economy and consumer practices that would ultimately destroy the planet.

The problem in recent decades has radically intensified as the economy has globalized, stagnation tendencies have increased because of lower wages and social benefits, and consumer culture has pulled out all the stops through a crazed blast of 24/7 electronic advertising at all demographics and age sectors. Juliet Schor, our leading critic of U.S. consumer culture, has titled a recent book *Born to Buy*.[48] And, indeed, we are. A daily splurge at the mall has become the regime's definition of the American Dream. On November 28, 2008, 2,000 shoppers trying to rush into a Long Island Wal-Mart as it opened on the day after Thanksgiving trampled a Wal-Mart employee to death, letting nothing stop them from grabbing the best bargains that day.[49] Nothing could better demonstrate the intensity of consumer passions (or better symbolize the mortal dangers that consumerism carries in the age of global warming). In early 2009, even in the depths of a scary recession,

Hollywood was reflecting and selling pent-up consumer fever in comedies such as *Confessions of a Shopaholic.*

Journalist Peter S. Goodman, reflecting on the trampling to death of the Wal-Mart employee, writes that "American business has long excelled at creating a sense of shortage amid abundance, an anxiety that one must act now or miss out."[50] And he captures perfectly the reality of coerced consumerism: "For decades, Americans have been effectively programmed to shop.... Financial institutions have scattered credit card offers as if they were takeout menus and turned our houses into ATMs. Hollywood and Madison Avenue have excelled at persuading us that the holiday season is a time to spend lavishly or risk being found insufficiently appreciative of our loved ones."[51]

Former Food and Drug Administration commissioner Dr. David Kessler proves that the U.S. food industry has perfected a new approach to coercing excess consumerism, in this case overeating.[52] Kessler shows that by layering on fat, sugar, and salt, food manufacturers can trigger brain mechanisms to increase our craving. The epidemic of obesity reflects an addictive reaction that the industry has bred by designing processed food to stimulate a chronic, incessant appetite that is intensified by the act of eating itself. Kessler says that Lay's Potato Chips' slogan "Betcha can't eat just one" is "scientifically accurate." He says, "The challenge is how do we explain to America what's going on—how do we break through and help people understand how their brains have been captured?"[53] This applies not just to food but also to all forms of consumption in America.

American-style consumerism is, we know now, violence against the planet. The great moral challenge of the green regime is to move us beyond the malls in our pursuit of happiness and a moral life. Millions of Americans seeking a retreat from the mall may be difficult to imagine. But to understand the possibilities here, we must return to our theme that our lifestyle choices—whether to drive to the mall, to live in the suburb, to drive a car, even to shop—are not "free" choices by each of us. Not all of us love to do these things. With more leisure, millions would spend more time with friends and family and community activities, but the corporate regime has made it extremely difficult to get off the work-and-spend treadmill.

The carbon-intensive consumer lifestyle in America is not an inevitable consequence of industrialism, as the European industrial alternative shows; rather, the American lifestyle is a result of the structural choices and coerced unsustainable consumerism that U.S. corporations imposed. But the current economic meltdown has suddenly made coerced consumption on its former scale impossible. As of early 2009, Americans are driving less, eating at home more, growing more of their own food, and keeping the house cooler in winter and warmer in the summer. Most of us just cannot afford $1,000 heating bills in the winter and the same hefty bill to pay for summer air-conditioning. We put on more jackets in the winter and less clothes in the summer, and we are fashioning more homemade Christmas gifts, maybe even recycling old ones, rather than buying expensive new stuff at the malls. The current crisis induces people to downsize and downshift, living leaner just to get by.

This is a coerced life shift for millions who would rather live higher on the hog. But it may instill new green habits now that are surprisingly pleasing and could lead to a voluntary long-term shift in the way people live and in the core values they uphold.[54] In early 2009, a furloughed mother said the new limits forced her to give up smoking, and others said they were enjoying the chance to spend more time with family. A simpler, more leisurely life can feel like a scary sacrifice at first—and it is not a long-term solution for millions who are poor and need living-wage jobs and benefits—but for a nation of involuntarily overworked Americans, it may come to feel like a gift from heaven.[55]

Personal stewardship disappeared in the third corporate regime, as the "now" of fantasy consumption drove individuals as well as businesses into short-term liquidity and credit crises. The debt-driven road to consumerism and life—enabled by the credit cards sent for years by the credit companies to nearly everyone—is another tragic/virtuous casualty of the economic meltdown. The current crisis has eliminated easy credit. As credit dries up, so do reckless borrowing, mindless consumption, and the short-term time frame that are wrecking our personal lives and planet. The new austerity is bitter medicine, but it may be just the medicine needed to help move us toward a sustainable American Dream built on saving and long-term personal and social stewardship.

Real Wealth: From the Religion of Growth to Quality of Life

Several countries and many analysts have decided to set up alternatives to gross domestic product or growth as a measure of economic and societal health. One measure that may be right for the green regime is called the "Happy Planet Index."[56] Despite its touchy-feeling sound, it points to the need for a new measure based on ecological sustainability and what David Korten calls "real wealth" rather than "phantom wealth."[57] Korten means wealth measuring the well-being of Main Street rather than of Wall Street, based on real social needs rather than money created out of thin air.

Redefinition of wealth is essential to solving global warming. Corporate capitalism defines wealth as commodities or services sold on the market. Such wealth is measured by market value and profit. But true wealth is measured by what Karl Marx called "use value," anything that provides for the well-being and satisfaction of people and communities.[58] This includes the fresh air we breathe, a beautiful sky, delicious water, all parts of the environmental commons, as well as social affection and intimacy, part of the social commons. Although water or air rights can be legally privatized, nature is an indivisible whole, with pollution of even privatized water or air spilling over and contaminating the commons. Until we change the way we define wealth, the commodities model will drive economics and keep intensifying the tragedy of the commons.[59]

The Happy Planet Index is calculated as a ratio of "life satisfaction" indicators multiplied by life expectancy with the total divided by ecological footprint. Korten argues that creating measures of these social and environmental indicators would allow us to redefine wealth in a truer sense: an economy delivering us the goods, services, and lifestyles that create genuine well-being and are sustainable.[60] This is common sense but completely at odds with the economic doctrine at the core of all American corporate regimes. Nonetheless, the economic meltdown has opened a new opportunity for paradigm changes in values and lifestyles, just at the moment that environmental survival requires it.

In a green regime, growth as the ultimate economic aim has to be replaced with sufficiency, a quality of life sufficient to sustain social well-being but not marked by our current excess promoting the tragedy of the commons. This seems the toughest aspect of moral regime change, because growth has become godly among economists, politicians, and consumers alike. In much of the world, including China and India, growth will remain important for some decades to come, and we will need new global economic policies to ensure that the poor and middle class in all nations—especially the global poor in developing nations—have enough to live a sustainable high quality of life. But in the United States, growth cannot be the ultimate aim if we want to sustain the planet. As part of a moral and spiritual transformation, we are likely to see a slow turn away from the monotheistic religion of quantitative growth and toward a focus on quality.[61]

A national happiness index—a simplified version of the Happy Planet Index—will help make clear that more growth and more consumption are not correlated with happiness, at least among the middle and upper classes. A person does not need to be rich to be happy; indeed, the rich get some short-term indulgences but are not happier than those who are just middle class. Studies show that once a person has a modest amount of money, marriage, jobs, and friendships make the difference.[62]

"It's all about the community, stupid." That will become the election slogan in the new green regime. And it reflects a regime change in morality from today's hyperindividualism, greed, and wilding to community, social solidarity, and interdependence. This regime change shifts from the morality of the invisible hand to the stewardship morality required in the age of climate change.

But that will take years. Yes, it will, but remember that all nations, including the United States, are built on competing moral narratives. The United States has always been individualistic, but it also has a historic and strong moral strain of community.[63] Individualism has been dominant, but we have seen many eras in which community has moved to the foreground as the reigning discourse. This happened in the progressive era and the New Deal, and community is ripe for resurgence today.[64]

And it may already be happening, just in time. In his inaugural address, President Obama signaled that the age of unlimited growth must end. He said that the United States can "no longer consume the world's resources without regard to effect." No president has said that before, and that he did so is immensely hopeful. Famous Harvard biologist E. O. Wilson said that Obama's talk "was like blinds being opened to let light beam into a dark room."[65] Journalist Derrick Z. Jackson said that "Obama became the first president to admit on a global scale that we have limits to live within."[66]

Obama's rhetorical willingness to challenge the religion of growth is a thunderbolt. Americans have long wrapped themselves in their divinely sanctioned "manifest destiny" to expand and grow beyond all geographical and material limits. It has been the main tenet of U.S. capitalism, global U.S. hegemony, and the American Dream. But as E. O. Wilson put it, Obama's challenge to the growth religion creates a shock "like a car stopped dead on the prairie."[67] Whether we go from this dead stop toward a regime change of sustainability and sufficiency—from the invisible hand to the common good—will help determine humanity's future and just might prevent the looming tragedy of the commons.

12

Through and after Depression

How Long-Term Climate Change Solutions Are the Best Medicine for Our Four Other Biggest Short-Term Crises

The last chapters would suggest that I am betting the ranch on the idea that the economic meltdown is good timing of very bad news. It could be the unwelcome gift propelling a green regime change to promote short-term economic recovery and save us from a new great flood. I am hardly comfortable, however, with the idea that our economic crisis is going to be the magic carpet on which we all climb and escape the burning flames of an overheated future world. For one thing, as I have already mentioned, the economic crisis could derail many crucial green initiatives on the grounds that we cannot afford them. Passing a gas or broader carbon tax in the United States is one critically important likely casualty—and spending enough money quickly on green jobs and infrastructure is another. Even though I am hopeful that, on balance, the paradoxical effect of the economic crisis will be to help promote green regime change and ward off climate change, I realize that this is not a sure thing.

Even if Barack Obama actually leads the world toward massive green stimulus to solve the global economic meltdown, and then invokes the powers I have described in the last two chapters, we cannot rest comfortably. At some point, the economy will recover and the sense of crisis may fade. But the threat of global warming and the need for urgent action to save future generations will be greater than ever. And at that point, the perversity of the timing crisis described throughout this book will rear its head again. How will we resist our deeply conditioned tendencies to focus on the short term even when we are still facing a long-term catastrophe that could end the human experiment as we know it? If the economy has recovered, what are the new short-term crises that could continue to catalyze and inspire more public support for green action big enough to defuse the climate change time bomb?

Even though climate change will loom very large for a long time, I still see hope. This is because global warming is deeply intertwined not only with the current economic meltdown but also with a series of other short-term crises that demand action from leaders and social movements now. The best solutions to these other crises are precisely the policies that we need to put in place now to solve climate change. Global warming may prove for decades to be the umbrella for pursuing social justice and for remaking the economy.

In the rest of this chapter, I want to briefly identify four urgent short-term crises and show how they are golden green opportunities to survive better today and make the world more survivable for future generations. But the president and the rest of us must take notice and act with unwavering dedication.

The Four Short-Term Crises

1. Global competitiveness
2. Energy independence
3. Oil wars and militarism
4. Jobs and social justice

Global Competitiveness

In late 2008, a journalism student asked Ted Turner about how young people like himself could make money fast. Turner did not blink or hesitate. Invest in green energy businesses, he replied, and the student would make a bundle. Ted said that clean energy is *the* economic future and *the* solution to the U.S. crisis of global competitiveness. Turner said he personally planned to invest big-time, blanketing the 3 million acres he owned in western and southern states with solar panels so that he could "heat Chicago."[1]

Turner's comment reminds us that we are dealing not just with severe recession but also with a newly urgent problem of global competitiveness. There are many causes of the current meltdown, but they are all related to the decline of U.S. global economic dominance. As soon as we "recover," we will find ourselves dealing with the deeper structural crisis of competitiveness that even now is pulling us into what we might call the "Detroit" malaise. The United States is no longer on the cutting edge of a globalizing economy in which more and more of the action lies in a very innovative and high-tech China and East Asia.[2]

Getting competitive in the twenty-first-century global economy is going to be front and center in U.S. politics, as part of the current recovery effort and beyond. If we recover without getting competitive, it will be a short recovery, leading to new downturns or long stagnation. If we find the key to competitiveness, we will speed the recovery and make it more sustainable.

The competitiveness issue is short term, midterm, and long term, but its short-term impacts are so enormous that politicians and the public cannot ignore it. Without immediate action, there will be huge ramifications throughout the United States: continually falling wages, more insecure jobs, growing inequality, an increasingly frayed physical infrastructure and safety net, and a more dismal standard of living.

Business as usual will intensify the competitiveness undertow, helping to make the current crisis worse and the recovery far more difficult. But Turner, along with many other environmentalists, especially Thomas Friedman, are right. The green policies to deal with long-term climate change are precisely what will help solve the short- and longer-term competitiveness crisis.[3] This happy coincidence—the source of new green ways to "trick time"—is a reflection of the growing scarcity of fossil fuels, their inevitable increase in cost, and the necessary consequence: that nations holding on to twentieth-century energy systems will become increasingly noncompetitive. Economies compete based on many factors, but the energy powering them is a foundation stone of competitiveness itself. The most competitive sector of the global economy is going to be clean energy technology and the entire broader matrix of green social and political innovations that move economies from twentieth-century brown to twenty-first-century green.[4] Any country that either creates a major breakthrough in new clean energy technologies or rapidly brings existing clean energy systems to scale is going to achieve instantaneous competitiveness. The competition around clean energy innovation—technologically, socially, and politically—forces countries for short-term competitive reasons to go green. It pushes leaders thinking only in the short term to embrace policies essential for the long-term prospects of humanity.

Thomas Friedman has advanced an important but truncated version of this idea, arguing for a green revolution precisely because he sees it as the best way to achieve global competitiveness now.[5] Friedman makes this argument as well as anyone, showing that it is self-interest, rather than altruism or visionary idealism, that will get us moving green. And he shows that the United States can persuasively argue to Chinese or Indian leaders that if they do not move green even faster than we do, we will "clean their clock" economically, essentially showing that it is in the economic self-interest of all major nations to engage in this kind of time trickery and go green as rapidly as possible.[6]

Friedman fails to highlight that competitiveness will hinge as much on green social and political innovation as on green technology. The truth is that the solutions do involve technological breakthroughs, but only ones wrapped in the deep economic, societal, cultural, and political regime changes described in the last two chapters. Competitiveness will go not simply to the countries with the best engineers but also to those with the most innovative architects, urban planners, community organizers, and citizens with the right political activism and cultural genius, including the genius of their presidents or leaders. Here is the kind of equation Friedman likes to write about: Competitiveness = green tech innovation + green social-political-cultural activism. But Friedman misses most of the second half of this equation. He argues that "there is only one thing bigger than Mother Nature and that is Father Profit," arguing that the green revolution for competitiveness requires American-style innovation: "The only thing that can stimulate this much innovation ... is the free market."[7] He realizes that government will have to help create market incentives for "crazy, wild—off-the charts demand" for green energy,[8] but he sees the climate and competitiveness solution all possible only within the context of U.S. capitalism. He overlooks all the ways in which U.S. capitalism systemically engenders the consumerism, reckless financialization, short-termism, lack of stewardship, and denial of limits and finitude that are at the core of the climate change crisis.

Nonetheless, Friedman is correct that green public and private investments are the key to twenty-first-century competitiveness. And he is also right that in the short to midterm, concerns about global competitiveness will likely be the most powerful mainstream short-term force helping the president and the rest of us trick time and lock in now the long-term green policies that we would otherwise delay until it is too late.

Energy Independence

In the 2008 when gas prices skyrocketed to more than $4 a gallon, the issue of energy independence became central to the presidential campaign. Both Democrats and Republicans made it an emotional focus, but the Republicans used the issue most effectively by reducing it to the mindless slogan shouted over and over at the St. Paul Republican National Convention and McCain-Palin rallies everywhere: "Drill, Baby, Drill." The GOP got so much traction out of the issue that Democrats, including Obama, backed off their opposition to offshore drilling, fearful that being blamed for high gas prices could be the secret weapon delivering John McCain into the White House.

Drilling for oil in fragile ecosystems is a crazy idea in the age of global warming, when all our efforts should go to kicking our addiction both to oil and the fossil fuel automobile and larger economy. Nonetheless, the issue of energy independence—and dependence on Middle East oil—is not going to go away, with growing oil scarcity and volatility of oil prices likely to be front and center on the roster of unavoidable short-term crises facing every president going forward, starting with Obama.

He has the opportunity to do his own brand of green time-trickery on the energy independence issue, and he has begun to do so.[9] Drilling for oil and continuing our larger dirty-energy addiction will only make our energy dependence on unstable Middle Eastern and other areas more severe and costly. The real solution to energy independence is a massive systemic shift to clean energy produced in the United States itself with the help of government incentives and entrepreneurs such as Ted Turner and T. Boone Pickens. If that shift is begun now to deal with the short-term costs of energy dependency, it will prove one of the most effective arrows in the green time-trickster's quiver, because it deals with energy dependency by kicking in policy solutions to long-term climate change.

This shift is already happening in Congress, where the 2009 Democratic climate change bill, led by Representatives Edward Markey and Henry Waxman, is framed around issues of energy independence and security, the short-term issues that seem to generate the greatest resonance and momentum for global warming action in Congress and the nation. In 2007, Speaker of the House Nancy Pelosi established a select committee on energy independence, chaired by Markey and featuring a Web site highlighting the intertwining of the issues: "Welcome to the Select Committee on Energy Independence and Global Warming website. This unique committee was established by Speaker Nancy Pelosi in early 2007 to add urgency and resources to the commitment of this Congress to address the challenges of America's oil dependence and the threat of global warming.[10]

The energy independence issue has to be treated carefully because it evokes images of national self-reliance in an age of global warming in which the reality is global interdependence. The United States and many other countries, even with rapid and huge shifts toward clean energy, will not be able to move entirely off of imported oil for decades. The economic and military issues connected to energy interdependence are not going to disappear by our pretending that we can construct a world of energy-independent countries. Energy independence can easily be exploited to move the world toward more insular, jingoistic, and environmentally destructive policies that will hasten, rather than solve, climate change.

Nonetheless, a progressive, nuanced approach to energy independence is something the green movement needs to ward off the abuse of the issue by hypernationalistic politicians, and big oil and coal, and to make good use of the opportunities to trick time for green aims. One of the early tests of Obama as green time-trickster will be how effectively he can exploit energy independence as a short-term lever for green policies warding off long-term climate change. The emphasis should be on massive subsidies to the clean energy sector at home, the broader green regime changes discussed in the last two chapters, and global trade and carbon agreements discussed shortly.

Oil Wars and Militarism

In the age of global warming, traditional national security ideas are becoming obsolete. Even though nuclear and conventional wars remain a huge existential threat, the other great threat to global national security has become climate change. Ultimately, the Department of Energy in countries around the world will become as important to preserving security as the War Department.

National security issues are always front-and-center crisis issues that dominate short-term U.S. politics. Middle Eastern wars, linked to the broader war on terrorism, are likely to be the short-term drivers of any U.S. administration, including Obama's. As the global hegemon, the United States inevitably is enmeshed in military actions that put lives at risk and destabilize strategic regions of the world. The crisis of the permanent U.S. war state, a nation constantly engaging in military interventions, is an unwelcome but major short-term opportunity for the green time-trickster. That is because the short- to midterm polices required to end U.S. wars are intertwined with a shift away from oil, an immediate shift from military to green stimulus of the economy, and a long-term construction of the green regime described in the last chapter. Any genuine green movement would make American demilitarization one of its first demands.

Foreign policy analyst Michael Klare argues that U.S. wars are increasingly for cheap oil.[11] With the discovery of massive oil reserves in the Arabian Peninsula in the 1930s, the United States began to cultivate strong ties to major oil sheiks, such as the royal Saudi family, and build political ties enabling Exxon and Chevron to displace the British oil giants and move into the oil fields in Saudi Arabia, Iran, and Iraq after World War II.[12]

Saudi Arabia, Iraq, and Iran have three of the greatest proven oil reserves in the world. In 1953, the CIA overthrew the democratically elected Iranian president, Mohammed Mossadegh, who was nationalizing British and U.S. oil firms, and replaced him with the shah of Iran, thereby instantly cementing ties among U.S. oil firms, the Iranian government, and the treasure trove of Iranian oil.[13] Bob Woodward has documented that President George H. W. Bush waged the 1991 Gulf war against Iraq to deal with concerns about Saddam Hussein's policies on oil and oil pricing, also obviously a major concern of President George W. Bush and Vice President Dick Cheney in their 2003 invasion of Iraq.[14] Klare's historical account of U.S. intervention, political alliances, and military bases across the Muslim world is powerful evidence that the United States fights for the world's biggest oil fields, oil refineries, and oil pipelines. This is hardly surprising: When I ask my students to raise their hands if they think the United States would be fighting wars in the Gulf and Middle East if there were broccoli fields instead of oil fields, I do not see any hands go up.

Klare's argument about oil wars does not tell the whole story. As I show in later chapters, the United States operates as the world's hegemon; it manages the world's broader military, political, and economic arrangements, largely in the service of global corporations that may use oil or fossil fuel but are not just energy or military companies.[15] The United States is often involved in wars that are not related to oil or scarce resources. The role of a hegemon is to maintain credibility and power in every part of the world, even where there are no resources directly at stake, as in the case of many of the poorest countries, such as Haiti, where the United States has sent the marines.[16]

Nonetheless, Klare's argument is important because it documents the growing connection among natural resources, energy, and war in the age of climate change. Although Klare does not emphasize the timing paradox at the center of my argument, he makes clear that the crisis of unsupportable wars on our country's short-term political agenda provides yet another opportunity for dealing with long-term climate change.

The astonishing economic costs of U.S. wars—Nobel economist Joseph Stiglitz calls Iraq "the $3 trillion war"[17]—along with the cost in human lives and in U.S. global moral standing, have made U.S. militarism, and specifically the Iraqi occupation, a short-term crisis. U.S. wars are overstretching the United States both militarily and economically, a form of what historian Paul Kennedy has called "imperial overreach," the historic recipe for the collapse of Great Powers.[18] Obama was elected on the promise of ending the war in Iraq and bringing a new philosophy to U.S. foreign policy. Here is another critical opportunity for time trickery, leveraging short-term peace initiatives to help implement long-term policies for climate change.

In the short term, a major U.S. shift toward green stimulus, conservation, energy efficiency, and clean energy—a shift already promised by Obama—would reduce incentives to continue current oil wars or wage new ones. If energy needs are reduced in the short term through efficiency and conservation, and met increasingly through efficient renewable systems in the mid- to long term, the arguments for current military intervention in the Gulf and larger Middle East would dramatically weaken. As public pressure builds for reconstruction at home—and as the cost of oil wars in a time of recession and massive deficits becomes politically unsupportable—we can see a transformation occurring. Short-term massive green investment and stimulus initiatives simultaneously act to (1) promote short-term economic recovery, (2) reduce short- and midterm needs for oil imports, and (3) thereby make it easier for Obama to withdraw from Iraq, limit his new war in Afghanistan and Pakistan, and resist entrenched militaristic pressures coming from U.S. energy companies as well as the military itself. The shift from military hegemony to global sustainability as the world's greatest security crisis is within Obama's rhetorical reach, but his expansion of troops in Afghanistan and strikes into Pakistan raise serious questions about whether he will deliver at the level of rhetoric or the level of policy.

A second quite different green time-tricking opportunity, however, arises from a crucial root of U.S. wars that Klare does not discuss. For decades, as discussed in the last chapter, the United States has relied on *military Keynesianism* (high government spending on the military) to stimulate and grow the economy, both in good and bad times.[19] Except in the New Deal era, U.S. capitalist ideology has rhetorically rejected Keynesian thinking as socialist. But because the U.S. economy requires massive government pump-priming and subsidies, U.S. leaders before, during, and especially after the New Deal turned to a "back-door" form of Keynesian thinking. The one legitimate form of permanent massive government spending—accepted by both conservatives and liberals—has been for the Pentagon, reflecting the ideology of "national security" as the only true national interest (all popular economic or social needs are viewed as parochial, or "special," interests). The national security consensus opened the door to huge defense budgets that for decades became the U.S. major government economic stimulus program to catalyze new technologies—including the transistor, computer, and Internet—and to spur economic growth.[20]

Military Keynesianism is thus a core economic policy in the United States, but it can be sustained only when there are wars to fight. An underlying systemic cause of U.S. militarism is the need to create environments in which large military budgets can be legitimated as necessary for military victory, requiring enemies to be found and fought, whether communists or terrorists. The real aim is not only winning wars but also keeping the economy humming.[21]

Here is where a green time-trickster such as Obama can employ his magic again. Ending unsupportable short-term wars could threaten the U.S. economy unless military Keynesianism is replaced with alternative massive government investment in the civilian economy. A president can reduce systemic pressures to fund the military and fight costly wars by showing that there is greater economic bang for the government buck in green domestic stimulus. *Green Keynesianism is the alternative to military Keynesianism—and it is a key foundation for a new politics on climate change.*

Obama was elected to end the war Iraq in the short term, which opens up this second way to trick time. Getting out of Iraq is a first step in shifting from military Keynesianism to green Keynesianism. If Obama could achieve this change as part of his exit strategy from Iraq—showing that green government civilian investment can boost the economy better than Pentagon spending—his legacy in history would be assured.

Ending costly wars and the military Keynesian philosophy behind them immediately frees up massive funds for nonmilitary ends. Ending the Iraq war opens up a short-term bonanza for government green stimulus of the U.S. economy. The idea of redirecting war funds toward green stimulus and regime change rather than simply lowering taxes or reducing the deficit comes both from the gravity of the current economic crisis and the need for massive stimulus, the seriousness of the global warming emergency, and the fact that climate change has itself become, along with nuclear proliferation, the ultimate national security issue.

Peace and green are becoming almost synonymous. The green regime has no need for oil wars, which would begin to end most of our military involvements in the Islamic world. A United States operating on clean energy, rather than fossil fuels, would develop a less militaristic foreign policy and would lose the major incentives that drive not only its oil wars but also much of its larger hegemonic policy. Meanwhile, a less militaristic United States that rejected military Keynesianism could redirect billions of dollars toward conservation, energy efficiency, research on new energy sources, and the social and political changes that will defuse the climate time bomb.

Jobs and Social Justice

The greatest crisis in the United States is the social injustice that has created what Chuck Collins, an expert on inequality and tax policy, calls "economic apartheid."[22] Long before the current economic meltdown, the United States was pursuing social and economic policies that deepened terrible race and class divisions. What Collins calls the policies of "extreme inequality" led the top 1 percent of the population to own more than 40 percent of the nation's wealth while the bottom 90 percent own less than 10 percent.[23] Despite working almost a month more each year, often in multiple jobs, the ordinary U.S. worker saw virtually no gains in real wages from the 1978 to 2008. Declines in pay, loss of job security, cuts in benefits such as health care and pensions, and spikes in personal debt and bankruptcy created a massive anxious class, once proud of its middle-class standing but now a paycheck or pink slip away from poverty, hunger, or homelessness.[24] We have at minimum 40 million poor people in this very wealthy society and perhaps as many as 75 to 100 million, depending on the various statistical measures economists use.[25]

The 2008 crash drove much of the anxious class over the cliff into the valley of the poor, leaving millions of others hanging by their fingertips.

Millions now are losing their jobs, their homes, and their pensions all at the same time. Meanwhile, the number of billionaires in the United States grew to include more than 400 superrich families.[26]

None of this is an accident. It is the inevitable outcome of the third corporate regime.[27] Reagan and his conservative successors initiated huge tax cuts for the rich, across-the-board cuts in social programs, a ruthless attack on unions, a vast increase of subsidies to big business, and trade policies that weakened workers and the environment. The social welfare of the New Deal was turned into a system of corporate welfare for the rich.[28] Such policies all converge to create economic apartheid, a society so deeply divided by class and race that it rivals Third World nations where the rich gate themselves off from the slum populations and employ private armies to protect their homes from the unwashed masses.[29]

I have written several books about our current corporate regime,[30] but a personal experience brought home to me in a new way just how deep its injustice has seared the soul of our nation (even before the current meltdown) and how this terrible systemic inequity is yet another potentially fruitful opportunity to trick time and solve long-term climate change with policies dedicated to fighting short-term injustices. I have long been involved in teaching a course to midlevel business managers dealing with business and society. My focus in recent years has turned increasingly to environmental issues and sustainability as core social justice issues. But the more traditional definition of the crisis of social justice—in particular the extreme gap between the rich and the poor—was what many of these managers saw as the big social question, far more important than climate change. They supported environmental sustainability but thought it meant putting too much attention on polar bears and not enough on poor people, fearing that the environmental movement would divert focus and actually make the crisis of social injustice worse.

When corporate managers want a sociologist to focus on economic inequality, then there is a truly serious crisis of injustice in the nation. And my manager-students were correct that the environmental movement has a history of elitism that has contributed to economic apartheid and has done little to promote broader social justice. Environmentalism in earlier incarnations has sometimes promoted its own eco-apartheid, creating a society where the affluent could afford organic food, clean water, and environmentally safe neighborhoods, while the masses of workers and the poor lived near industrial plants spewing out poisons into their local rivers and toxic waste into their backyards.[31] Early environmental movements often ignored the fact that the poor bore the biggest brunt of pollution and that calls for ends to growth preserved the affluent lifestyles of the Western comfortable classes while locking millions of working and impoverished people around the world into poverty.

But if my managers are rightfully focused on dealing with economic inequality, now made worse by the economic crisis, they have not seen clearly that climate change is piling more misery onto the poor and intensely deepening the crisis of social injustice. Former UN secretary general Kofi Annan has said: "Climate change is the greatest humanitarian challenge of our time, causing suffering to hundreds of millions of people world wide.... The first hit and worst affected are the world's poorest groups, and yet they have done the least to cause the problem."[32] A report commissioned by Humanitarian Forum, based in Geneva, calculates that poor nations suffer 90 percent of the burden of global warming, but the fifty most impoverished countries create less than 1 percent of the world's total carbon emissions.[33]

My managers also did not understand the newest incarnation of the green movement emerging in recent years and crystallizing around the ultimate issues of both climate change and social justice. It is a movement that not only is beginning to reject eco-apartheid and focus on environmental justice, but is also now offering a ripe opportunity to restructure the entire movement for social justice in the United States and the world by intertwining itself with ecopopulist green regime initiatives for social justice that will in the long run ward off global warming, end poverty, and create jobs for all who want them.

A leader and chronicler of this new wave of environmentalism in the United States is Van Jones, an African American green activist from Oakland, California; a climate change adviser to President Obama; and author of the influential 2008 book, *The Green Collar Economy*.[34] Jones argues that we are entering the third wave of the environmental movement, the first being the conservation movement championed by Teddy Roosevelt at the beginning of the twentieth century and the second being the regulatory movement inspired by Rachel Carson's book *Silent Spring* in the 1970s.[35] Jones suggests that both earlier waves made contributions to the environment but, ironically, helped build a form of white affluent environmentalism in which well-to-do whites ran the movements and reaped the benefits, while ordinary workers and poor folks, particularly minorities, played little role in the movements and received few of its benefits. They increasingly became a population left behind economically and used as a dumping ground for the pollution created by the larger society, leading to what Jones calls "eco-apartheid."[36]

Jones argues that the newest green wave is different. Rather than being focused on conservation or regulation, this environmental movement is focused on "investment."[37] Its new aim is to build a new green economy that has two intertwined aims: (1) to ward off and solve the climate change crisis and (2) to do so by bringing the poor and working classes of all colors back into the mainstream of society by employing them in millions of new green collar jobs.[38]

Jones talks about a green new deal, and he is implicitly talking, as I have advocated earlier, about replacing "free-market," or laissez-faire, economics with green Keynesianism as the governing U.S. economic doctrine.[39] His argument is that the green economy is labor intensive and creates a new demand for the huge anxious class that is currently seeing its jobs outsourced, downsized, or taken over by machines. The core insight is that the green economy—one with a massive enough green public investment to ward off global warming—will be a full employment economy composed of jobs with a huge variety of skill sets that millions of poor and working-class people have or can learn quickly. Many of these jobs will be in their own poor communities, involving weatherizing their own homes or those of neighbors, installing solar panels on local homes and offices, building a new "smart grid," and cultivating local gardens and farmers markets.[40]

I love Jones's way of defining the "green collar job" on the frontpiece of his book. It is worth quoting in full:

> Green-collar job, noun
> : blue-collar employment that has been upgraded to better respect the environment
> : family-supporting, career-track, vocational or trade-level employment in environmentally friendly fields
> : examples: electricians who install solar panels; plumbers who install solar water heaters; farmer engaged in organic agriculture and some bio-fuel production; and construction workers who build energy-efficient green buildings, wind power farms, solar farms, and wave energy farms.[41]

What is clear here is that Jones sees the new environmentalism as a full employment movement that can lift the poor and working classes into a dignified life. It will help both liberal and conservative working people, even "Joe the Plumber," who became John McCain's symbol of right-wing populism. Even though the new movement's long-term aim is preserving the planet, it works immediately to alleviate America's largest current social justice crises. By mobilizing the masses for full employment, it can build the political support necessary for the vast public and private investment policies required to jump-start the green collar revolution, which Jones sees as creating 5 million new jobs over the next few years.[42]

Jones does not focus on the time paradox at the heart of this book, but his analysis offers one of the most potent ways to trick time. The scale of injustice and the depth of populist pain are such an intense, short-term emergency—particularly in the current meltdown—that it will be difficult for politicians to ignore, especially in an Obama-led Democratic Party. Jones's policies to alleviate poor and working-class pain today are precisely those necessary to ward off the long-term threat of the Great Flood, a masterful model of green politics.

Jones is an optimist, and he is infectious—and now Obama seems to be taking note and proposing initiatives in the ecopopulist spirit. Obama has put Jones in the White House as a top energy adviser and has adopted some of Jones's green jobs vision in his own stimulus. Obama shares many of the social justice concerns and solutions Jones shows to be intertwined with the climate crisis. If I have any quarrel with Jones, it is that I think he underestimates the economic and political resistance that his ecopopulist revolution faces from the corporate powers that be if it seeks to get big enough to deal adequately with either our social inequities or global warming, something already evident in the 2009 huge rise of corporate lobbyists, especially from the oil and coal industries, to fight Obama's energy initiatives.[43] Jones offers no systemic analysis of the roots of our current social injustice in the reigning corporate regime—and appears, if anything, relatively sanguine about the movement of large sectors of big business to his green collar revolution.[44] True, many small and large businesses are trying to go carbon neutral and can make a contribution, but the larger corporate system will not embrace ecopopulism.[45] Without a more fleshed-out analysis of the corporate systemic power blocking the gates to ecopopulism, Jones also cannot offer a persuasive analysis of the political movements that can create green regime change.

Jones is a gentle evolutionist seeking to include everyone in his revolution. He is a prophet, a twenty-first-century green Martin Luther King, but he will need to match his largeness of heart and spirit with a recognition of the entrenched powerful interests that will not gracefully make way for him, anymore than they did for King. Nonetheless, there is no more compelling and magical green time-trickster than Van Jones—and he has articulated beautifully the possibilities of defusing the long-term climate time bomb with policies to heal the short-term pain of America's diverse and abandoned working poor. His analysis can also be applied to the world at large and suggests an approach to creating a more socially just globalization through global green initiatives, the subject of our next two chapters.

PART III
Green Globalization

13

The West and the Rest: One

Why It Takes a Global Village to Cool the World

Consider this possibility: President Barack Obama leads a green revolution in the United States and engages in all the time tricks required to create a new sustainable America.

An astute reader might say: "Yes, but China, India, and the rest of the world have to paint their own houses green if we are to save humanity. And that doesn't look like it's going to happen. China and India alone are hell-bent on rapid dirty growth using lots of coal, even though both are also investing heavily in wind and solar. No matter what we do, China, India, and other huge economies such as Japan and Russia are going to spew out enough carbon in the next ten or twenty years to sink the planet."

I reply: "Yes, yes, that's absolutely right. The green revolution must go global, fast, or it's useless."

The reader says: "There is no sign that is about to happen. China, India, and other developing nations are racing toward maximum growth, whatever the environmental costs."

I reply: "That is not true, as I show here, but they have good reasons to tell the richer nations to stop preaching. Their poor now bear the brunt of global warming created by the West—and colonialism locked them into their poverty as well as horribly polluted slums. We have to own up to our responsibilities and finance green development throughout the developing world to get the extremely ambitious global climate change agreements we need."

And the reader replies: "Well, tell us how all that's going to happen. You have focused on the United States, which doesn't have a lot of money to give away in aid and ignored all the problems in getting the rest of the world on board."

And I say: "That's what this and the next chapter are for. Buckle your seat belt."

I have focused this book on the United States because a green revolution here will be a shot heard round the world. It would catalyze global greening faster than anything else. This reflects not only our nation's enormous leadership powers but also the reality that the United States is 4.5 percent of the world's population and spews out 20 percent of the world's greenhouse gases.[1]

The United States has opted out on climate change, with George W. Bush evolving reluctantly from a stage 1 to a stage 2 denier president. President Bill Clinton himself, with Al Gore by his side as vice president, refused to commit the United States to the Kyoto Accords, the first global effort to deal with climate change; Clinton's action was an epic mistake. But Barack Obama's election could make the United States a leader on climate change and could forge new global policies and agreements—starting at the crucial 2009 Copenhagen meetings—that could dramatically shift the development strategies of China and India if we offer them the financial incentives and technology to help them do it.

Of course, we can imagine a very different scenario. The world moves forward to solve the climate change crisis, and the United States, even under Obama, still opts out. That, too, would sink humanity. Or China and India could refuse to go green fast enough, no matter what we do.

The lesson is obvious. Climate change is a global crisis and has only a global solution. This is the greatest unifying issue of all time. If it does not bring us together in a new world system, we are all condemned. The good news is that there is reason to believe a new green global system could arise from the ashes of our current ravaged globe. Climate change, global recession, and the erosion of faith in American economic and military policies all suggest the prospects of a global regime change, parallel to the green regime change that may emerge in the United States. The bad news is that this regime change is at least as hard to achieve in the world as in the United States. At least we know, however, the outlines of a global solution. That is the subject for the rest of this chapter and the next one.

Separate and Unequal:
Why Hegemony Cannot Be Green

I spend a lot of time teaching my students about the idea of hegemony. Few have heard the term or thought much about it. I tell them that if they have not thought about hegemony a lot, they should not consider themselves literate because it is the governing principle of our current world order.[2]

Since at least the rise of the European empires a few centuries ago, the world has been organized on the hegemonic principle, which dictates that the world be ruled by the strongest nation or nations. Hegemonic nations (or "hegemons") police the world, usually in the name of providing security, civilized order, and prosperity for all peoples.[3] In the last five hundred years, the West—including the British, French, Germans, and Americans—has been the hegemon. Today, the United States is the sole global hegemon, even though many believe it is declining and that rising powers such as China might replace it.[4]

Hegemony is rule by "the boy with the biggest toy" (the nation with the biggest guns and dominant military power). It has proved to be an immature and dangerous principle, now suicidal because it undermines the possibility of solutions to global warming and wars with weapons of mass destruction.

Hegemony has different dimensions. There are economic hegemons, the nations that control the world economy. There are also military hegemons, which conquer and police through force of arms. The United States has been both the world's economic and military hegemon since World War II—and historically these two types melded in what we have called empire. Today, most Americans do not think of the United States as an empire. Unlike the Romans, we do not own slaves as property, and unlike the British, we do not have formal colonies. But whatever we call the United States, its hegemony is nevertheless a fact.[5]

The world will not turn green in a hegemonic order. At first, this assertion seems counterintuitive, because when a big change is needed quickly, one dictatorial power in the world might seem the only force capable of achieving it. But just as one superpower cannot end the global existential threat of nuclear war, a single superpower lacks the might to stop warming by itself, which requires the willing consent and robust cooperation of many states and peoples.

Fortunately, there are alternatives to hegemony brewing, as U.S. military and economic hegemony decline. One alternative is collective security.[6] The United Nations is a symbol of this new kind of world order. If we took its principles of global interdependence, cooperation, and human rights seriously, we would create a global regime change and have a far better chance of greening the entire world. It is far from certain that the world will embrace collective security, but the crisis of the hegemonic principle and the emergencies of both nuclear war and climate change could bring such a change faster than has long seemed possible. Meanwhile, even under the hegemonic system, we can fire up intensified diplomacy, something favored by the Obama administration, leading toward nuclear disarmament and "carbon disarmament" that start the world on a new path. I add the ideas of "green globalization" and "glocalism" as part of the alternative we need. They would put a lot more emphasis on local economics and communities while nurturing a different system of global economics.

Hegemony during the last five hundred years played a major role in creating global warming. Spanish, French, British, and now American empires exploited global resources to propel the Industrial Revolution that is now heating up the earth. Western hegemony gave birth and global license to the huge corporations—such as John D. Rockefeller's Standard Oil, which morphed into Exxon—that pursued profits and secured a high standard of living in Western societies at the costs of the rest of the world's subject populations, their resources, and the condition of the earth itself.[7]

Hegemony drives and divides the world in ways that worsen the climate crisis and make solutions hopeless. Hegemony is by definition a divider. It polarizes the world into two distinct camps: those with hegemonic power and resources and those without them, thereby undermining the values and unity needed to solve climate change.

The principle of hegemony is not sustainable in politics or nature. Based on domination and force, it cannot create willing consent by the governed. Historically, it has led to unfettered expansion and production, ripping fossil fuel and other finite resources from nations of the rest of the world to promote prosperity in the West.[8] Hegemony undermines cooperation and partnerships by substituting force. History shows that a hegemonic world is ruinous of cooperation, peace, and environmental sustainability.

The United States has been a special hegemon, internally democratic and liberal. It brings particularly high moral claims to its global power.[9] Yet like earlier Western hegemons, U.S. hegemony divides the West from everywhere else, with its own shameful neocolonial legacy of Western privilege and resulting poverty throughout the rest of the globe. That legacy blocks cooperative solutions to the two great existential threats to humanity: nuclear war and climate change. A quick look at the nuclear threat helps explain why.

The fundamental crisis stems from the fact that the Western powers with nuclear weapons have claimed an exclusive right to them on the basis of their hegemonic responsibilities to secure world order. That is no longer an argument that the rest accepts as either legal or moral. Non-nuclear nations believe that power and self-interest, rather than moral responsibility, lead the United States and former hegemonic Western powers to keep their nuclear weapons. This belief is so deeply entrenched in the global rest that a nonproliferation regime is unsustainable and is crumbling. The nonhegemonic world believes that its interests, as well as simple fairness, entitle it to the same military deterrents and power as enjoyed by the West. It is hard on principle to refute that position.

The conclusion drawn by many conservative as well as liberal Western analysts is that disarmament and *abolition* are the only solution to the existential nuclear threat. Conservative and centrist nuclear policy thinkers, including Henry Kissinger as well as former Georgia senator and senior defense specialist Sam Nunn, have moved toward the view that abolition is the only alternative to proliferation, a view that President Obama embraced in February 2009, declaring his goal of a "nuclear-free" world.[10] If the United States and other nuclear powers abolish their arsenals, a nonproliferation regime can be achieved. But the cost of this solution is that the West must abandon its hegemonic claim to privilege. Abolition requires the end of special moral arguments or military privileges for hegemons. The West will have to sign onto enforceable international legal and moral covenants treating the West and the rest equally, secured by the United Nations, and initiated now with intense new negotiations to create nonproliferation and disarmament agreements.[11]

Western hegemony stands squarely in the way of a sustainable clean energy regime, for much the same reasons that it dooms nuclear nonproliferation. The West has exploited hegemonic power over several centuries to achieve a high standard of living that spews out per capita carbon emissions far higher than the historically subjugated nations of the rest of the world. The West's colonial policies locked other nations into global poverty, and the West now exports polluting industries to the rest of the world. Now that many non-Western nations are in a better position to catch up economically, just as they are now in a position to develop nuclear technology, they see no just reason to accept limits on their own development while the West continues to enjoy the carbon-intensive fruits of its past and present hegemony.[12]

Carbon pollution and other dirty emissions are the metaphorical equivalent of nuclear weapons in the climate change crisis. Hegemony gave the West nukes and allows it to make claims to preserve them while others cannot get them. Likewise, hegemony, from the rest's point of view, shapes the West's untenable special claims on carbon emissions.[13] The West can keep living high off the hog on its high carbon footprint while the rest of the world is expected to deny itself equal treatment, as in the case of nuclear technology.

Abolition of dirty emissions is not possible for many decades, but drastic reduction or "dirty emissions disarmament," as close to abolition as possible, is the only real long-term solution to climate change. This means all nations must relinquish their right to spew out most of their current carbon emissions, which are as threatening to global and national security as nukes. Realistically, the rest of the world will never accept drastic carbon emission reductions until equity between it and the West becomes the governing principle of the solution. This requires the financing of green development alternatives in the West within a transformed global political and economic framework. In the next chapter, I investigate how green development can be financed even in this era of Western financial meltdown. We need to look first, however, at the economic face of Western hegemony, both past and present, to see how we get to a sustainable carbon-reduction global green regime.

Globalization is the economic face of U.S. hegemony, intertwined with the U.S. military but no less violent in terms of the environment and people.[14] Economic hegemony is as corrosive of global climate change solutions as is military hegemony. This does not imply that globalization must be abolished as a precondition of saving humanity. But any kind of salvation does require movement toward a new global economy that rejects the legacy and hegemonic privileges of the West over everywhere else.[15]

Globalization spreads U.S. capitalist principles (known as the "Washington consensus"): profit, privatization, speculation, deregulation, small government, competition, growth, and consumerism. The core animating principle is short-term profit created by hyperaccelerated global financial flows and financial markets. These principles have historically been applied in ways that created massive economic inequalities and injustices polarizing the West and the rest of the world. The latter has begun to catch up, but it sees the climate solutions the West is now proposing as a way to preserve its own long-standing hegemonic wealth and power.

None of the Washington consensus principles are green. All of them contribute to global warming and endanger not just humans but also thousands of other species seeking to cling to their own survival on this lovely planet. These principles have contributed to economic growth in sectors throughout the non-Western world, but this growth itself, in East Asia particularly, has become an integral part of the global climate crisis.

I have already described global warming as a *systemic* problem in the United States, reflecting the triumph of the U.S. third corporate regime. Globalization is the regime's effort to impose its core principles on the rest of the world, imperiling ecosurvival in the name of spreading democracy and prosperity. The fact that globalization can bring short-term both democracy and prosperity to some peoples in some nations makes the long-term threat far harder to grasp and solve.

Remember that per capita carbon emission is more than two times greater in the United States than in western Europe and far worse in comparison to developing nations, including China. If the United States—by far the world's worst carbon criminal (a harsh term but how else to brand behavior that threatens human civilization?)—is the model for globalization, all nations will be led along the same suicidal path of profiteering based on carbon burning. Even though the West is prepared to amend selectively the Washington consensus principles to begin creating a carbon nonproliferation agreement, it is making demands of other nations that appear to close off their own last chance to move out of poverty.

The only solution is to create new principles and bodies of globalization that promote sustainable development in a way seen as equitable to both the West and the rest, as fleshed out in the next chapter. However, we need to be precise about how U.S. economic hegemony and the U.S. rules of globalization are "antigreen." Consider the World Trade Organization (WTO), the International Monetary Fund (IMF), and the World Bank, the global bodies, historically crafted and controlled by the U.S. Treasury, that make and enforce the current rules. They have democratic facades, but these bodies have been the new tools of economic hegemony.[16] Let us be clear how their five basic principles or commandments, drawn from the Washington consensus, turn U.S. globalization into an enabler of climate change in both the West and the rest of the planet in the name of promoting global prosperity. All of the rules or commandments have one overwhelming disastrous consequence: a shift toward extremely short-term profit strategies and business visions that subvert the long-term thinking and policies necessary to stop global warming.

Globalization's Five Commandments

The Commandments in Brief

First Commandment: Thou shalt protect property rights above all else.
Second Commandment: Thou shalt privatize and shrink the government.
Third Commandment: Thou shalt not favor the home team.
Fourth Commandment: Thou shalt deregulate and free the markets.
Fifth Commandment: Thou shalt go forth across borders, grow profits, and consume your just rewards.

The five commandments are part rhetoric and part reality. The rich nations tend to observe them only when it is in their own interests while forcing poor nations to live up to them whatever the consequences for their people. Because these commandments are the gospel of globalization, I flesh out each commandment in the following paragraphs and show why they endanger the global economy and environment. Each commandment much be changed if we are to create a globalized green economy and survive.

The first commandment: *Thou shalt protect property rights above all else.* WTO rules make property rights king, with minimal accounting for environmental or labor rights. How can a global system that does not cherish and prioritize such rights save us in an age of climate change? The WTO has never recognized global warming as a cost or a harm relevant to global trade. WTO rules make deadly dirty energy pollution and all other externalities cost-free—and the WTO is not set up, by its own admission, to internalize externalities of any kind. The WTO treats environmental costs and regulations as nothing but potential trade barriers.[17]

Nations that have a different view must defer to the WTO. The WTO is constitutionally equipped to impose its view of property and "free trade" on all countries.[18] This emphasis on property over human or environmental rights helps create an overwhelming emphasis on short-term thinking and business practice. The purpose of property—especially the financialized form at the heart of the global corporate system—is to generate more property (money) as fast as possible.

WTO rules make it difficult to balance social considerations with property in a way that would slow down the hypermanic global financial markets. It institutionalizes the radical short-term profit emphasis incompatible with long-term business strategy and sustainability.

The second commandment: *Thou shalt privatize and shrink the government.* The IMF and the World Bank have made privatization a cardinal principle of their global financing and aid deals for poor nations.[19] If a country needs money, it has to sell off public enterprise to private companies and get the government out of the economy. This shrinking of government (what U.S. conservatives call "shrinking the beast") has devastating implications for climate change because government has to play a huge role in reorienting economies away from their toxic fossil fuel ways. There is no nation on the planet that can move toward clean energy and lighten its national carbon footprint without creative and major government intervention. The developed countries with the lowest footprints are European states such as Denmark, the Netherlands, and Germany. All see government in a positive way and rely heavily on it to design and subsidize both public and private green enterprises and markets.[20]

A world hostile to government will succumb rapidly to the fires of global warming. We have seen that a green future requires creative and robust government action in the United States—and this is true in all countries. That can happen only with a new *global* green architecture that is antihegemonic and subordinates business to society rather than the other way around, which is what the current global system does.

Governments are necessary to slow down and regulate the inherently speculative and short-term pathology of unregulated capitalism.[21] They are also necessary to internalize externalities of greenhouse gas pollution, move us beyond an invisible hand mentality, and invest in a green energy economy that will create jobs and decent wages for billions of people around the world. The financial meltdown of 2008 made abundantly clear how the demonizing of government strips us of the institutional capacity for long-term thinking, sustainable business practice, and social development that can preserve our precious planet.

The third commandment: *Thou shalt not favor the home team.* The WTO proclaims nondiscrimination as its cardinal principle.[22] This means that a government cannot play favorites with domestic or local producers. The WTO calls this restriction common sense: creating a level playing field and preventing protectionism.

It sounds good, but the WTO is inconsistent, permitting a double standard of subsidies and protectionism for rich nations, most obviously in agriculture, while preventing protection where it is needed most, in the infant industries of developing nations.[23] The WTO emphasis on export orientation and "openness" goes too far and subverts the localism and domestic markets that are vital to green economies. Local production is not always possible, but where it is, it is almost always greener, for reasons discussed shortly. By discouraging localism and hyping growth, the WTO undermines any serious effort to reduce our global carbon footprint. These policies also subvert the possibility of social development out of poverty for many nations by forcing them to compete with developed nations before they are prepared to do so. The United States itself, as well as Britain before it and Japan after it, developed only by first creating major protections for its own infant industries until they were in a position to compete. Even today, despite free-market rhetoric, the "open market" rules of the Washington consensus are violated by the United States and other rich nations, which protect their agribusinesses and many other industries through subsidies or direct trade barriers.

The fourth commandment: *Thou shalt deregulate and free the markets.* Nobody loves regulation and the bureaucracy that often goes with it. But the IMF and World Bank are implacable ideological enemies of all regulation and controls over capital flow.[24] Before they give money to nations in desperate need, they force them to strip away regulations that protect workers, citizens, and the environment.

Regulation, love it or not, is a cornerstone of any green society—and wholesale deregulation in an age of global warming is suicidal. Corporate regimes have made regulation a scare word, but it is nothing more than public oversight to ensure the public interest.[25] In an age of climate change, it is time to stop fear-mongering about government and develop the lean and clean regulation we need to protect ourselves and all the other imperiled species on the planet.

Regulation is especially important to slow the speed of global financial flows.[26] The WTO and IMF make it very difficult for countries to slow the tsunamis of money that may enter or exit their country with extraordinary speed. The consequence is a hyperacceleration of investments and disinvestments tied to extremely short-term economic returns.[27] This hyperacceleration forces corporations in all countries to adopt extremely short-term business models and eschew the long-term thinking essential to sustain both the economy and the environment.

Many other forms of regulation are necessary to green the world. These include regulation of labor standards in new trade treaties and, most clearly, global regulation of carbon and other dirty energy. Setting global caps on greenhouse gas emissions has become the most important global regulatory goal in the world. Current neoliberal global rules make this critical defense against our greatest existential threat extremely difficult.

The fifth commandment: *Thou shalt go forth across borders, grow profits, and consume your just rewards.* This is the philosophy or creed underlying all the other principles. Without profit and growth as ultimate goals, ones that raise living standards and allow all to enjoy the blessings of the American lifestyle, the preceding four commandments would not mean anything. These are the moral values of the U.S. corporate regime, and U.S. economic hegemony has created a globalization system that might be summarized as "Don't ask; tell." The presumption is that all nations share these U.S. values and are happy to be instructed in how to use them economically.[28]

Many peoples across the world have been attracted to the American Dream. But second-grade math shows that if all people lived the U.S. high-carbon life, we would pump so much carbon emissions into the atmosphere that we would all be choking to death on the brown carbon clouds now floating ominously over so much of Asia, Latin America, and the Middle East and already clogging the lungs and life prospects of millions of people. It would take more than five planets endowed with the current resources of the earth to support the entire world's population at the economic level enjoyed by U.S. citizens. And because global population is growing rapidly, economic growth in the developing world to match the U.S. carbon-intensive lifestyle and standard of living will rapidly deplete the earth's resources and burn us all up in the fever of fossil-fuel-driven growth.

Globalization is currently a systemic triumph of global greed over global green. It is the U.S. corporate regime writ large in hyperspace and hypertime. It seeks to brand a Planet, Inc. with the U.S. corporate economic rules and short-term business model that will overheat the planet on a seductively gilded path toward extinction. Globalization has attractions for both the West and the rest of the world, but the current global crisis has led the entire world to question the U.S. model and U.S. hegemony. This questioning opens the door to a new posthegemonic order of green security and globalization described in the next chapter.

14

The West and the Rest: Two

Green Globalization and a Global New Deal

It is going to take difficult, systemic change on the global level—meaning we must change the relation between the West and the rest of the world and the rules of the global economy—to save human civilization from global warming. We have little time to do it. Because it almost always takes time to make big change, I dearly wish there were a silver bullet—for example, a new technological breakthrough—that would solve our climate problem.[1]

But a silver bullet probably will not appear (at least not as rapidly as we need it), and even if it does, it cannot be put in place without the transformation that I have called green regime change—toward a new world that realigns power, responsibilities, and burdens as they currently exist between the West and the remainder of the planet. Global regime change aimed at long-term solutions to both environmental and economic crises is a revolutionary challenge when nations all over the world—and especially huge polluting countries such as China and India—are facing short-term economic crises and a legacy of extreme poverty that appear to overwhelm any focus on long-term system change, especially one that might limit growth.

This takes us back to a central focus of this book: the perverse timing that leads us to ignore even the most catastrophic long-term problems and dwell instead on the crises on our plates right now. Because of the hyperaccelerated global financial markets and the DNA of powerful global corporations and governing bodies such as the World Trade Organization (WTO), short-term thinking and short-term economic policies created by Western hegemonic nations are enshrined globally.[2] Equally widespread are the emotional forces leading people to deny or ignore the long-term deadly truths of climate change.

This global short-termism can lead to despair, but I have shown that the economic short-term crisis in the United States can be treated with the medicine that can solve our long-term climate emergency. This possible good timing of extremely bad news in the United States also is a potential, though far from certain, blessing on the global scale. The world faces the same long-term climate change crisis as the United States does, and China, India, and most other parts of the world are not a lot better than the United States in the way they tend to prioritize short-term problems at the expense of long-term crises. But the world as a whole is now facing the same deep, short-term economic crisis that began on Wall Street, whose toxic subprime mortgages began unexpectedly to show up and drag down banks in Iceland and Ireland and economies from Germany to China.[3] This globalized economic crisis is part of a short-term set of catastrophes that is shaking the U.S.-led world order and forcing new ways of thinking.[4] If we are lucky and act with a mixed brew of short-term and long-term wisdom, we might make possible a shift to a new sustainable green deal between the West and everywhere else.[5]

The hard truth for Americans is that U.S. hegemony is now eroding under the pressures of multiple military, economic, and political changes that have damaged U.S. credibility and power.[6] This weakening of the U.S. economy and military, along with rapid growth in recent decades of other powers such as the European Union, China, and Brazil, is already cracking the hegemonic world order and opening up possibilities for global green system change in the short term that could reconcile the growing green demands of the West with the imperatives of global growth elsewhere.[7] We must rapidly transfer global economic power and wealth from the West to the non-Western world to finance green development and jobs.

A perfect storm of military and economic problems is undercutting the United States as a hegemon. The U.S. military reversals, in both Iraq and Afghanistan, are showing the world the limits of U.S. armed power and of its hegemonic morality.[8] U.S. militarism has become a structural contributor to U.S. hegemonic decline, draining resources from the civilian economy for long and unwinnable wars and fueling unsustainable U.S. debt.[9] Military spending is used in the third corporate regime as a form of military Keynes-ianism, but it creates the opposite aim that John Maynard Keynes intended. Military spending for Iraq alone—which economist Joseph Stiglitz has calculated to ultimately reach $3 trillion—is contributing to the huge debt bringing down the U.S. economy.[10] The United States is skewered by the imperial "overstretch" that has brought down previous empires.[11]

U.S. hegemony is undermined not just by militarism and America's own economic crisis—rooted in speculative finance, excess debt, and long-term chronic underinvestment in public goods such as education, health care, and infrastructure—but by the severe global recession. Because it began on Wall Street, world leaders have condemned it as a product of flawed U.S. rules. French president Nicolas Sarkozy, a conservative U.S. ally on many fronts, clearly targeted the United States when he pronounced: "Laissez-faire, it's finished. The all-powerful market that is always right, it's finished."[12] Sarkozy and many other world leaders see the global economic crisis as "made in the USA," producing its own blowback against U.S. hegemony and economic rules. This blowback has already led nations around the world to adopt policies at odds with orthodox U.S. economic thinking and to begin developing alternatives to U.S.-sponsored globalization. The rest has new powers as China and Middle Eastern nations increasingly financing the U.S. $11 trillion debt; they could drive the U.S. hegemon into a ditch if they stopped buying U.S. treasuries.[13]

The crisis of U.S. hegemony is a consequence not just of U.S. policies and economic meltdown but also of the outmoded principle of hegemony itself. The United States has not proved itself capable of quelling terrorism, securing world peace, or ensuring environmental survival. Building a more peaceful and sustainable world will be a collective project involving new fundamental rules between the West and the remainder of the world, reflecting and repairing the troubled colonial legacies that shape the current economic and environmental global crises.

A New Green Deal Between the West and the Rest?

My local Whole Foods store has a declaration of interdependence on its wall. Those who regard this as softheaded had better think again. In an age of global warming, it is becoming obvious that we are all interdependent and will live or die together. Hardheaded self-interest, as well as moral ideals, requires new military and economic rules for the world and a fair solution to climate change and economic development for all nations.

For human survival, there is no long-term alternative to nuclear abolition and drastic carbon-reduction agreements. They can only be created by all nations in a new spirit of cooperation for common survival as well as new rules and power. The U.S. refusal to sign the Kyoto global agreements shows the inevitable clash between hegemony and cooperation. The Kyoto and Rio agreements immediately foundered on the obvious global divisions and power inequities created by the hegemonic system. The United States argued that it should be permitted to continue polluting at a far higher level than other countries because it was starting at a higher base.[14] As seen in the last chapter, China, India, and other developing nations argued that it was unfair to ask developing nations to jeopardize their development and be prevented in the future from emitting as much as the United States.[15] From the developing nations' standpoint, allowing high-polluting nations to continue polluting more was perpetuation of hegemonic logic. The Western hegemonic nations (1) had helped cause the problem by their own carbon-intensive industrialization strategies, (2) had polluted much more than poor nations in the past and exported much of their polluting industries to their colonies, (3) had enshrined colonial and neocolonial policies to lock into desperate poverty hundreds of millions of people in the developing world, and (4) were continuing to pollute the world on a per capita basis by five to thirty times the amount of other nations. As noted in Chapter 12, 90 percent of the current economic damage inflicted by climate change is affecting poor nations, while the fifty poorest nations emit only 1 percent of global carbon emissions. Climate change largely created by rich nations kills more than 315,000 people a year, mostly in poor countries, and creates economic losses of more than $125 billion, also mostly in poor nations.[16] The inequities involved are simply too stark to be ignored if we are to reach a viable global warming solution.

Figuring out the fair burden for rich and poor nations to solve global warming has become one of the world's great challenges. The United States and Europe will have to accept the moral responsibilities for having created the bulk of the climate crisis while exporting a model of fossil fuel development to poor nations that has devastated both the global poor and their local environments. China, India, and other developing nations, however, have to accept the truth that high carbon emissions will jeopardize all humanity and most of all their own citizens.

Any new spirit of cooperation and any true global warming solution will require, first, that the West take responsibility for the poverty and environmental degradation it has foisted on the rest of the world and finance massive aid and technology transfers that allow the remaining nations to develop a green strategy without giving up their rights to achieve a decent standard of life. But where will the money come from? I see several key approaches.

First, *end U.S. militarism, abolish military Keynesianism, and reduce military spending in the United States.* This approach simultaneously tackles the integrated problems of hegemonic wars, economic crisis, and environmental disaster. The United States commits many hundreds of billions of dollars annually to its hegemonic war system,[17] while relying on military Keynesianism to prop up economically the third corporate regime and ensure U.S. global competitiveness through Pentagon-funded innovation.[18] This policy has become dysfunctional for military, economic, and environmental reasons already discussed in earlier chapters.

The United States can increase its own security by cutting at least one-half of its bloated military budget. The United States needs to get out of countries where its presence is creating hatred and blowback.[19] It should be involved in the economic reconstruction of countries that it has devastated by wars and regimes changes, but the best anti-Islamic terrorist strategy is to get American boots off the soil of Islamic nations and other developing nations around the world. Cutting U.S. militarism and changing its imperial foreign policy will not just reduce hatred toward the United States but also free up massive funds for American green economic stimulus and for the global financial aid program necessary to get developing nations to embrace green alternative development strategies.

A perfect place to invest this money is in Brazil, where extreme poverty is leading many impoverished Brazilians to cut down the rainforests to settle, farm, and log there. They have no place else to go and no other way to survive. But one-fifth of the world's "climate sink," the resources that soak up carbon emissions from the atmosphere, comes from rainforests, and when rainforests are cut, massive increases in carbon emissions occur. In places such as Rondonia, a western state in Brazil, loggers, ranchers, and desperate poor people are moving in to clear-cut more than 700,000 acres of rainforest imperiled in Rondonia alone.[20]

The United States would increase its national security by removing its military forces and military assistance from governments in Latin and Central America and transferring the money to the impoverished settlers in the Brazilian rainforests. The same fundamental model—shifting military funds to green jobs for the global poor in regional green development funds—applies all over the world.

Second, *implement a green Tobin tax.* James Tobin was an eminent Yale economist who proposed a very small tax on very-short-term global currency bets and other speculative global financial trades. This tax could generate hundreds of billions of dollars while slowing down the hyperaccelerated and speculative global financial system that is driving the world toward both economic and environmental disaster. The money generated by the Tobin tax could be shifted toward financing green jobs as alternatives for the poor cutting down the Brazilian rainforests or for the squatters in Johannesburg and Soweto who are planting trees and building parks in their own "dustbowl" slums as part of a South African government program for environmental justice. The Tobin tax could help put thousands of slum dwellers in Soweto and other parched treeless slums to work beautifying and greening their own neighborhoods.[21]

Third, *cancel dirty debt in exchange for green development.* Most developing nations are burdened with high debt and poverty created by rogue deals among their own corrupt leaders, Western banks and corporations, and the International Monetary Fund (IMF). In the last decade, the international community has recognized that much of this is "dirty debt," as unscrupulous as the shady loans created by Wall Street bankers and leading to the huge housing and mortgage crisis. Just as the U.S. government is moving to clean up this dirty debt by renegotiating the mortgage terms, so, too, should the international community renegotiate Third World debt to help these nations escape national bankruptcy and move toward green development.[22]

The West has already extended debt forgiveness to some of the world's poorest countries, with the banks long ago writing the loans off their books as uncollectible. A much larger fraction of the developing nations are carrying debt that should be forgiven in exchange for commitments to invest in green development and stimulus plans.[23] The money that the developing nations would pay back to Western governments and banks would instead be committed to green job creation and green infrastructure in their own countries. This would help save their economies while also helping preserve the planet, a win-win for the West and the rest.

Fourth, *create a clean energy/technology commons.* The West can save the developing nations vast funds if it agrees to a new "commons" of clean energy technology. This would put all publicly funded or subsidized green energy technological breakthroughs or major clean energy products into a shared global commons available for use at reduced price by all countries. This also would finance a substantial amount of green development in poor countries, which do not have the resources to develop or pay for many of these technologies.

There are two precedents for this. The WTO already permits nations to declare emergencies to produce generic drugs still under patent by Western pharmaceutical firms.[24] Southern African nations in the heart of an AIDS plague have used these provisions to deal with a medical emergency of biblical proportions. Global warming is a longer-term emergency of cosmic proportions that requires immediate remedies not possible under current intellectual property rules. The emergency WTO provisions on generic drugs mainly help the poorer nations, but a clean energy commons would benefit both rich and poor nations, because dirty energy used in one nation ultimately imperils all the others. This policy would apply to energy breakthroughs and clean energy products created by publicly run energy companies in government laboratories and would therefore not undercut incentives for research and development. Private entrepreneurs could still retain a profit on clean energy products and breakthroughs, but after ten years the products would become part of the clean technology commons. They would be the equivalent of generic drugs, making them accessible to everyone.

There is also a history of technology transfer long used by countries such as China to ensure their own development—and one that China today still sees as essential to any viable global and Chinese climate change strategy.[25] A clean energy commons would be another way for the developing countries to get fair compensation—and historical remedy—for the economic environmental damage caused by colonialism and current corporate globalization rules. Under the current rules, Western corporations can invest in the rest and repatriate profits to the West, often leaving pollution and impoverished workers behind. A clean energy commons would reward these nations with a tangible benefit for the privilege of investing in their country, while also giving all nations easier access to clean energy technology.

A Global Carbon Tax

A new set of transformative green policy possibilities are beginning to crystallize. Even though a global cap-and-trade agreement is one possibility, an enforceable global system of carbon taxes is preferable. Nobel laureate economist Joseph Stiglitz argues that the tax uses a simple incentive that can avoid initially some of the burden-sharing conflicts between the West and the rest and also create immediate and substantial reductions in carbon use.[26] Unlike the Kyoto cap approach, a common tax does not require agreement first on emission targets among the United States, China, India, and other nonsignatories to Kyoto—thus avoiding contentious arguments about the legacy of hegemony and which nation should bear the biggest burden of emission reductions.[27] And a tax allows each nation to levy and collect the revenue from its own tax, possibly refunding it to national consumers in a progressive fashion (as discussed in Chapter 9 with the U.S. cap-and-trade program) that reduces the burden on the poor while protecting the planet.

Such a common global tax would mean that no country would lose competitive advantage by cost increases associated with the tax. It would also give each country freedom to use other additional means of reducing carbon (for example, through energy efficiency gains, conservation, and investments in green infrastructure). Each country would also retain the freedom to use the tax revenue as it pleases.

Lester Brown, an environmentalist who helped found Earth Day, has proposed a global carbon tax that would start at $20 a ton and increase each year to $240 a ton by 2020.[28] Brown views this as the only way to prevent climate catastrophe, arguing that this tax level could reduce carbon emissions by 80 percent by 2020, a target we have to meet. He would make the carbon tax "neutral" for ordinary citizens by corresponding reductions in income taxes or increases in cigarette taxes. Brown argues that spending an additional $190 billion a year, a tiny fraction of global gross domestic product, could get us to climate stability.

Getting a sustainable common carbon (or "dirty energy") tax approved as soon as possible in new global negotiations is the single most important thing we can do to solve global warming. Although the political hurdles remain formidable, the election of Barack Obama and the new receptivity of the central Chinese leadership make some form of carbon tax a real possibility.

Eventually, however, even with the carbon tax, there remains in the end the question of how to allocate the burdens of climate reduction, which comes down to the need to set ultimate targets for rich and poor countries and to figure out how the costs of implementing the tax rates that could get each country there should be shared. One emerging principle is "contract and converge,"[29] meaning that rich Western nations will have to set accelerated targets relative to poor ones, giving them more flexibility to develop and get out of poverty, even though that means carbon emissions will be a terrible consequence of their early development strategies. But over time, the targets should converge to a common per capita burden, with all peoples and companies accepting the same tax rate and emission target consistent with a 350 parts per million of CO_2 globally.[30] The ultimate goal is drastic carbon reduction in both the West and the rest.

This contract and converge approach has no chance of working except within the broader context of a shift in power and wealth relations. The West will have to agree to restrain its own dirty energy emissions drastically during the next few decades while signing on to far more liberal emissions elsewhere in the world. The more aid and technology transfer the West offers the developing nations, the faster the rate of convergence can be. But even with massive Western aid, which is essential, the solutions will not arise without larger shifts in the globalization rules that I spell out later in this chapter.

Global Hope: Green Beginnings in Both the West and Rest

Serious hurdles remain before new climate and globalization agreements are reached, but I want to highlight four reasons for hope that global change is possible. A first is the new factor of President Obama finally bringing the United States on board, making international cooperation a signature of his policy and creating a shift in the hegemonic model of the West. As spelled out in the next chapter, Obama is working with a genuine green vision and a new all-star energy team seriously devoted to solving climate change. Green change in the West, led by an inspirational new U.S. president, is good news for the prospects of change elsewhere.

A second hope is that the global economic crisis will kick-start, rather than derail, green stimulus plans across the world. As in the United States, the global recession may inspire green global time trickery rooted in a big green global stimulus, a global extension of the model earlier described in the United States. A third closely related hope is for a global economic regime change growing out of the collapse of faith in U.S. neoliberal policies and a shift toward a more public, regulated, and democratic world economy based on green Keynesianism.

A fourth and surprising hope is the new green approaches taken by the biggest emerging market nations, especially China, but also India and Brazil. Chinese national leaders seem to have realized that they risk social disruption, economic decline, and political instability if they do not get serious about climate change. In 2002, China passed an environmental impact assessment law; in 2003, a national renewable energy law; in 2007, a major national climate change plan; and on October 29, 2008, a new ambitious white paper on climate change.[31] In late 2008, Premier Wen Jiabao announced a 4 trillion yuan financial stimulus plan with 350 billion targeted to green jobs and infrastructure and to the growing solar, wind, and geothermal clean industry within China. As discussed in Chapter 10, China is surpassing the United States in wind and solar production, will direct more money to renewable than fossil fuel electrical power development in the coming decade, and is on track to become the biggest clean energy superpower in the world, despite its continued growth in carbon emissions making it the world's largest greenhouse gas polluter. China's leaders seem to increasingly believe that the way out of their current crisis and into assured global Chinese competitiveness is to rapidly green their own economy. They seem to have partially bought Thomas Friedman's argument that the United States will "clean their clock" economically unless they move as fast or faster than the United States to promote clean energy technology, the most profitable sector of the twenty-first-century world economy.[32] China has become a world leader both in solar energy and in wind turbine production. Although the Chinese still struggle with difficult potential trade-offs between growth and climate protection, the most important hurdle to a green China has shifted from the will of national Chinese leaders (although more is still needed here) to the local and regional leaders who are devilishly clever at circumventing the national mandates.

The green shift in China is immensely important and largely ignored in the West. Along with Obama's victory, this shift makes possible a new perspective on global agreements and green globalization. Carbon-rationing agreements will increasingly become possible because leaders in both the West and the rest continue to see that many of their own short-term economic and political interests lie in green initiatives.

These sources of hope will have little impact without an all-out mobilization by global movements, civil society, and political leaders to make climate change agreements and green globalization the immediate and top priority for the world, showing that this is not only a moral imperative but also the way to deal with the global economic crisis through massive investment in green development. After decades of obstruction, the United

States—meaning the Obama administration; U.S. social, environmental, and labor movements; Congress; and the public—will be judged by history as to whether it made the heroic efforts necessary to save the planet. This will mean moving heaven and earth to set the foundations of a solution in the December 2009 Copenhagen meetings. The extent to which the United States brings the intensity of focus—and the generosity of spirit—necessary to reach the comprehensive and ambitious agreements the world needs will likely determine the prospects for future generations.

Green Globalization

Solving global warming requires swift changes in the West's economic globalization system, especially in its capacity to operate on long-term social needs rather than short-term profits. This shift will be made easier by the fact that the governing Washington consensus rules (discussed in the last chapter) are losing global credibility.[33] Nearly all nations, including the United States itself, are looking for a new global economic road map.

From the ashes of the current global economic meltdown and the overwhelming emergency of climate change we can see five new core green globalization policies emerging, which might be called the new five commandments of green globalization.

Five Green Global Commandments

1. Create slow-mo capital: Regulate and slow down global money.
2. Know and show that government is cool: Encourage smart government intervention.
3. Globalize the commons: Protect our shared precious common wealth.
4. Race to the top: Create green and socially just trade agreements.
5. Build a new great wall between corporations and government: Enact global campaign finance reform.

The commandments must operate in addition to and intertwined with the common global carbon tax and rationing system and Western financing of green development in the developing world. The five new commandments are already remaking globalization faster than I ever thought possible, moving toward what might be called "green globalization." They may reduce the hyperspeed of the global financial markets just enough—and invite just enough major new government intervention—to permit longer-term planning both for social development and for a green global economy.

The five new core globalization commandments, leading to global regime change policies, work immediately on the short-term economic global crisis while simultaneously greening the world:

1. *Create slow-mo capital: Regulate and slow down global money flows.* This is the key to "slow globalization" because it involves policies that restrain the hyperacceleration of capital in today's global financial markets. Slowing capital flows is the most important thing we can do to adopt longer-term thinking and sustainable policies. Regulating hyperspeculative global finance is also the most important immediate requirement for stabilizing the world's financial crisis.[34] The easiest approach to slow-mo capital is to tax short-term money trades.[35] This incentivizes longer-term sustainable investments and generates a global revenue stream that can be reinvested in social and green development. As discussed above, it is a green version of a Tobin tax. Indeed, for years a proposal has been circulating to put a 0.25 percent tax on very-short-term capital flows and trades. It will create the space desperately needed for long-term economic thinking and generate many billions of dollars for the other green globalization principles and projects.

   Slow-mo capital taxes should be combined with other rigorous global regulation of the egregious financial speculation that precipitated the 2008 Wall Street meltdown and poisoned the entire world financial system. This means systemic regulation especially of global hedge funds, derivatives, offshore or underground financial exchanges, and many other speculative drivers of today's corrupted global finance. Rigorous global financial regulation through a new financial global regulatory and watchdog agency is the time-trickery politics that President Obama has already begun to propose. This regulation immediately addresses the short-term crisis while putting in place conditions to permit the longer-term sustainable economics that speculation has made impossible.[36]

2. *Know and show that government is cool: Encourage smart government intervention.* With strong pressure from President Obama, the IMF and World Bank should rework loans (and their entire structural adjustment programs) to ensure green development through green public investment and stimulus.[37] Because of the seriousness of the short-term crisis facing most countries, the loans should be large and linked to major internal government spending on green jobs, infrastructure, and clean energy. Every proposal would be based on an assessment of the carbon footprint of the development or financing project, and no

project would get approval without being within the cap approved in the larger common cap and target framework. This would involve a dramatic makeover of current structural adjustment programs because it encourages government investment both for short-term stimulus and long-term sustainable development. Remember the new defining globalization motto of green Keynesianism coined by Obama himself and embodied in much of his early actions to both the economic and climate change crises: "Government is cool."[38]

3. *Globalize the commons: Protect our shared precious common wealth.* Corporate globalization's aim is to strip away the commons and turn all natural resources, including water, land, and air, into commodities. This is the ultimate extension of what Karl Marx called the "fetishism of commodities," the ideology at the heart of capitalism.[39] In fact, privatization of the commons ensures the opposite—the degradation of common wealth and the unsustainable exploitation of the environment—because it subjects all resources to the pitiless logic of profit and consumption. Green globalization depends on rebuilding a global commons and ensuring that the biosphere is protected from predatory profit-seeking.[40]

   We need to start with new enforceable global conventions defining water and air as public trusts owned and governed by the public.[41] Public trusts should also manage land where private development creates unacceptable risk of flooding or drought; rigorously protect forested areas, which are among the world's most important carbon sinks; and help protect and regulate other land hosting the 40 percent of world species currently in danger of extinction. I have already argued that green energy technologies should also be part of a new global commons. The environmental standards governing water, air, and land will need to be integrated within the larger framework of the global common tax and cap system, with countries or companies going greener than the common framework standards rewarded with funds from the green Tobin tax.

4. *Race to the top: Create green and socially just trade agreements.* Globalization is now a race to the bottom, as corporations chase the cheapest labor in nations with the lowest social and environmental regulations.[42] Neoliberal trade agreements lock in this "downward leveling" and make impossible the creation of a green world. Green globalization and new green trade agreements must turn the race to the bottom into a race to the top by (a) creating new trade agreements with labor and environmental regulations at the heart of the agreements themselves and (b) rewarding nations if they increase labor and environmental standards—especially those involving carbon emissions and caps—

above that required by the green trade agreements and by the common global tax and cap framework. Those racing to the top should be rewarded financially from the green Tobin tax as well, making their greener regulations more cost-efficient.

5. *Build a new great wall between corporations and government: Enact global campaign finance reform.* Big oil and big coal, along with global banks, global giant hedge funds, and many huge global companies with a lot of short-term profit to lose, will oppose some or all of green globalization. The only way to implement the principles outlined here is to limit the overwhelming global corporate power that has poisoned democracy as well as the environment in the third corporate regime.[43] Green globalization is, as already emphasized, a global regime change requiring a change in systemic power relations. Today, both rich and poor nations are held hostage to financial markets and global corporations that create a "pay or play" mentality for world political leaders. To get elected, they need the cash, and to continue governing, they need to play by the rules put in place by the corporate lobbyists and corporate leaders often sitting at the top perches of government. We need new global rules strictly limiting the influence of corporations and lobbyists not only in national governments but also at the WTO, IMF, World Bank, and other global governance agencies. The aim must be a huge wall that cannot be crossed: a true separation of corporation and state that allows government to serve the people rather than play handmaiden to the world's richest financiers, corporations, and oligarchs.[44] Building this wall is essential to the populist politics of green justice that I take up in the last few chapters.

There is one other green principle for both the West and the rest: *Go local.* This is different from the other principles because it challenges the very concept of globalization. It proposes greening the world economy by localizing it to the greatest degree possible. Going local does not abolish globalization, but it does reduce the pace and space of globalization and moves us toward carbon abolitionism in the long run. This brings us to the final subject of this chapter.

Glocalism

We cannot save ourselves from climate change even with green globalization unless we add the principle of *glocalism*. This is the effort to shift as much production as possible away from the global level and toward the local level, partly because doing so is the greenest way to produce and because it has other benefits of democracy and community. Glocalism is not pure localism, but it favors local economies wherever possible, reserving global production for only those areas where local production cannot work.[45]

In our current global corporate regime, the guiding systemic imperative is to maximize profit in global markets as local markets saturate. These policies are unsustainable, and the United States is now in a phase of hegemonic and economic decline as the global manager of that system. There is no prospective new hegemonic power to take its place. The astonishing volume of global criminal and immoral "hot money"—invested in sex trafficking, biopiracy, blood diamonds, drug trades, slave workers, and mafia enterprises—grows as hegemonic power declines. As the chaotic and frenzied pace of unregulated financial markets intensifies, the prospects are reduced for sustainable international governance or long-term planning that can solve either the short-term moral crisis of what Loretta Napoleoni calls "rogue economics" or the long-term climate change crisis.[46]

The global corporate regime's local as well as global affairs throughout the world are in disarray, a symptom of the need for glocalism as part of an alternative global model. Enabled by the collapse of the hegemonic order; the selective application of the rules of the WTO, IMF, and World Bank; and the global financial markets and global companies, global greed and wilding and rogue economic entrepreneurs have torn holes in the social and local community fabric of most nations. Corporations have become absentee owners of global neighborhoods, and not surprisingly, they treat their tenants poorly. This is, after all, the aim of a global corporate regime: to help global corporations make money by extracting surpluses from the masses of people living far away from corporate headquarters, in what world system economists call the "periphery."[47]

Glocalism dictates that economic production and political decisions should be pushed down to the lowest feasible level. This reverses the fundamental premise of our current globalization system: that fully globalized markets are the most efficient and democratic way to organize twenty-first-century economics. A model of glocalism that preserves a framework for democratic and equitable governance at the world level but shifts the locus and control of some markets to regions and communities offers one powerful way to curb global warming and build a new green economic system.[48]

Glocalism requires a major shift in the current balance among global, regional, and local scales. The corporate regime has been catapulting us at lightning speed from local to global. Green regime change will shift the balance back toward the local, because localism builds community, is economically beneficial in many sectors, and will become increasingly cost-efficient as the price of oil and other energy inevitably rises. The local is also good medicine for global warming in many sectors. This point has been argued persuasively by Bill McKibben and others writing about local food.[49] Their arguments for localized agriculture apply across many, though not all, industries.

Globalization makes the entire food and larger economy a distance race, requiring global transports, packaging, storage, refrigeration, and marketing. Globalization loads on carbon emissions like so many toppings on an ice cream cone from each point of production to each point of distribution and sale. Local economies immediately eliminate this suicidal "carbon topping" of global production, and they can be the new building blocks of a new green economy.[50]

The core principle of green glocalism is the subsidiary principle.[51] It argues that we should make decisions at the lowest level consistent with efficient, democratic, and sustainable production. We cannot make global warming decisions only in local communities, however, because warming is a global problem; that is why green regimes need a clear vision of a global world order and of green globalization. But as local farmers markets show, there are many ways we can move toward locally based economies that are going to save us money, save us time, make our life more tasty, and—not a minor matter—reduce energy use and help preserve our species.[52]

Local farmers markets help make the merits of economic localism clear to a first grader. At the farmers market, producers do not have to use energy to refrigerate the product or to preserve it—it is eaten the day it is picked, making it greener and tastier at the same time. Producers do not have to use trailer trucks or cargo plains to fly the food across the country or across the border, another huge oil drain that will become ever more expensive. They do not have to package the food in plastic containers made from petrochemicals. There are no bins at a supermarket to heat or cool. And customers can often walk to the local market (although this is true mainly in pedestrian-friendly cities, meaning customers do not have to burn gas in the tank). Moreover, citizens can participate in their local city council to help regulate the local market on community friendly terms, meaning that they are getting practice in the democratic spirit that will be necessary to fight the big power battles coming up over the future of the corporate regime.[53]

It is hard to believe that anyone opposes local farmers markets. For people who like them, exactly the same logic applies to supporting local markets in crafts, small-scale manufacturing, local retail, and everything else that makes local community possible. I am not, to summarize, endorsing localism but glocalism, that is, moving toward the local when possible but recognizing that many economic sectors cannot be localized and that global community is becoming as important as local community. Climate change itself is inherently global and cannot be solved only by local communities or particular nations and economies. But in the age of global warming, the words *community* and *green* are becoming indistinguishable. This is good for our connections to people—the ultimate source of our happiness—and might just mean that we will not suffer, as many do, from loneliness quite so often. And glocalism might help save human civilization.

PART IV

When the Grass Roots Grow Green

15

And Along Came Obama
Yes, We Can!

In a 2006 popular film called *Along Came Polly*, Ben Stiller, who plays a buttoned-up insurance salesman named Reuben, finally finds his perfect wife, gets married, and goes for a honeymoon on a Caribbean island. A handsome islander with rippling muscles and a sleek boat comes up to the happy couple on the beach and offers to take them snorkeling. Reuben gets seasick on boats, but his new wife is so eager that he agrees to her going off for a solo lesson. When she does not get back on time, he goes to the beach and sees the boat docked near shore. Climbing onto the boat, he finds his perfect wife making passionate love to the island hunk.

With his wife wanting to test out this new relationship, Reuben leaves and heads back to the city, emotionally crushed. He feels he has lost his last opportunity for the marriage and stability he has always wanted. But as he is sinking into total despair, along comes Polly. Played by Jennifer Anniston, Polly is an old grammar school friend whom he has not seen in years. She is beautiful, funny, quirky, and smart. It is love at first sight for Reuben, and they end up happily together.

After eight years of George W. Bush, many Americans were sinking into a despair like Stiller's. Would they ever find a president they could love? Or just respect? At just that moment, along came Barack Obama. He inspired the passion and hope that many Americans were losing in the country. In Chicago's Grant Park, when Obama's victory was announced on November 4, there were tears of joy flooding the huge crowd and a sense of a new awakening love for both the man and the country.

Excitement rippled across the progressive community. This seemed more than a politics-as-usual shift back to the Democratic Party. The symbolism and substance of this new African American president hinted at what I have called "regime change at home." Obama might not just displace Bush but lead us out of the desert of the Reagan Revolution and the third corporate regime.

Those who had some of the highest hopes for regime "overthrow" were the folks of green America. During the campaign, Obama spoke passionately about climate crisis and a green revolution. We were witnessing a shift from a stage 1 denier president to one passionate about clean energy jobs, smart energy grids, and new electric cars.

Many believe that Obama could be the green Polly for America. He came at the last moment, as hope was running out, to save us—or help us, as he would say, save ourselves. I believe Obama is the genuine article when it comes to climate change. His speeches and energy appointments indicate that he sees the urgency of the existential threat—and the day after his election he updated to his Web site even bolder green pledges than he had made during his campaign. His early economic policies suggest he has a genius for time trickery that could lead a short-term nation in economic crisis toward a long-term green future. He has promised America that he will lead us out of the fossil fuel age into a sustainable future, that "we will harness the sun and the winds and the soil to fuel our cars and run our factories."[1]

But will Obama prove to be a green Polly or simply a Pollyanna? Obama is a cautious politician, and he came into office backed by Wall Street investors who contributed massively to his campaign. He is confronted by so many short-term emergencies that his long-term visions could easily be blindsided and deferred. Political realities and his centrist advisers make it difficult for him to invoke the bold responsibilities essential to a climate solution. Within two months of his inauguration, he responded to corporate pressures by weakening his climate change program in both the House and Senate versions of his budget.[2] In June 2009, when the House of Representatives passed the first climate change bill in U.S. history to reduce carbon emissions by 83 percent by 2050, Obama gave strong support—but even before it reached the Senate, where it faced tougher sledding, the cap-and-trade legislation had been weakened to the point that Greenpeace and other environmental organizations opposed it.[3] Obama will not achieve a green revolution on his own steam, a proposition made increasingly clear by his corporate-friendly bailouts in the earliest months of his administration. The transformative potentials of an Obama presidency will require a mass mobilization by the grassroots movements that helped elect him—the subject of the next chapter. In this chapter, I show how and why Obama may be laying the groundwork to make possible the green regime change we need, a reason for hope and inspiration. I also show why he cannot succeed on his own and might not try.

The First Green President

Just one week after inauguration, Obama had already introduced an economy recovery plan built around green jobs and a clean energy revolution. On January 26, 2009, Obama issued two major climate change executive orders. One directed the Environmental Protection Agency (EPA) to review the Bush administration's denial of California's waiver request to cut car emissions in the Golden State, a major shift making it likely that states could move rapidly on their own to create new carbon standards. The second ordered the Department of Transportation to creates rules on new fuel efficiency. *Time* proclaimed these two moves on one day a "Clear Win for Greens."[4] Shortly thereafter, the Obama administration's EPA ruled that carbon dioxide was a hazardous pollutant and would be regulated under the Clean Air Act, making possible robust action by the executive branch even if Congress failed to pass legislation.

These are early indications that Obama is the first U.S. president to take global warming seriously and to see its urgency. Obama minces no words about the perils of climate change: *"What we can be scientifically certain of is that our continued use of fossil fuels is pushing us to a point of no return. And unless we free ourselves from a dependence on these fossil fuels and chart a new course on energy in this country, we are condemning future generations to global catastrophe."*[5] No other president has been as definitive about global warming, with Obama being the first president to mention the scary concept of a "point of no return." In his short inaugural speech, he made three different references to the climate change crisis, resolving to "roll back the specter of a warming planet."[6]

Within days of his swearing-in, Obama introduced his Energy Plan for America, updated with ambitious and far-reaching beginnings of a global warming solution:

- Implement an economywide cap-and-trade program to reduce greenhouse gas emissions 80 percent by 2050
- Help create 5 million new jobs by strategically investing $150 billion during the next ten years to catalyze private efforts to build a clean energy future
- Save more oil within ten years than we currently import from the Middle East and Venezuela combined
- Put 1 million plug-in hybrid cars—cars that can get up to 150 miles per gallon—on the road by 2015
- Ensure that 10 percent of the country's electricity comes from renewable sources by 2012 and 25 percent by 2025
- Weatherize 1 million homes annually

- Establish a national low-carbon-fuel standard
- Crack down on excessive energy speculation
- Prioritize energy efficiency and conservation
- Offer a new $7,000 tax credit for purchasing advanced vehicles[7]

Obama also pledged that 100 percent of greenhouse gas emissions would be auctioned in his cap-and-trade program and be paid for by the polluter (although he later retreated on parts of this promise). He will invest $150 billion over ten years in "advanced" energy technology, including a vast new "smart grid." He pledged to make the United States a leader in combating climate change and to reengage with the UN Framework Convention on Climate Change. And he also promised to create a new forum of largest greenhouse gas emitters, based on the G8 and five other countries—Brazil, China, India, Mexico, and South Africa.[8]

Throughout his two-year presidential campaign, Obama promised a transformative climate change agenda. On October 27, 2008, in a *Time* interview with journalist Joe Klein, he said his highest goal as president would be to launch an "Apollo project" for a new clean energy economy. Obama was explicit that the rationale was to "transform our nation from the leading global polluter to the leader in solutions to our global climate crisis."[9]

Obama was crystal clear that creating a green economy was his *top* priority: "There is no better potential driver that pervades all aspects of our economy than a new energy economy.... That's going to be my No. 1 priority when I get into office."[10] No U.S. president has ever had this vision, let alone put it at the center of his presidency.

Obama's Truth

Why has Obama become so deeply committed to solving climate change? I believe it is based on his respect for science and truth, in this case perhaps the most consequential truth science has ever delivered. In his inaugural speech, Obama promised, "We will restore science to its rightful place."[11]

Obama was signaling that his predecessor, George W. Bush, denigrated both science and truth, something he found intolerable. This was a widely shared view. Al Gore's book *Assault on Reason* traced the Bush administration's failures to its unwillingness to engage with scientific truth.[12] Prominent journalist Chris Mooney, in his book *The Republican War on Science*, argued that the Bush administration had brazenly subordinated science to its own ideological ends, partly to appease his Christian Evangelical base.[13] Obama signaled in his inaugural address that the war on science would end.

Obama is an intellectual who combines his idealism with a political pragmatism grounded in scientific evidence. Science and truth clearly help define his worldview, and Bush's looseness with truth offended Obama personally. He was explicit that he would act to change this: "The truth is promoting science is not just about providing resources. It's about protecting free and open inquiry. It's about ensuring that facts and evidence are never twisted or obscured by politics or ideology. It's about listening to what our scientists have to say, even when it's inconvenient. Especially when it's inconvenient. Because the highest purpose of science is the search for knowledge and a greater understanding of the world around us. That will be my goal as President of the United States."[14]

Obama's reference to the special importance of "inconvenient truth" made clear that he believed that the most important truth-telling was about global warming. Obama has said explicitly that scientific evidence would drive a bold and truthful climate policy: "To protect our climate and our collective security, we must call together a truly global coalition.... My administration will not deny facts—but be guided by them."[15]

Obama virtually drained Harvard of its most eminent scientists to staff his entire administration, but his most important scientific appointments were in the Department of Energy, the EPA, and the Office of Science and Technology. He chose scientists who had devoted much of their own careers to truth-telling on global warming, hinting that Obama saw that the most important scientific truth we must act on now is climate change. His appointments along with his speeches suggest this is gut truth for Obama.

His secretary of energy, Nobel Prize physicist Steven Chu, reorganized the famous Lawrence Livermore Laboratory at the University of California, Berkeley, to focus on global warming. Chu has repeatedly emphasized the extreme urgency of global warming. He has said that global warming is already breeding disease epidemics "killing millions more per year and creating water shortages that will affect "most people in the world."[16] He added, "I don't think the American public has gripped in its gut what could happen." "We're looking at a scenario where there's no more agriculture in California.... I don't actually see how they can keep their cities going."[17] He also said that "coal is my worst nightmare," a strong statement in a country getting the majority of its electricity from coal.[18] Perhaps most revealing from a regime change perspective, he observed: "We share a common Earth. [Climate change] is the ultimate commons problem. Free-market incentives will not take care of this."[19] Chu's view on climate action is that "what the world does in the coming decade will have enormous consequences that will last for centuries. It is imperative that we begin without further delay."[20]

Obama also tapped an eminent scientist, John Holdren, to be director of the Office of Science and Technology. Holdren has written that "the ongoing disruption of the Earth's climate by man-made greenhouse gases is already well beyond dangerous and is careening toward completely unmanageable."[21] He has also said that "a massive campaign must be launched ... to de-develop the United States in order to conserve energy."[22] This is one of the first times a leading public official has questioned the "growth religion" and embraced a "sufficiency" alternative, although as noted earlier, Obama himself has declared that it is time to recognize the "limits of growth."

Obama as Green Time-Wizard

The simultaneity of the economic collapse and the global warming crisis created possibly the greatest time challenge ever faced by a president. On the one hand, he faced a catastrophic short-term economic crisis. On the other hand, he came into office precisely when scientists told him that he had to act decisively now to solve the most catastrophic long-term threat to human civilization.

Obama's speeches suggest he has a long-term time frame. His urgent warnings and ambitious policy pledges on global warming, even as he tried to win and keep the support of America's pale green voters, show a resolve to see and act on long-term truths. He explicitly and repeatedly talks about "future generations" in his public addresses. And he has promoted more ambitious climate initiatives even as an economically desperate public goes even paler green.

It is true, of course, that Obama's main public focus from day one was the economy, not climate change. Because he is a savvy politician, Obama knows that he has no choice but to prioritize the economy. But rather than abandoning the long-term climate crisis, he showed a genius for time wizardry, wrapping his solution to the short-term economic crisis around initiatives designed to solve long-term global warming.

As Obama began his trip to his 2009 inauguration in Washington, D.C., his very first stop was at Cardinal Fastener and Specialty Company, a company making wind turbine parts, in Bedford Heights, a suburb of Cleveland. While the Rust Belt economy in Ohio was tanking, Cardinal Fastener was hiring new people to catch up with the demand for windmills. Obama spoke of the plant as hope for the future. "The story of this company—which began building wind turbine parts just two years ago, and is now poised to make half its earnings that way," said Obama, "is that a renewable energy isn't something pie-in-the-sky, it's not part of a far-off future. It's happening all across America right now." Obama made clear that his stimulus plan would help Cardinal and other clean energy businesses hire more workers. "We're looking to create good jobs that pay well and can't be shipped overseas. Jobs that don't just put people to work in the short term but position our economy for the long term. That starts with new, clean sources of energy."[23]

Here, Obama explicitly melds short- and long-term solutions, displaying his skills as a green time-trickster. The trip to Cardinal was to build support for his economic recovery plan, but he made clear that recovery would come by green policies also designed to solve global warming. The economic crisis had his primary attention, but he was telling the public that the crisis had a silver lining because it was an opportunity to solve global warming. This became a signature of his presidency.

Before the economic collapse, candidate Obama had practiced a reverse time trickery—arguing that spending big money now to solve climate change had a silver lining because it offered a way to solve shorter-term problems of energy dependency and economic competitiveness. That led to this framing by candidate Obama: "Let's be the generation that finally frees America from the tyranny of oil.... We can set up a system for capping greenhouse gases. We can turn this crisis of global warming into a moment of opportunity for innovation, and job creation, and an incentive for businesses that will serve as a model for the world. Let's be the generation that makes future generations proud of what we did here."[24]

A few weeks after the Wall Street implosion in September 2008, Obama reversed the time-trickery equation. Recognizing that a short-term nation demanded the economic crisis as its overwhelming priority, he reframed his presidential discourses. We must focus on the short-term immediate economic meltdown, but it offered the opportunity to solve longer-term crises such as climate change.

Obama's first major accomplishment was the massive $787 billion stimulus plan signed on February 16, 2009. It was Obama's first giant step toward walking his green time-tricking talk. The legislation invested $45 billion in energy efficiency and new renewable energy, including $13 billion to weatherize as many as 1 million homes, $10 billion for a "smart" electricity grid, $8 billion for light rail, $6.9 billion for public transit, and $20 billion in tax incentives for renewable energy production. Experts predicted the stimulus would produce 500,000 green jobs.[25]

Eventually, Obama moved into a time-wizardry discourse for much of his agenda beyond the economic crisis. He presented long-term climate change solutions as a way to address all the short to midterm issues discussed in Chapter 12: energy dependency, global competitiveness, Middle Eastern wars, and social injustice. Obama seems poised to be the president most capable of leading a short-term nation to solve long-term global warming by aligning the pressing needs of current generations with those of the future.

Obama's Green Sociological Imagination

Obama brings another unusual strength to the table. He is one of our few presidents to have what sociologist C. Wright Mills called "a sociological imagination."[26] And he is almost certainly the first president endowed with what I called in the Introduction a "green sociological imagination." Mills saw the sociological imagination as the gift of the best sociologists to connect the deepest structurally ingrained problems of society with both personal biography and social change. But a person does not have to be a sociologist to have a sociological imagination. Leaders and ordinary citizens can have talents for the same kind of thinking. Certainly, Martin Luther King, a preacher and great civil rights leader, had a sociological imagination, using his own biography to analyze and fight racist institutions and power elites. And so did Franklin Roosevelt, who fought his own rich ruling class to solve the Depression and create a new and more just socioeconomic order.

Obama combines features of King and FDR. He shares King's gift for inspiring hope and belief in change, and, like King, he understands that we need to change social institutions to ensure rights and opportunities for all. Like FDR, Obama is a terrific communicator who is using Keynesian pump-priming, new regulations, and forms of nationalization—all major changes in the current corporate regime—to solve a massive economic crisis.

Obama adds to these earlier leaders a powerful melding of personal biography to social and political change. Mills called the sociological imagination the artful linking of personal problems to social issues.[27] Obama has written two books about his own life story, making clear he has used his own identity struggles to work out his political philosophy of social change.

Obama has also added the color green to his sociological imagination. This is a product of historical timing and the exploding awareness of global warming as an existential threat. Obama's green sociological imagination seems especially ripe, for he repeatedly discusses global warming as a drastic and systemic problem than can be fixed only by economic, political, and social change.

Obama cut his teeth as a community organizer in Chicago. Every good community organizer has to have a sociological imagination because the work involves (1) analyzing the power structure that the community confronts and (2) inspiring the community to act and change. Obama took his mind-set and skills as an organizer and turned them into his new brand of politics. He saw his candidacy and now his presidency as an extension of his community organizer mission, often referring to his Chicago organizing as prime evidence of his qualifications to lead. A community organizer in the White House seems a perfect recipe for bringing the sociological imagination to the national stage.

A sociological imagination, especially a green one, goes hand in hand with both long-term thinking and time trickery, skills we have seen that Obama possesses. The sociological imagination requires the ability to stand back from the present with the historical insight to figure out how we got here and the long-term focus to create major social change. Global warming is the ultimate social problem demanding an imaginative gift for seeing the future and leading a short-term public toward long-term solutions.

A sociological imagination also tends to create a mind-set of regime change. Mills argued that the imagination required a critique of power elites and a commitment to a systemic shift in power and governing values. Martin Luther King and FDR had sociological imaginations and supported regime change, but the evidence is not yet in on Obama.

Obama was elected on the promise of change, but not necessarily regime change. He has moved toward the center since his community organizing days, and he has surrounded himself with pragmatic advisers, many from Wall Street, disciples of Citigroup's Bob Rubin. Wall Street financed much of Obama's campaign, contrary to the image of small donors. There were millions of such small contributors, but 60 percent of the money came in big bundles from corporate elites. According to political scientist Tom Ferguson, politics works by an investment theory, with history bearing out the fact that those who invest in a campaign get a return on that investment.[28] Obama wants to change much of the Bush administration's policies, but he came with no promise to change the third corporate regime. The investment theory would suggest that Obama is not likely to seek regime change.

Nonetheless, history delivered Obama a double whammy of economic and environmental crises that could well take him toward regime change. The fixes to both crises must be extremely bold and will ultimately require regime change. It remains unclear whether Obama will move boldly and fast enough and fight hard enough against all the entrenched interests to deliver regime change solutions.

Much depends on how Obama and his team calculate the risks of too much action versus the risks of too little. Regarding the economic crisis, the Obama team said early on that the risks of excess timidity on the economic crisis outweighed the risks of excess boldness. Treasury secretary Tim Geithner expressed this view at his January 2009 Senate confirmation hearings: *"In a crisis of this magnitude, the most prudent course is the most forceful course."*[29]

Obama seems to share this same risk calculation on global warming, although the "most forceful course," as he currently defines it, is far from forceful enough. Nonetheless, Obama's time trickery, massive green stimulus, tilt toward financial nationalization, and repeated alarms about the potential catastrophes of the interlinked crises of the economy and climate change improve the prospect of his turning into a green regime changer.

I find special hope in some of Obama's comments to David Leonhardt, a *New York Times* reporter. He recommended to Leonhardt that he look at Robert F. Kennedy's quote on the problem of measuring wealth by gross domestic product (GDP). "Well, I'll send it to you," said Obama, "because it's one of the most beautiful of his speeches." In it, Kennedy argued that a country's health or true wealth should not be equated with GDP. That measure, he said, "counts special locks for our doors and the jails for those who break them. But it does not count the health of our children, the quality of their education or the joy of their play."[30]

Obama had a particularly important reflection on climate change. He said we need a "paradigm shift" in economics—and soon. If we wait another ten or fifteen years, he told Leonhardt, it might be too late.

Caution: Obama Needs a Big Push

Despite the objective conditions favoring green regime change—and Obama's green sociological imagination—Obama is far from having executed regime change. The public should not confuse his repudiation of Bush with regime change. President Bill Clinton repudiated many of President George H. W. Bush's policies but operated well within the third corporate regime. Obama could do the same, creating important reforms of Bush-era policies but not systemic change that would solve either the economic or global warming crises.

The scale of both crises requires far bigger and more systemic changes than Obama has implemented or contemplated for the future. The problem is especially dire for climate change, with its existential threat to global humanity and its unrelenting time constraints imposed by planet earth. Even as Obama took office in January 2009, the National Academy of Sciences was warning that we were approaching levels of CO_2 atmospheric concentration—between 450 and 600 parts per million (ppm)—that seemed inevitable on our current course and would be "irreversible," at least for a thousand years. The academy report warned that carbon emissions are like nuclear waste, toxic for millennia whatever we do. We are on a path, the report said, to "inexorable sea level rise" and dust-bowl droughts for the next millennium.[31]

Obama's climate change initiatives are far from bold enough to forestall this terrible fate. There are several reasons for this failure. Obama has numerous crises on his plate. All cost money. The public strongly supports bold action on the economy—as well as on health care, education, and other short-term crises. But even though the public also supports action on global warming, its support is pale green. The public's own short-term focus does not offer Obama the same strong climate springboard that it does on the economy and health care. Early polls after Obama's election showed that the public prioritized climate change solutions far lower than it had even a year earlier, as it refocused entirely on the short-term crisis of the economy and jobs. Environment ranked sixteen on a list of issues, topped by the economy with the environment below, among others, terrorism, social security, deficit reduction, crime, military, tax cuts, and flag burning.[32]

Obama is an inspiring and potentially transformative president but also a cautious politician. He wants to unify the nation and put partisanship behind him, a strategy that may ensure his popularity in the mainstream but could lead him to take moderate positions when climate change and other crises require urgent radicalism. Within days after his inauguration, liberals were worrying that Obama was taking a year to close Guantánamo, fudging on his promise to get troops out of Iraq in sixteen months, sending 17,000 new troops into Afghanistan, offering business new tax cuts to appease Republicans, and listening mainly to Wall Street insiders and mainstream economic advisers to deal with the economy. As for global warming itself, Bill McKibben, one of the leading green writers and activists, called for civil disobedience to get Obama to commit to more radical action on everything from shutting down coal plants to capping emissions at 350 ppm.

To ensure enough boldness on warming by Obama, it will take massive mobilization by large-scale social movements that are bright green and farsighted. This includes not only the environmental movement itself but also the broad justice movements focused on human rights, labor, equality, peace, gender, and race. History—and especially the story of regime change in the New Deal—tells us that these movements must massively mobilize the public and push the president far beyond his political comfort zone to meet the climate crisis.

Do we now have social movements capable of rising to this historical challenge? That is the subject of the next chapter.

16

Blessed Unrest Revisited

Existential Threats and the Reinvention of Social Movements

Blessed Unrest, the title of a book by famed ecologist Paul Hawken, brings hope and a smile to those on the brink of despair.[1] "Blessed unrest" is Hawken's description of the thousands and thousands of rising nonprofit organizations and social movements with a new mission. They aim to make a new world free of the scourges of global warming, poverty, and corporate rule.

Hawken brings sunlight to the grim realities of climate change, seeing a renaissance of unstoppable grassroots groups sprouting up to save us. He subtitles his book *How the Largest Movement in the World Came into Being and Why No One Saw It Coming*. Composed of millions of people remaking their own lives and communities, the splendidly diverse forces he describes are a mighty multitude.

How could such a huge new force not be noticed? Sometimes, the biggest things are the least visible. Hawken writes: "Describing the breadth of the movement is like trying to hold the ocean in your hand. It is that large. When an iceberg rises above the waterline, the massive ice beneath is unseen."[2]

Hawken sees "the movement" as a global immune reaction to a deepening global illness. "If we accept that the metaphor of an organism can be applied to humankind, we can imagine a collective movement that would protect, repair and restore that organism's capacity to endure when threatened. If so, that capacity to respond would function like an immune system, which operates independently of an individual person's intent. Specifically, the shared activity of hundreds of thousands of nonprofit organizations can be seen as humanity's immune response to toxins like political corruption, economic disease and ecological degradation."[3]

Hawken sees the movement as miraculous. "At the core of immunity is a miracle of recovery and restoration.... The ultimate purpose of a global immune system is to identify what is not life-affirming and to contain, neutralize or eliminate it. Where communities, cultures and ecosystems have been damaged it seeks to prevent additional harm and then heal and restore the damage."[4] Hawken recognizes that the movement could still fail because it lacks the power to combat the entrenched interests that prop up the current regime. He writes that "as yet there has been no coming together of organizations in a united front that can counter the massive scale and power of the global corporations and lobbyists that protect the status quo."[5] But he returns to his message of hope: "Critics of the environmental movement have taken it to task, citing the worldwide collapse of ecosystems as proof of its ineffectiveness. What may be happening is the opposite. Although the momentum of damage and exploitation continues to accelerate in both the social and environmental arenas, the activity addressing it is increasing exponentially and has broken out of its traditional institutional boundaries."[6]

Using biological metaphors to explain social forces is all too common among environmentalists. Such rhetoric tends to make assumptions about the morality of nature (which is amoral) and to turn sociology into sociobiology, something that misses the heart of the best sociological analysis. Nonetheless, Hawken has done something that many other environmentalists have too often missed. He recognizes that social movements are at the heart of any solution to global warming and that these movements are not just environmental but are also focused on everything from women's rights to workers' rights, from climate change to change in corporate charters.

Hawken is certainly right that grassroots social movements remain the last and best hope for saving us in the age of global warming. And he is also right that these are groups focusing not just on climate change but also on all kinds of social justice causes. These grassroots groups are emerging in new forms—highly decentralized and localized, networked electronically, and ideologically less codified in grand doctrinal "isms." They are focused on change in their own lifestyles along with larger system change, and they operate globally. They carry the spark of the younger plugged-in generation.[7] Climate change has catalyzed a huge new energized global movement with a yearning to remake the world.

But Hawken has given us only a glimpse of what the movement must do to solve the overwhelming challenges it faces. It must create overwhelming global system change in an almost impossibly short period of time—requiring brilliant long-term vision in a world with intensely short-term focus. And pulling off such a "miracle," which indeed it would be, requires transformation in the world and in the movements themselves. Although Hawken certainly knows many of the environmental movements, he does not appear as intimately familiar with the history, strength, and weaknesses of their sister social justice movements—labor, peace, feminist, antiracist, anticorporate, and antiglobalization. The truth is that these movements are both the core of any hope to stop global warming and yet so weakened in the current era that they need to reinvent themselves. We need to look at the strengths and problems of these movements and then show how they can rapidly reinvent themselves to pull off the miracle we need.

What Are Right and Wrong
with the Movements?

Today's social justice and environmental movements are the best last hope for solving global warming on the urgent time scale required. I have highlighted the president's role in educating and mobilizing the nation. But the truth is that social movements have always been the social institutions that awakened the country to urgent systemic crises—whether of slavery, women's disfranchisement, or the capitalist exploitation of workers—and they have always mobilized both the public and the president to make the drastic emergency changes necessary.[8]

Every American should read historian Howard Zinn's classic book, *A People's History of the United States*.[9] Zinn vividly shows how abolitionists, suffragettes, populists, labor movements, and peace activists have been the true heroes of our nation, taking power into their own hands to solve collectively—often with remarkable speed and power—the great crises of their times. Social movements are the soul of democracy, the banding together of inspired ordinary folk to rise to the most urgent crises.

The unique attributes of movements fit the unique challenges of the age of global warming. Movement activists urgently seek to topple the reigning ideas of the ideological apparatus and the power relations of the existing order.[10] They operate outside conventional restraints of the "bubble" in which all corporate regimes seek to lock their citizens, especially in the midst of the deepest crises. They are the social institutions best designed to craft radical change in a hurry.

The emergency of global warming can never be addressed from within the system itself. It requires movements that break out of the bubble to articulate a vision radical enough to address the overall system crisis and to act with the lightning speed and power that an emergency requires. Movements often must endure for decades or centuries to succeed, but when an existential systemic crisis such as global warming requires immediate emergency action, only social movements can act with the blazing pace necessary, because they operate outside the system and refuse to be slowed or chained by its rules.

To solve global warming, we need the huge diversity of people, movements, and visions that Hawken describes as our "blessed unrest." But solutions will arise only with the movement of those who see the existential dimension of the climate change emergency and are capable of taking the most radical action in the shortest time period to mobilize the largest number of people, including the president. Fortunately, there are radical traditions within the history of American movements seeking to do all these things, and these traditions are arising today to cope with global warming and injustice.[11]

One such tradition is nonviolent civil disobedience.[12] It is a kind of "emergency" politics suited to dealing with existential threats and yet, despite its radicalism, carries a measure of legitimacy in the nation as a whole. This is because its historic philosophers and movement practitioners—such as Henry David Thoreau and Martin Luther King—are iconic figures in U.S. history. Green activists are beginning to embrace this tradition and may help produce the emergency mobilization that an existential threat requires.

Even though movements are the only hope, they have major weaknesses in the United States today. The problems are so serious that, taken together with the uniqueness of the climate crisis, their solution requires reinvention of the movements themselves. First, the movements face big problems about how to engage both the population and the president. They are relatively disconnected from the mass public. The public has lived since 1980 inside the third corporate regime's bubble, lulled into the seductive creature comforts of couch potato land.[13] The corporate regime's ideological apparatus—including the mass media, the conservative churches, the corporate ad world, and the political leaders themselves—has immobilized much of the public with fears of job loss, bankruptcy, and terrorism, as well as love of "free markets" and consumer delights, all combined with distaste for political activism. The public's passivity has been aggravated by overwork and excess stress, with the majority of Americans too exhausted after long work hours to drag themselves to political meetings.[14]

The ideological apparatus of the corporate regime has been demonizing social movements since the 1960s.[15] The sixties student and antiwar movements got caught in the fire of the culture wars and helped trigger the religious fury of the Bible Belt. In the 1980s and beyond, corporate and Christian conservatives successfully branded progressive or liberal movements as unpatriotic, hedonistic, and even terrorist.[16] This backfired, but social movements in the last few decades still carry what sociologist Erving Goffman calls a "spoiled identity,"[17] disgraced in the eyes of millions in the center and the Right and disconnected even from many mainstream liberals.

The public disconnect reflects not only the well-funded corporate regime's ideological blitzkrieg but also real problems in the movements themselves. Millions of Americans see progressive and Left movements as angry and divisive—and, in fact, many of the movements fit the bill. They are often dogmatic, polarizing, and elitist; too many lack the welcoming style and positive spirit that the public seeks. Some mirror the ideological rigidity and hierarchical structure of the regime they seek to overthrow, a tragic historic pattern.

Moreover, the movements are divided across issue, class, and race lines.[18] They only weakly support each other's work, leaving them unable to build a vast coalition with a broad political vision. After the 1999 "Battle of Seattle," antiglobalization movements began to develop a common framing that brought together labor, environmental, and peace groups, but much of this coalescing dissipated after 9/11.[19] As a result, much of the public fails to connect the dots, with no larger movement showing how our environmental and social justice crises are rooted in the common soil of the third corporate regime.[20]

Beyond these internal problems of the movements are the external problems tied to the crisis itself. Movements, other than the peace activists focusing on all-out nuclear war, have never faced an existential threat to humanity such as global warming, whose scale and timing are uniquely and overwhelmingly dangerous. Nor have movements ever had to mobilize such massive emergency remedies. Movements have always lived with a vision of enduring human history and the belief that they will persevere for generations and centuries to solve the problem. But global warming threatens the end of history and thus renders obsolete the very idea of history on which movements have always depended.

Movements suffer from a time frame pathology mirroring that of the society that they are trying to change. Because of shortages of money and staff, and the intense pain of the vulnerable populations they serve, grassroots movements tend to lurch from one short-term crisis to another. They throw themselves into solving daily problems and are reactive in the short term rather than proactive for the long term. They lack the luxury to develop long-term strategies for climate change, even though it is the crisis that produces the greatest need for emergency action now.

What Movements Must Do

1. Face the existential truth of the emergency.
2. Reinvent radicalism for survival.
3. Become time tricksters on a multi-issue agenda.
4. Fight for green regime change.
5. Let labor lead.
6. Pursue positive politics.
7. Use emotional intelligence.
8. Integrate personal and system change.
9. Master the art of cooperating with and confronting presidents (in this case, love Obama; push Obama).

The scale of the problem and the internal crises of the movements both imperil their ability to address existential emergencies. In the following pages, I suggest the key themes and changes needed to reinvent themselves.

The Existential Truth of the Crisis

The movements have to face the existential truth that we are confronting the possible end of history. This is extremely difficult for movements, perhaps more so than for the general public. Whereas the public commits to private lives largely in the present, movements live in and for history.[21] Contemplating the end of history contradicts the very idea of movements as we know them, because they have no purpose without history. Movements cannot live for the present.

This truth of a looming end-of-history scenario reframes everything about how social movements must act. It explains the need for each of the other transformations I outline here. But, most obviously, it means a shift in the philosophy and timing that movements embrace. Because the time window is closing on action to preserve history, the movements must shift from normal to emergency "movement politics." They must move from short-term reactivity to long-term proactivity. Movements must become social magicians, masters of time wizardry and of melding short-term reactions to single-issue politics with long-term emergency strategies to save the planet.

The Need for Greater Radicalism

On March 2, 2009, a coalition of environmental organizations, led by environmentalists such as Bill McKibben and Wendell Barry, organized a mass nonviolent civil disobedience action at the coal-fired Capitol Power plant in Washington, D.C., very close to Capitol Hill. Several thousand high-spirited protesters mobilized to shut down all five entries to the power plant, and hundreds were ready to commit civil disobedience in support of radical climate change legislation. Barry and McKibben proclaimed, "There are moments in a nation's—and a planet's—history when it may be necessary for some to break the law in order to bear witness to an evil, bring it to wider attention, and push for its correction." They emphasized that "clean coal is a lie," that "coal is driving climate change," and that catastrophe looms unless we stop using coal to generate electricity within ten years. Barry and McKibben say that they break the law reluctantly but that the emergency is so great that global witness and personal sacrifice are called for, including "a trip to jail."[22]

Al Gore has also called for "creative nonviolence" outside coal plants, lending his own authority to a new phase of radicalism and emergency politics in the movement.[23] Once the existential threat to humanity—and the short window of opportunity is understood—there really is no choice but to radical-ize the movement's vision and strategy. This is what great historical movements such as the abolitionists, the civil rights movement under Martin Luther King, and the anticolonial Indian movement under Mahatma Gandhi did. The cli-mate change emergency dwarfs even the challenges King and Gandhi faced.

The movements must use a wide array of strategies, including mass civil disobedience, to move the 2009 Copenhagen meetings toward a successful and radical global agreement. Overcoming the resistances will be difficult, despite the new efforts by the United States and China at the highest level to facilitate dialogue between themselves that might set new models for agree-ments between the West and the rest of the world. These global meetings are among the most important in history, and the movements must concentrate all their emergency powers and strategies to move the politicians to create a framework for the coming decades that can truly solve the crisis.

It is extremely important that this new radicalism remain nonviolent. Doing so is the only way to preserve the moral integrity of the movements and win support from the public. But the movements must move rapidly toward the most radical phase of their vision and strategy. Civil disobedience is only one approach, and less radical strategies should also be ratcheted up and used far more widely. But the movements need to signal the public in every way possible that time is running out and that even in the midst of economic meltdown, there is no choice but to make all necessary sacrifices to create the most radical and effective nonviolent means commensurate with the existential threat.

At this writing, the need for radicalism becomes urgent as the December, 2009, international climate meetings at Copenhagen take shape. As discussed further in the next chapter, these meetings are the most important ever to take place, where restrictive global greenhouse gas caps must be embraced in a post-Kyoto framework involving all nations, including the United States, China, and India. In mid-2009 leaders do not appear to be moving toward the radical steps necessary to meet the global existential threat. This is a crucial moment for global movements to come together and "demand the impossible," a set of drastically binding carbon and other greenhouse gas agreements leading toward 90 percent reductions over the next few decades. These reductions are possible if we have the will. Global movements will also have to move rapidly to consolidate and sustain links among communities all across the globe to sustain radical agendas.

Time Wizardry and Multi-Issue Organizing

A friend told me that it hurt his head to think about the grim realities of climate change now. He was having enough trouble getting his head around the enormity of the current economic crisis. This feeling is widespread, with public priorities on climate change dipping during the economic meltdown, especially among Republicans.[24]

This means the movements have no choice but to employ the time trickery that I have described throughout this book. The economic meltdown is so painful to so many people that they cannot think about anything else, especially anything long term. The only hope for climate change is to promote the green solution as a "two-fer," solving the economic and environmental crises together. The first steps required to fix the planetary emergency are the best fix to the economic meltdown today.

For the movements, this "two-fer" strategy means moving beyond linear time and shedding the single-issue pathology fragmenting the movements today. Time wizardry requires focusing on multiple issues with different time dimensions simultaneously. But the movements operate in their own silos and come together only sporadically in coalitions for large protests. I have been working with Boston-area activists to try to inspire such multi-issue coalitions, and it has been hard going. The movements are inwardly focused and do not trust each other. They do not appreciate enough the importance of other issues or see how solutions are intertwined. But we are beginning to see national efforts to bring together the labor, peace, and environmental movements to help move the Obama administration toward a green stimulus and broader green economic and peace agenda in the early period of his administration.[25] This could blossom into a new era of multi-issue movements of "turtles and teamsters," as the early environmental-labor coalition in antiglobalization movements was dubbed, that have pulled down their walls and work together on multiple problems and time frames. Nothing may prove more important than the ability of global labor movements to work with the global green movements in simultaneously transforming the economy and the environment.[26]

Green Justice and Regime Change

Moving away from single-issue politics involves taking the holistic approach to social justice—linking labor, environmental, peace, and civil rights issues—that activists understand in their bones but have abandoned in their organizing strategies. Most social justice movements know that they confront a capitalist order that operates systemically to perpetuate economic injustice, inequality, racism, sexism, war, and environmental degradation.[27] These movements implicitly understand that it takes a regime change to address all these issues. But they have taken the view that fighting their own struggles, often purely on a local basis, will create the blessed unrest leading to systemic change.

Within this model is an implicit view of an invisible hand in movements whereby each movement operating on its own issues will transform the system. But justice is indivisible and requires indivisible movements. That does not mean returning to a single ideology or central party—the spontaneous near-anarchy of Hawken's blessed unrest is better than that.[28] But it does mean building strong and enduring coalitions capable of acting in concert to create regime change in Washington and the world.

No issue, not even global warming, deserves to be singled out for exclusive attention. But given the closing window of time for action, all movements may begin to reimagine a green vision in which a form of justice is wrapped around and integrated with global warming solutions. *There can be no justice on any issue—race, sex, economy, war—if there is no viable future for human civilization.*

Leadership by the Labor Movement

The labor movement is at the intersection of the economic and environmental crises that make a green revolution possible. I have argued that climate change is capitalism's time bomb and that solving global warming means remaking the economy. Labor has always been a core social movement in any effort for economic change and justice, and its energizing role in climate change movements is indispensable.

With the labor movement's decline, we have been able to ignore its importance. But there are reasons for hope that labor will play a key role in green regime change, both in the United States and much of the world. The labor movement has begun to advocate strongly for green economic solutions to the current crisis, as well as to remake the economy and ensure full employment for the long term. We see in many U.S. states the growth of groups such as the California Green Stimulus Coalition, an alliance of many of the Golden State's most influential labor and environmental groups to promote green stimulus and a green economy. The labor groups include the California Labor Federation and the California Building and Trades Council as well as the César Chávez Institute representing agricultural workers.[29]

For several years, the U.S. labor movement has been building its own new national and global "labor war on global warming."[30] The Sierra Club joined forces with the United Steelworks in 2006 to create the "Blue-Green Alliance."[31] Its call was to create "Good Jobs, a Clean Environment and a Safer World." Its strategy was to focus on "those issues which have the greatest potential to unite the American people in pursuit of a global economy that is more just and equitable and founded on principles of environmental and economic sustainability." Steelworker president Leo Gerard said, "Secure 21st century jobs are those that will help solve the problem of global warming with energy efficiency and renewable energy." Sierra Club executive director Carl Pope confirmed that "our new alliance allows us to address the great challenge of the global economy in the twenty-first century—how to provide good jobs, a clean environment and a safer world."[32]

In the United States, we can see at least two key reasons that labor has such an important role to play and has already begun to fight "labor's war on warming." First, it is the social movement with the greatest organizational, financial, and electoral strength, despite its relative decline over recent decades. Labor is a key part of the base that got President Obama elected and is one of the few social movements with the clout to help Obama achieve the transformative green regime change we need.

Second, labor has a new stake in environmental change. Historically, the labor movement opposed environmentalism, seeing it as a movement inherently opposed to creating jobs to protect the environment. But green investment, as outlined in Obama's economic plan and described in the last chapter, is now the foundation for millions of new good jobs and the rebuilding of a secure life for millions of outsourced, underrepresented, and displaced workers. The creation of a green collar economy ensures a "butter-oriented" full employment economy and represents the best hope for a new economy ensuring living wage jobs that cannot be outsourced.[33]

For this reason, we saw U.S. labor movements play a major role in helping President Obama pass the green stimulus, which ensures billions of dollars for new jobs, as well as for the health care and education that workers need. Similarly, labor is now seeking to help pass Obama's 2010 budget to provide the systemic change that can ensure the comprehensive health care, education, economic, and environmental transformation at the heart of green regime change.

More broadly, both U.S. and international labor organizations have been forceful players in recent years for global climate change agreements. The Energy Task Force, created by the American Federation of Labor–Congress of Industrial Organizations (AFL-CIO) in 2006, published a 2007 report, "Jobs and Energy for the 21st Century," asserting that "human use of fossil fuels is undisputedly contributing to global warming, causing rising sea levels, changes in climate patterns and threats to coastal regions."[34] Labor's Bob Baugh, who leads the AFL-CIO's Task Force, says that "over the past year, the AFL-CIO's position on climate change has moved much closer to the ongoing efforts of the ITUC."[35] The ITUC, or International Trade Union Confederation, is the international association of trade unions that worked hard to advance the Kyoto and subsequent global climate change agreements. In 2008, AFL-CIO president John Sweeney told the UN Summit on Climate Risk: "The global labor movement is proud to have been among those who called for decisive action at Bali. [In December 2007, the United Nations sponsored international climate change meetings in Bali, Indonesia, to lay the ground for major progress on carbon agreements at Copenhagen and beyond.] ... Global warming means global depression, food and water shortages and drowned cities. I have stood in New Orleans' Ninth Ward and seen that future."[36]

Throughout this book, I have argued that the U.S. capitalist model must be transformed rapidly if there is to be any hope of solving climate change. This requires blessed unrest from the entire range of grassroots movements, both in the United States and the world, but the movement historically positioned to benefit and fight for systemic economic change has always been the labor movement. Where labor movements have been strong, as in Europe, we have seen the most enlightened climate change and broader environmental progress. The future of climate change and of labor are tightly entwined, and the future strength of the turtles and teamsters coalition will in large measure determine whether the planet has a future.

Positive Politics

Given the grimness of climate change scenarios, it is extremely important that movements embrace a positive and hopeful vision. Depression creates paralysis, not activism. This is only one of several reasons that movements need to sustain a positive solutions-oriented approach rather than a purely critical and negative tone.[37]

Today's movements are too often overwhelmingly negative rather than positive, a historic problem with social justice movements. The nineteenth-century populists were inspiring models of corporate regime activists struggling for democracy, but they poisoned their politics with the negativity of racism, anti-Semitism, and xenophobia.[38] They sometimes appeared to demonize all business enterprise, although they strongly supported cooperatives and local firms. More recently, New Left movements of the 1960s, while inspiring and preaching democracy, created hierarchies based on charismatic white male leaders and organizations permeated by political correctness, egotism, and competitiveness. Their negativity reflected the pathologies of the larger society, and it has persisted in many justice movements today. Negativity leads to burnout and contributes to failure to win over the mass public.

A new and more positive green populism is emerging based on what Van Jones, the inspiring African American green leader we met earlier, calls the "Noah Principles."[39] As Jones sees it, a Noah movement focuses more on "goals" than "demands." It works more with "partners" than against "targets" or enemies. It aims to create "solutions" rather than define "issues." It has less "accusations" and more "confession." Overall, this "Noah" style is less divisive, less ideological, more collaborative, and more harmonious than that of the movements of the sixties.[40]

The movements embracing the Noah Principles must create an artful balance between confrontation and cooperation, especially in the Obama era. They must speak truth to power and mobilize the righteous anger always necessary to win struggles against power elites, which now include the Obama administration. But the movements must also sustain the generosity of spirit and positive energy that can win over much of the mass public. Terrible injustice and the prospect of civilizational catastrophe lead activists toward confrontation and anger, but history suggests that they will succeed as a mass movement only if they balance these impulses—which can lead to self-destruction—with generosity and love.

As noted earlier, this less angry and divisive spirit does not imply less radicalism. To the contrary, it permits the greater radicalism we need. Activists should reflect on this equation: Greater movement radicalism + lesser movement anger and divisiveness = movement success. More radical visions require greater public receptivity on both emotional and ideological levels. But anger, dogma, and polarization shut people down. This is the emotional intelligence that movements need: to approach the intensely radical politics that existential threats require with the gentle and loving style that disarms and opens people rather than leading them to barricade themselves.

Emotional Intelligence

High emotional intelligence for movements is especially important on a subject as overwhelmingly depressing as global warming. In a recent workshop of global warming community activists that I attended, the leaders asked people at one point to describe their feelings after hearing more of the scientific prognoses. The room went dead silent, and then a series of emotions were named and claimed by participants: *depression, despair, hopelessness, paralysis, powerlessness, grief.*[41] I have already described my own grief and the issues of mortality that climate change inevitably creates.

Such emotions are rational responses to global warming realities. But they can breed self-fulfilling defeatism, crippling the hope and energy that the movement needs to succeed. Movements must spend time and develop skills in nourishing the spirits of their participants and the public. This requires the positive politics just described. It also necessitates a new sensitivity to the way politics operates at the emotional and psychological levels.

Psychologists, grief counselors, and spiritual teachers, as well as sociologists and organizational consultants, have developed approaches to dealing with grief and other incapacitating emotions. Movements must incorporate what they can from these "emotion specialists." They must realize the importance that personal emotions have in all movements and especially in green movement politics.[42] This recognition requires personal and collective commitments to emotional self-reflection and healing in the movement community. Music, poetry, dancing, fun, and hugs can help, as shown in the next chapter.

Existential politics is inherently a deep politics of emotion and the spirit. Distress is inevitable if we stay focused on the real prospect of the end of civilization. Movements have always had to foster the kind of community that can collectively sustain the spirit and nourish the heart.[43] Green movements need this community more than any others.

Lifestyle Politics and System Change

I have been part of one of several "eco-teams" in my town where we "diet" to shed "carbon pounds" and lighten our homes' and community's carbon footprints. We playfully dubbed our group the "clothesline" gang because to cut emissions, one of us now uses her grandmother's clothesline rather than a gas dryer. Some of us are beginners on the carbon diet, but an "advanced" member took us on a tour of his basement to show us how he has rigged up his superefficient German oil burner and hot water tank that stores electricity from his roof solar panels. To diet, we talk about everything from recycling (easy) to composting (a bit more effort), to doing home energy audits (free from our local utility), to using power strips and unplugging electronic devices (a pain), to eating less meat (healthy), to flying less on vacations (almost impossible), to lowering temperatures and taking shorter showers (inconvenient but doable). Our personal biographies also come up, because one member is doing penance for his grandfather's operation of a very dirty coal plant and another participant talked about her childhood where a river she swam in turned black from factories on the other shore running sewage right into the water. She now has asthma as a reminder.[44]

The lifestyle changes we discuss take the green revolution into the kitchens and basements of our own homes. It creates interesting new collaboration and conflicts among family members. But our eco-team finds that as we change our households, we need to know more about the energy grids and water zones in the town. We ask questions about the way our local utilities, development and zone boards, and city council operate. We cannot separate our own carbon diet from the carbon footprint of the town, and we find ourselves quickly discussing carbon diets for our state and the nation at large. We start talking about our water heaters one minute, and the next minute we are talking about joining mass civil disobedience to protest coal-fired power plants on Capitol Hill.

Our conversation shifts back and forth quickly from our grandparents' sins and our own health to presidential and global politics. The group is spontaneously playing out Mills's sociological imagination—connecting personal biography, personal troubles, and lifestyle with social problems and power elites.[45] As a sociologist, I find this exhilarating!

The group also struggles with the real meaning of recycling and taking shorter showers. Can these small personal lifestyle changes really make a difference when we need to change drastically national and global political rules of the game—and very rapidly? This is a very big question in the global warming movement. Is this a countercultural movement or an emergency transformation in global capitalism and politics? Or is it both?

Closely connected to this question is whether we can even make lifestyle changes that matter without big changes in social policies. Even the greenest activists all live contradictions, which may include driving long commutes or living in suburbia. But because of the lack of good public transportation and the shortage of decent urban housing, we may have few options. So lifestyle politics quickly moves us to reflect on government and corporate policies that lock us into our heavy carbon footprints.[46]

Lifestyle changes in our own homes will not solve global warming. But personal changes play a key role in building the political movement for green regime change. For one thing, they help people, including many with no political background, become part of neighborhood groups that are fun and educational. Lifestyle changes create a sense of mutual support and personal empowerment that is essential for and often breeds a new political consciousness among former couch potatoes. The conversation about personal biographies and personal troubles, as sociologist Mills would have predicted, leads naturally toward political activism.[47]

As the women's movement taught us, the personal is political. This is intensely true not only in the battle of the sexes but also in the politics of climate change. Personal and lifestyle changes—as well as community service—are the preferred approaches of millions of Americans worried about global warming. These micro and personalized approaches *cannot* stop climate change. But the lifestyle changes and the neighborhood groups people are joining in large numbers nurture a more collective political consciousness and activism.

There is a danger that much of the movement will not move fast enough to spur the systemic change we urgently need. But without the emotions bred by the personal stories and neighborhood connections overcoming our isolation, it is unlikely that mass political activism will be catalyzed and sustained. The green revolution is truly an exercise in the sociological imagination—enabling and bridging personal and societal transformation.

Cooperation with and Confrontation of Presidents

All relationships involve some mix of cooperation and conflict. A successful marriage involves an artful balance of the two. So, too, does the movements' relation with President Obama and with future presidents. Movements must always be confrontational to create the change that political elites resist.[48] But they must also offer the olive branch of support and cooperation with presidents who are expressing many of the values and ideals for change that they support.

Obama presents a particularly interesting paradox. He was elected on his soaring rhetoric of change, and he is more committed to a green revolution than any other president. The movements love this Obama. But as a cautious politician beset by multiple crises and financial constraints, Obama also operates inside the Beltway bubble, his action not yet matching his rhetoric or the emergency we face. The movements want to push this Obama to walk the talk of green regime change.

The relationship of progressive movements to presidents has always been complicated, depending on the president and the era.[49] The movements were totally confrontational with George W. Bush, seeing no common ground for cooperation. Social movements in the Great Depression, in contrast, had a more complex relation with FDR, as did movements in the 1960s with JFK. In both cases, they were inspired by the hope offered by these new presidents but also needed to prod them to move from liberal reforms to regime change (successfully with FDR, aborted by John Kennedy's assassination).

Obama deserves both more cooperation and more confrontation from social movements than any prior president. On the one hand, he offers hope and a program of green economic transformation that the movements must do everything possible to support and expand. It is not an exaggeration to say that Obama holds the future of history to some degree in his hands, and he may be the best U.S. president the movements could hope for at this moment of destiny.

On the other hand, the best is not good enough. We are not living in ordinary times, and Obama will invoke the emergency powers and measures humanity requires only if the movements find a new kind of relation that they have never had with earlier presidents. They must be radically confrontational enough to force Obama to contemplate the emergency measures that he will never consider without being pushed. But they must present themselves through this confrontation as partners in his call to change politics and change the world.

Such adversarial cooperation—or cooperative opposition—is delicate, and never has it been more important. The movements must steer Obama toward a truly radical emergency agenda on global warming and global justice without appearing hysterical, crazy, or totally out of touch with the sensibilities of the public and the political realities that Obama confronts. They must help him see them as partners even as they are relentless in pushing him toward actions that are politically risky and unorthodox. As they push, they must promise that they will help him cross over the political chasms that he faces.

This will be an improvisational dance between the movements and the president—and the public, too. The movements are now trying multiple methods—from forming radical caucuses and organizations inside the Democratic Party to engaging in civil disobedience and other actions that show unwillingness to compromise on the future survival of human civilization. There is no tried-and-true formula because an existential emergency of this kind is totally unprecedented. In this sense, Hawken may be right that movements need to be spontaneous and experimental and as flexible and fluid as the new online technologies they increasingly rely on. Some sectors of the movement will be mercilessly confrontational on the streets, spending lots of time in jail. Others will be operating in the caucuses of the Democratic Party and testifying to congressional committees to sound the call of the emergency within the marbled corridors of power. At this writing, the most important test will come in Copenhagen, where activists must mobilize in multiple movements with multiple strategies to move Obama to embrace an extremely comprehensive global agreement, at minimum embracing the 80 percent carbon cut by 2050 Obama endorsed in his 2008 campaign. All methods except violence, which should be avoided for the means must reflect the ends we seek, have to be entertained. When it comes to preserving human civilization, nobody has a monopoly on strategies of salvation.

17

Making a Life and Making History
From Bowling Alone to Bowling Green

On the first day of my classes, I often warn my students that they might need some industrial-strength Prozac by the end of the semester. That is because social topics can be truly depressing. We sociologists show that today's problems are big and frightening and are wired into our social systems. It is not easy to find solutions or to see how one person can do anything about them.

This seems true in spades about global warming. A pessimist could easily conclude that we are creating our own specieswide holocaust, gassing ourselves to a collective death with carbon emissions. She could look at her own child or grandchild or great-grandchild and conclude that the whole family tree is cooked. An optimist can, of course, come to a different conclusion: that because humans created this crisis, we still can solve it. Most climate scientists are telling us that time has not yet run out. But they are also warning us that the window for action is closing rapidly.

This leaves each of us with an overwhelming responsibility to make global warming a gut truth and devote as much time as we can to solving it. This is the biggest moral obligation humans can have: saving our precious human species as well as many other species with whom we share this beautiful planet. If that sounds too idealistic or softheaded, it is also the most hardheaded, self-interested thing we can do: act to ensure our own survival and that of our children.

But it is one thing to say this, quite another to get off the couch and try to make a real difference. This book has offered many reasons that people might choose to remain couch potatoes and slouch toward an overheated future of collective disruption, despair, and death. Even though Americans and many others in the world have become worried about global warming, it is not yet on the front burner. We have turned pale green, but we will have to act bright green if we are going to survive. On some days, this moves me back toward

Prozac. But on other days, I see that green awareness has grown faster than I ever imagined possible—and that there are so many people and movements and leaders who are beginning to take creative, contagious action.

The situation reminds me of the film *Pleasantville*, where everyone is living in a 1950s world of living death, without any color in their conformist, doomed universe (filmed in grainy black and white). But a few people, including a time traveler from the future, rise up against this dead world and start to break the lifeless, authoritarian rules. They begin to see and paint colors—orange and red and, yes, green—and then they themselves begin to turn from pale white to the vibrant flesh color of truly living beings. All of Pleasantville eventually blossoms into radiant color.

So we need to reenact our own real version of Pleasantville, the world of grim and compliant global warming, and break its tight, deadly hold on us. In this chapter, I look at a few people who have begun to struggle against their own pale green—and against the paleness of our whole society. They are not necessarily leaders or heroes, just ordinary people, some of whom have done extraordinary things. My hope is that seeing some of their failures and obstacles will make us feel less guilty about our own weaknesses or couch potato inclinations. More importantly, some of their ideas and successes may inspire us to believe that we can make a difference. They may help us think about what we can to do to help stop global warming and propel us off the couch.

In the service of truth in advertising, I want to say something first about myself. People rightfully want to know whether authors and teachers walk their talk. A lot of us do not. I see myself as a mixed case, not a couch potato but not a hero-activist or a great charismatic leader. I am one of many in my generation struggling to balance the demands of a busy career and personal life with my values and my desire to make a better world.

I am a child of the 1960s and 1970s, part of the generation that actively rebelled against the literal Pleasantville of the 1950s. This makes me a classic baby boomer. I was a young activist who landed in jails protesting segregation in the South and agitating against the Vietnam War at huge Pentagon rallies. Some of my brother and sister protesters ended up dropping out of conventional careers and becoming full-time activists. My route was somewhat different. Even as I was registering black voters in Mississippi summers, I was eager to get on with school and my intellectual career. I lived in tension between the demands of my personal ambitions and of my activist politics.

My dissertation adviser, sociologist Richard Flacks, wrote a book that captured this tension.[1] Flacks distinguishes between "making a life" and "making history." Making a life is focusing on the hard challenges of creating a personal life and a career that work. Making history is working to change society, as full-time activists do. Flacks concludes that most of us will always be focused on the challenges of personal life, but he remains optimistic. Great change can come when just a small minority decides to make history.

My own path was to try bringing the two life tracks together. I did not want to give up either my career or my political commitments. But although the tension was real, and it still creates a tug of war inside of me, there were ways to do both together. As an academic, I had a lot of freedom to teach about political subjects and encourage my students to believe in their capacity to change the world. I could write about the big social justice questions that were central to my academic discipline and to my activism. I could use my standing and resources in the university to help community activists wage their social justice campaigns. As I became more aware of the urgency of the global warming issue, I integrated it into my teaching and writing, helped my university think about how to build sustainability into the whole curriculum as well as the physical operation of the university, ran workshops on climate change with community groups and managers, did media shows on global warming and social justice, and worked with community, national, and global activists to push the Obama administration and global social movements to stop climate change and heal our planet.

A big life lesson for me has been that I cannot ignore my own psychological needs or force myself to give up my career ambitions. Although I still wrestle with this issue, I have largely accepted that my personal needs and career aspirations are going to drive much of my action. What gives me some peace has been my ability to harness a huge amount of my career energy into teaching, writing, and engaging in actions that advance my social justice aims. This is no perfect solution—I wish I could give up self-interest and focus only on the larger good. I have evolved a little more in that direction but not enough to satisfy my conscience.

Is my imperfect solution relevant for others? Academics have unusual freedom to meld work and politics. But if others share some of my dilemma, they can integrate political education and activism into nearly any profession or job. A journalist can make sure to deliver the news about green products, policies, debates, and movements. A lawyer can work in the growing field of environmental law and justice and represent environmental activists who need legal help or companies seeking to go green. An architect, carpenter, electrician, mechanical engineer, or plumber can help design or build the greenhouses, offices, cars, mass transit, and power grids needed to lower our carbon footprint. Each of these workers makes money and a career by making green social change.[2]

The green revolution is an open door for almost everybody to blend personal and political lives. After all, going green is partly a matter of personal lifestyle. A person can recycle, insulate the house, install solar panels, buy a hybrid car, and make other lifestyle changes, all both personal money-saving lifestyle choices and a micro form of green political activism. I have made small personal steps of this kind and want to make more. I recently went to a local community meeting about how to shed 5,000 pounds a year of carbon emission in my daily life at home. I am now part of a neighborhood "eco-team" working together to keep ourselves on a "carbon diet." I have also started going to a committee of my local city council exploring how the schools, heating and water systems, and overall carbon footprint of my town can be reduced. Seeing my neighbors come out in large numbers to meetings like this has been a source of hope. I have made new friends while learning about reducing my own carbon footprint.

Do personal lifestyle changes really make a difference? The truth is they will not by themselves stop global warming, which can be solved only by the big system changes I have described. But they have symbolic and strategic value that should not be minimized. When a person recycles, remembers to turn off the lights when leaving a room, unplugs a cell charger when not in use, or insulates the house, she is becoming more personally committed to the larger green struggle. I find that my own growing awareness about these little daily decisions increases my commitment to do more in my community and more with green political activists in national struggles. Lifestyle changes also have effects on the people around me. I can inspire others to think about living greener, too. This green "social contagion" is a major benefit of personal lifestyle changes.

The biggest lesson of my own story is that political action—or making history—can enrich our personal lives. Flacks emphasizes the tension between making a life and making history, but his historical analysis shows that a big reason people become and stay activists is because doing so is personally rewarding.[3] That has certainly been true for me. One of my great personal and professional pleasures is writing. It is a meditation for me and concentrates my mind and spirit, distracting me from personal anxieties while also giving me the simple joy of crafting artful sentences. Much of my writing has been about politics and social justice and is one form of activism, thus allowing me to indulge myself personally, deal with my psychological needs, and make my very small contribution to history.

There are many other ways besides writing books to indulge a passion for writing or other creative expression while moving the green revolution forward. A person can blog for green Web sites or write letters to the editor or op-eds about local and national green issues. I have a friend Ken who loves to write and formed a one-person writing company. He educates young people and companies on how to think, write, and communicate about the green issues (mostly about water use) that are his professional specialty. He also writes his own personal column on the environment in his local community newspaper.

Many of the most interesting people I have encountered—and some of my good friends—are people I meet in activist circles. We all have a hunger for community, and activists have often satisfied that very human yearning through their social movements. Historians write about the "romance" of communism during the Great Depression because so many activists fell in love with other activists, some marrying and creating "red diaper" babies. Left activists lived together in cooperative apartments, sent their kids to the same summer camps, came together around folk music and political poetry, and built long-term friendships and community that nonactivists often lacked.[4] More recently, activists in the New Right have found a similar sense of community in Evangelical churches and politics. The Obama "permanent campaign" and groups such as Moveon.org have virtually revolutionized politics in this spirit, with heavy reliance on the Internet. They have used MySpace, Facebook, and meet-ups in kitchens and dining rooms to ignite the chemistry of personal relationships that builds political movements. Politics becomes intertwined with helping an increasingly disconnected population connect, make friends, and build a personal community.[5]

My own life experience supports this so strongly that I feel truly sorry for the majority that never gets politically involved. For me, politics has always been a route out of America's Pleasantville and a road into excitement, adventure, new ideas, fascinating people, and strong communities and friends. The fight for a better world has made my personal life so much more interesting and "connected" that I can make a case for political engagement on purely personal or selfish grounds. I think the personal payoff of green politics is especially big; it can connect a person with good people, welcoming local community groups, lifestyle adventures, new ideas, and life-saving national and global political movements.

Peter Crawley: A Businessman Who Stopped a Dam and Turned Green

I turn now to my friend Peter, because he inspires me and may inspire others.[6] He is in his late forties and originally hails from Plymouth, Massachusetts. He has worked in his own family's small real estate business and is now married and raising a young son. He is not an academic, he is not famous, and he is not a self-identified political activist. But I have watched him evolve in his own green life adventure and seen him turn people on—really move them off the couch—to start their own green adventures. There is something about him that makes others want to make a difference and believe in their own ability to do it. I wish I could bottle Peter and clone him because it might be one of the surest ways to ensure the success of the green revolution.

I became most impressed with what Peter has to teach us when I watched him lead a workshop session with mainstream managers who did not think of themselves as political activists. Peter's workshop was about getting involved in one's own local community as a form of green activism. He made it very personal. He told a story about his own decision to get involved in a battle with a local real estate developer who dammed up a river to build a condo complex. The project would make the developer a lot of money but damage the ecosystems of the marshlands nearby and the fish migrations in the river.

This was happening in the town in which Peter had grown up, and although he had moved to a nearby town, his parents still lived there. It was not an easy decision for Peter to get involved. He had recently started his own business and was raising his young son. He had also begun to take some classes to prepare for his new career. Money was tight, and he did not have a lot of free time. He would likely choose to make a life rather than to make history.

But Peter decided to get involved. Some of his friends from the community invited him to conversations about the dam problem. His parents had moved to a place on the river itself and told him about their own concerns. He began meeting with a few of the community folks. Because he knew the town and the main players so well—the concerned people living on the river, members of the town government, and various people in the local real estate business, including his own father and the developer who had dammed the river—he became a logical person to try starting negotiations among the various groups to find a solution.

The negotiating was not fast or easy, but Peter eventually helped build a set of community partnerships and activists who succeeded in getting the dam removed. People trusted him because he is a reconciler without an ax to grind and with the good of the community clearly at heart. He is honest, open, and driven by strong values. Peter was good at working across differences to find points of agreement, while also learning how to rally people and use the regulatory system when necessary to be effective in confrontations with the developer and votes at public committee meetings. Peter was becoming one of America's thousands of green community activists—whose focus, as I show shortly, would expand to state and then regional, national, and global issues.

Peter told his story in a way that riveted the workshop participants—probably because of his quiet authenticity and unpretentiousness. The participants talked a lot about that authenticity, his heartfelt community values, and how he made the idea of activism seem personally relevant and even exciting to them for the first time. Peter converted some couch potatoes that day into people who would no longer ridicule protesters and would begin to think about stepping up.

What the participants wanted to know was what made Peter decide to get and stay involved, given his time and money constraints. It was the same thing I wanted to know, because I am constantly dealing with competing demands on my own time—and I always want to know what moves people to choose activism. Peter thought it was not any one factor but had to do with his very personal ties to the place and the people, as well as his core values. He had grown up in this community and played as a boy near the river. He had spent his boyhood years in Plymouth on the ocean and in the bay where the river flowed out; he loved the outdoors, water, wind, and sun. The folks living near the proposed dam were his friends or his family. Maybe the most important thing was that his parents had lived much of their lives in the town and were upset about the dam project; they could look out their window in their current house and see the river. Peter's father, as a real estate developer and longtime resident, felt a stake in the fate of the community—and that had helped shape Peter's own strong feelings about the local environment. Peter said that his feelings for his elderly parents played a big role in tipping him to do something.

To me, this reveals the strong connection between personal life and political action. A lot of invisible emotional and personal threads tugged Peter toward his community activism. He would not have decided to spend so much time if he did not have such a strong identification with his family, friends in the community, and the river. His activism was a way of defending his personal life and community. It also was a clear expression of his deepest values.

When Peter talks about his growing political identity as an environmental activist, anyone listening will soon be deep in conversation with him about culture, community, and values. He is a progressive, but his cultural approach to politics reminds me of Evangelical conservatives who come to politics driven by their own brand of morality and spirituality. Peter's community-oriented, value-driven approach tells us that green politics may become quite different from much traditional liberalism and leftism and may motivate a new breed of activists who are disconnected and often alienated from traditional progressive politics. A closer look at Peter's values suggests that the green movement may begin to activate millions of liberal people who are turned off by the conflictual, angry style of Left-leaning movements and who are looking for something more "positive." The green movement may also attract surprising numbers of value-driven and community-oriented conservatives.

Peter is a homespun philosopher. Raised in a traditional Catholic family, he grew up with a strong religious feeling. In college, however, he took classes in Eastern philosophy that appealed to him as his Catholic faith waned and led him to begin a Buddhist meditation practice. He backpacked several times around Asia—Cambodia, Laos, Thailand, and rural China—and was drawn spiritually to traditional Chinese culture and its worldview. He liked the culture's emphasis on harmony with community and nature. The Chinese view of morality and community, balance and harmony, seemed very appealing.

Peter eventually married a Chinese woman, whom he had met in the United States. Peter moved deeper into a life bridging Western and Eastern values of family, community, and compassion. I find him one of the more harmonious people I know and one who naturally thinks about the good of the community and the environment. Finding balance seems at the center of Peter's life adventure—and as he gets more deeply into green politics, it seems natural to me that he would be focused on lightening his own carbon footprint while helping his community and society live in harmony with nature.

Peter revealed to me, however, that he had not always had these values. He had grown up as a conventional American guy interested in business and socializing. He described himself as competitive, aggressive, and wanting to make a lot of money. After working in his family business, he had gone to work for John Hancock Insurance and some other big financial service companies. He made some money, kept partying, and was getting into a high-consumption lifestyle.

But his introduction to Eastern philosophy in college and his repeated backpacking excursions in poor areas in Asia began to shift his thinking about life. He noticed in rural Asia that people lived more simply, with a respect for the land they farmed and the community they belonged to. They lived more in tune with nature in a way that probably resonated with his own boyhood love of the outdoors. Peter felt that even though these people enjoyed none of the pleasures of the Western consumer lifestyle, many of them seemed to be living on the land and in their communities in peace. Their lifestyle was simple, even grindingly poor, and he did not romanticize it. He was keenly aware of the disregard for nature and human rights displayed by modern Asian business and government. But through his rural travels and readings in Eastern philosophy, he developed a vision of life based on not doing violence to the land, community, and environment that one operated in and loved. This would become a tenet of his green philosophy and politics.

He saw a materially poor life in many communities in Asia, but one lived simply and "from the heart," illustrating a moral philosophy that he had read about in Buddhism and that was becoming more attractive to him as he found himself falling away from his consumerist lifestyle. His childhood religiosity was evolving into a new personal ethics of simplicity and compassion. All of this began to create big changes in Peter, even as he continued to work in business.

His drive for money lost its appeal, and he began to question his lifestyle and U.S. consumerism itself, which contrasted so deeply with the simplicity and respect for nature he had found in Asian villages. He increasingly felt that American big houses and cars were unnecessary and artificial, even a type of violence against the natural world. This personal change in thinking was converging with the growth of the U.S. environmental movement and a Western culture increasingly concerned about climate change and sustainability. Peter found himself getting interested in green thinking and community action, one of the reasons behind his decision to get involved in the dam project. That decision was a reflection of the new green direction his life would take, anchored in the community values of his boyhood and family and bolstered now by his new Eastern moral interests and the new Western green culture.

At midcareer, Peter is now in an educational program to retool and work in the field of environmental science and management. He has gotten more involved with other community social justice projects. Peter's personal green adventure symbolizes to me a green turn in American lifestyles and politics that integrates personal life and politics. It spans traditional ideological divisions and also melds local and global issues.

Peter's political activism has been mainly at the community level—something hardly new but perhaps more central to green politics than to other progressive politics, because building local economies is so inherently essential to stopping climate change. He is also becoming interested in the national and global politics of global warming, a natural extension of his concern for the preservation of his local community. He feels that the local and the global are intimately connected but that global activism must start with personal values and always be anchored in one's own life and community. Otherwise, it risks becoming as impersonal and disconnected as the corporate system it is trying to transform.

His green politics is an expression of his Eastern values but is also very American in its community spirit. Peter gives me optimism that all kinds of Americans, whether liberal or conservative, may become green activists. Watching Peter and the workshop participants makes me hopeful that millions of people who have never been politically active will join Peter, himself not an activist until now, and turn bright green in their own fight against Pleasantville. The emerging green majority may find green politics a new just-right type of activism.

The biggest lesson I take from Peter is that making heartfelt connections to people and nature—especially family and friends and newcomers on the shared common ground in a community—is one of the biggest incentives to become an activist today, especially a green activist. The community spirit that Alexis de Tocqueville described as so defining of Americans is what pulled Peter—along with his changing value system, his love of nature, and his desire for a "life of the heart"—off his couch and into activism on the dam project.[7] The connections he deepened with family and old and new friends— and with nature—were some of the biggest personal rewards. Preserving the river and local environment was a way of saving his own community and expressing his core values. Peter has found a way to make a life and make history at the same time through his green activism.

Making friends and building community are increasingly important for the millions of Americans who political scientist Robert Putnam describes as isolated and "bowling alone."[8] Peter's example suggests that green politics may be fueled by a new search and respect for community. Rather than bowling alone, Peter is "bowling green," his way of finding and preserving common ground with other people and our imperiled natural world.

Bill McKibben: A Writer and His Students Step It Up

The last person I want to write about is Bill McKibben. He is an influential environmental writer and activist whose book *The End of Nature* helped in- spire the climate change movement.[9] I do not know McKibben personally, and I do not know enough about him to offer a good biographical snapshot. But I want to turn briefly to his "Step It Up" campaign, a 2007 project that began with McKibben and a few of his students. It evolved in a few months into one of the largest and most intriguing national campaigns to stop global warming. Step It Up shows how a few people without money or prior political experience can make a huge impact.[10]

An intriguing fact about McKibben, which he confesses in the book he coauthored with his students, is that he had had almost no prior experience in political activism. He was a writer and a public figure, but he was a political novice and knew almost nothing about activism. Many environmentalists are like this and have never been that comfortable with either Left or Right politics. In this sense, they are like Peter and may take new ideological di- rections that break the mold of familiar liberal/conservative divisions. They may also, as McKibben and his students did, invent new kinds of political strategies that work well for the millions of other Americans who have been turned off by politics and have never been activists.[11]

McKibben and his students wrote a book about Step It Up, with the specific goal of showing how one person can make a difference.[12] They proved that political amateurs without experience, money, or high-powered connections can actually create quickly a local and national climate change initiative that grabs headlines across the country. Step It Up was a campaign for a day of action in more than 1,400 local communities to put pressure on Congress to cut carbon emissions by 80 percent by 2050. The day of action was April 14, 2007.

The idea started with McKibben's own personal frustration that time was running out to solve global warming. Not having been an activist, he decided he should do something, anything, that he thought might focus people's attention on climate change. He figured he would walk across Vermont to the steps of the city hall in Burlington, the state capital, where he would sit until he was arrested. But then he learned that the police would be perfectly happy to let him sit there as long as he wanted.

McKibben shared his story with a small group of students, who began to meet regularly in a "Sunday evening club" to figure out a better strategy. Most of the students were no more politically experienced than McKibben, but they shared his passion and urgency about global warming. They decided to create the Step It Up campaign as way to capture media attention and put pressure on nearly every congressperson by organizing coordinated local events in the 1,400 local communities. They hoped this would trigger new action and begin a newly focused national movement to stop global warming.

Knowing so little about movements, they decided the best thing was to "just move." In a few weeks, they organized a short walk in Vermont that drew a lot of support and was a lot of fun. The number of people who joined in—and the coverage—convinced them they should think bigger. In a few months, on April 14, they would get the whole country moving—or at least so they dreamed.

After the huge success on April 14 that they never really expected, they decided that even though they had obviously not stopped climate change, or created a true national movement to sustain the struggle, they had done far more than they expected. Their plan had spread across the country. Local organizers they had never heard of joined in from towns and cities from Alaska to Florida. Community activists very much like my friend Peter had decided that it made sense to Step It Up together. Each local community group designed its own typically very creative, colorful, and charismatic event and created a national mosaic described in thousands of newspaper stories around the country. Moreover, important figures in Congress had taken note and publicly endorsed the project, including Steny Hoyer, one of the Democratic leaders in the House of Representatives. Hoyer signed on when one of the local Step It Up groups in his own town organized an April 14 canoe ride up a brook to his backyard, giving the powerful congressman a local taste of their global warming passion.

The McKibben group in Middlebury decided to interview many of the local organizers to see why and how they had pulled off these community actions. The group figured this might help an emerging global warming movement devise strategies to grow fast and to refrain from constantly having to reinvent the activist wheel. What group members wrote will look naïve and obvious to some veteran activists, but the truth is that their naïveté may have been an asset, forcing them to create a different kind of politics for a new era, part of the reinvention of movements discussed in the last chapter.

* * *

Their experience punctuates many of the ideas of movement renewal I have already described and adds some hopeful conclusions. I take from their success, first and foremost, that a small number of ordinary people working together with hardly any money can quickly pull off dramatic climate change actions that affect the nation. That should give hope to every individual or small group that it can make a difference.

Second, I see evidence here of a new generational politics. The McKibben core of Sunday night activists and the majority of the Step It Up local organizers around the country were young. Their visions, goals, strategies, tactics, and general way of being activists were new. This reminds me of the shock of the new youth politics of the 1960s, but this new generation's approach is unique.

Third, this new generational politics—and the green issue itself—seems to be breeding a new movement philosophy discussed in the last chapter as the "Noah Principles."[13] It focuses on partnerships and flexible positive solutions and is driven as much by hope and love as by anger or dogma. Overall, this Noah style is less divisive, less ideological, more collaborative, and more harmonious than the movements of the sixties.

I regard all these factors as improvements on my generation's movement style, but this new style is not a perfect model and is still evolving. Solving global warming means confronting huge corporations and entrenched political elites that will fight against green regime change with everything they have. The new movement must be mobilized to overcome this resistance. It must know how to confront as well as collaborate.

The green movement is also more localized and decentralized and loosely networked than the sixties movements were. And the environmentalists who have chronicled the new movements, such as Paul Hawken, see this localization as the natural outcome of the issue itself.[14] Global warming is such a huge and urgent global crisis that there is no time to create a single party or a single ideological doctrine. We need millions operating now on their own steam, using the Internet to network, to ensure that as many can get involved now, locally, in every corner of the world with their own approach. Saving the splendid diversity on the planet requires a splendid diversity of movements.

One of McKibben's group's own conclusions is that the Internet and electronic networking are key to this new generational politics. This is the first generation that has grown up on the Web and has made online communities and friends. This Web savvy logically translates into a politics that can use the Internet for global movement networking in a way that no prior generation could.[15]

I see the localized, decentralized, and electronically networked style of organization to be another major advance of the young green movement. But, again, it has some of its own problems. One is that localized and decentralized movements sometimes have trouble networking with enough clout to create systemic change in Washington and the other global centers of power. We will not solve global warming without a strategy for overcoming the centralized power of fossil fuel capitalism—which is going to require some centralization of power in the green movement.

The local will have to be integrated with a global political vision and strategy. This global challenge to global capitalism and its fossil fuel foundation must deal with power as well as love. The new politics cannot ignore the fact that capitalist realities are extremely resilient and entrenched in national and global institutions and treaties. Localist politics must have a serious, hardheaded vision of how to confront and change corporate power beyond the local level. It must be prepared to do real regime change and transform the U.S. and global capitalist order.[16]

In 2009, McKibben and his colleagues took the Step It Up model to the global level. He called for October 24, 2009, as an "international day of climate action" focused on the Copenhagen meetings. Using much the same approach as the Step It Up campaign, this new movement will be a crucial test of the efficacy of the emerging movement's Internet savvy and sophistication, with McKibben using his organization's Web sites 350.org and 350.org/oct24 as home base.[17] Given that the Copenhagen meetings are the most important meetings ever held on global climate change, the world's future hangs in the balance. Success at Copenhagen will require the kind of grassroots mobilization that McKibben is trying to catalyze, and the early efforts, at this writing, seem to parallel the successful community spirit and innovative use of technology that led to the Step It Up campaign's earlier achievements. Nonetheless, mobilizing now on a global scale, with so much at stake, will require a far greater engagement and collaboration with the vast and diverse movements that Paul Hawken describes in *Blessed Unrest*. And this means linking innovative climate change movements like McKibben's with all-out participation by global labor and peace movements, which must be collectively focused on the common goal at Copenhagen of saving the planet.

All of these goals will also require a special new relation between the movements and the president, as well as with leaders in other countries.

Neither the movements nor the president and other world leaders can succeed without each other. Only the president has the moral authority and the constitutional emergency powers to create the systemic changes we need in the United States. But only the movements will offer the push and the pull that will move him to live up to those constitutional responsibilities. The same is true on the world stage, where the demands of movements must collectively focus on all the world's leaders. Copenhagen will be a crucial test, where the rubber meets the road. Leaders may well fail to achieve the radical greenhouse gas global caps and carbon tax agreements we need. Global movements will have to redouble their efforts—not just for and at Copenhagen but for years afterward—partly by linking local communities in nations across the world as part of a new "glocalist" movement.

The new green movement—full of the creativity and exuberance of youth—has yet to prove that it is up to the huge challenge it faces. But the green movement is growing faster than any movement I have seen. It gives me hope that we have a chance to solve global warming and in the process remake our economy and renew our community and harmony with one another and the earth.

Notes

Notes for Introduction

1. "Time bomb" (noun), http://www.thefreedictionary.com.
2. "Doomsday Clock Overview," *Bulletin of the Atomic Scientists,* http://www
.thebulletin.org/content/doomsday-clock/overview.
3. See Chapters 2 and 3 for a discussion of the scientific consensus.
4. Harry Frankfort, *On Bullshit* (Princeton, NJ: Princeton University Press, 2005).
5. For a most persuasive argument on the Bush administration's manipulation of and contempt for science, see Chris Mooney, *The Republican War on Science* (New York: Basic Books, 2005).
6. See Chapter 15 for President Barack Obama's own pronouncements on science, truth, and evidence.
7. C. Wright Mills, *The Sociological Imagination* (New York: Oxford University Press, 1959).
8. Mills focused specifically on the intertwining of economic, political, and military elites as the structural foundation of the "power elite" organized to harness society to its own narrow ends rather than to the public interest. See C. Wright Mills, *The Power Elite* (New York: Oxford University Press, 1956).
9. John Bellamy Foster helped pioneer the most critical and illuminating sociological and neo-Marxist approach to environmental sociology and justice. See John Bellamy Foster, *Ecology against Capitalism* (New York: Monthly Review Press, 2002). See also John Bellamy Foster, *Marx's Ecology: Materialism and Nature* (New York: Monthly Review Press, 2000).
10. The three most important works of these sociological founders on political economy are Karl Marx, *Capital,* vol. 1: *A Critique of Political Economy* (New York: Penguin Classics, 1992); Max Weber, *Economy and Sociology* (Berkeley and Los Angeles: University of California Press, 1978); and Emile Durkheim, *The Division of Labor in Society* (New York: Free Press, 1997).
11. See Paul M. Sweezy and Paul Baran, *Monopoly Capitalism: An Essay on the American Economic and Political Order* (New York: Monthly Review Press, 1966). See also John Bellamy Foster and Fred Magdoff, *The Great Financial Crisis* (New York: Monthly Review Press, 2009).
12. See Chapter 9 for a discussion of our current "tragedy of the commons."
13. Chris Hedges, "Are We Breeding Ourselves to Extinction?" *Alternet,* March

11, 2009, http://www.alternet.org/environment/130843/are_we_breeding_ourselves_ to_extinction/.

14. Thomas Friedman, *The Lexus and the Olive Tree* (New York: Anchor Books, 2000), 104.

15. Ibid.

16. Thomas Friedman, *Hot, Flat, and Crowded* (New York: Farrar, Straus and Giroux, 2008).

17. Ibid.

18. Ibid.

19. For a classic discussion of the relation of structure and agency, see sociologist Anthony Giddens, *Central Problems in Social Theory: Action, Structure, and Contradictions in Social Analysis* (Berkeley and Los Angeles: University of California Press, 1979).

20. For Adam Smith's classic treatment of the invisible hand, see Adam Smith, *The Wealth of Nations* (New York: Bantam Books, 2003).

21. See my arguments about such systemic changes in the "rules of the game" in Charles Derber, *Corporation Nation* (New York: St. Martin's Press, 2000); and Charles Derber, *Hidden Power* (San Francisco: Berrett-Koehler, 2005).

22. This argument has made forcefully by a leader in the environmental justice movement, Van Jones. See Van Jones, *The Green Collar Economy: How One Solution Can Fix Our Two Biggest Problems* (San Francisco: HarperOne, 2008).

23. See Derber, *Hidden Power.* See also Charles Derber, *Regime Change Begins at Home* (San Francisco: Berrett-Koehler, 2004).

Notes for Chapter 1

1. The "boiled frog" story is used in many different contexts, with its origin in scientific research done by G. Stanley Hall in the 1880s. Hall was studying the neurological reactivity of frogs to environmental changes, including changes in temperature. Later, Al Gore used the boiled frog story in *An Inconvenient Truth: The Planetary Emergency of Climate Change and What We Can Do about It* (Emmaus, PA: Rodale Books, 2006). For Hall's work, see G. Stanley Hall and Yuzero Motora, "Dermal Sensitiveness to Gradual Pressure Changes," *American Journal of Psychology* 1, no. 1 (1887): 72–98, at 72–73.

2. For Gore's view of the importance of science and its credibility crisis in the United States, see Al Gore, *The Assault on Reason* (New York: Penguin, 2007).

3. See Thomas Kuhn, *The Structure of Scientific Revolutions* (Chicago: University of Chicago Press, 1966).

4. Polls show the majority of Americans respect science but reject it when it conflicts with their religious beliefs on matters such as evolution. See Pew Forum, "Science in America: Religious Beliefs and Public Attitudes," December 8, 2007, http://pewforum.org/docs/?DocID=275.

5. For a classic discussion of social construction arguing that all knowledge, including science, is socially constructed, see Peter Berger and Thomas Luckmann, *The Social Construction of Reality* (New York: Anchor Books, 1966). For a provocative discussion of the social construction of science, see Paul R. Gross and Norman Levitt, *Higher Superstition: The Academic Left and Its Quarrels with Science* (Baltimore, MD:

Johns Hopkins University Press, 1998). See also Kuhn, *The Structure of Scientific Revolutions.*

    6. Michael Polanyi, *Personal Knowledge* (Chicago: University of Chicago Press, 1974). For a view of the postmodern philosophy of knowledge, see Stephen R. C. Hicks, *Explaining Postmodernism: Skepticism and Socialism from Rousseau to Foucault* (Tempe, AZ: Scholargy Publishing, 2004).

    7. See Pew Forum, "Science in America."

    · 8. Richard Hofstadter, *Anti-intellectualism in American Life* (New York: Vintage Books, 1966).

    9. Kuhn, *The Structure of Scientific Revolutions.*

    10. Ibid.

    11. For the survey data on these subjects, see Chapters 4 and 8. See also the Pew Global Attitudes Project, December 18, 2008. http//pewsglobal.org/.

    12. The classic founding work in the sociology of knowledge is Kurt Mannheim, *Ideology and Utopia* (New York: Harcourt Brace, 1936).

    13. For a discussion of the ideological apparatus and its operation in the United States, see Charles Derber and Yale Magrass, *Morality Wars* (Boulder, CO: Paradigm Publishers, 2008), chap. 3.

    14. George Orwell, *1984* (New York: Signet Books, 1977).

    15. See Noam Chomsky and Edward Herman, *Manufacturing Consent* (New York: Pantheon, 2002).

    16. See Chapter 7, which focuses on the ideological apparatus of denial in the United States on the climate change issue.

    17. See the work of Robert McChesney on this point. See, for example, Robert McChesney, Russell Newman, and Ben Scott, *The Future of Media: Resistance and Reform in the Twenty-First Century* (New York: Seven Stories Press, 2005).

    18. See Derber and Magrass, *Morality Wars,* chap. 4.

    19. See Chapter 7. For the seminal work on the denial industry, see Ross Gelbspan, *The Heat Is On* (Reading, MA: Perseus Books, 1998).

    20. For a discussion of the structural bases of time orientations in the United States, see David Harvey, *The Condition of Post-modernity* (New York: Wiley-Blackwell, 1991).

    21. George Monbiot, *Heat: How to Stop the Planet from Burning* (Boston: South End Press, 2007), 204.

    22. Ibid., 206.

Notes for Chapter 2

    1. This consensus is developed in a series of reports by the UN Intergovernmental Panel on Climate Change, discussed throughout this chapter. See Intergovernmental Panel on Climate Change 2007, *Mitigation of Climate Change: Working Group III Contribution to the Fourth Assessment Report of the IPCC* (Cambridge, UK: Cambridge University Press, 2007).

    2. The data on public opinion are discussed in detail in Chapter 4.

    3. For a discussion of the irreversible character of warming associated with carbon dioxide already "in the pipeline," see Susan Solomon, Gian-Kasper Plattner, Reto Knutti, and Pierre Friedlingstein, "Irreversible Climate Change Due to Carbon

Dioxide Emissions," *Proceedings of the National Academy of Sciences* 106, no. 6 (2009): 1704–1709.

4. International Symposium on the Stabilization of Greenhouse Gas Concentrations, Report of the International Scientific Steering Committee, Hadley Centre, Met Office, Exeter, UK, February 1–3, 2005. See also Martin Parry et al., "Millions at Risk: Defining Critical Climate Change Threats and Targets," *Global Environmental Change* 11 (2001): 181–183.

5. Günther Fischer, Mahendra Shah, Harrij van Velthuizen, and Freddy Nachtergaele, "Global Agro-ecological Assessment for Agriculture in the Twenty-First Century" (International Institute for Applied Systems Analysis and the Food and Agriculture Organization, Vienna, Austria, July 2001).

6. James Hansen, "Global Warming Twenty Years Later: Tipping Points Near," testimony to Congress, June 23, 2008.

7. IPCC 2007, *Mitigation of Climate Change.*

8. See ibid. for a discussion of the research contributors, scholarly editors, and rigorous process of compilation of the IPCC reports.

9. For the actual statements of endorsement from these professional associations, as well as a list of all signing governments and organizations of the 2007 report, see Wikipedia, "Scientific Opinion on Climate Change, 2008," http://en.wikipedia.org/wiki/Scientific_opinion_on_climate_change.

10. Naomi Orenski, "The Scientific Consensus on Climate Change," *Science* 292 (December 3, 2004): 1686.

11. See Chapter 7 for a discussion of the "denial" community and industry.

12. IPCC, Working Group 1, "Fourth Assessment Report: Summary for Policymakers," November 2007, 5, http://www.ipcc.ch/pdf/assessment-report/ar4/wg1/ar4-wg1-spm.pdf.

13. Ibid.

14. Ibid.

15. Ibid., 2–6.

16. IPCC, Climate Change 1, Working Group 1, "Third Assessment Report," 2.3.5 summary, http://www.grida.no/publications/other/ipcc%5Ftar/?src=/climate/ipcc_tar/wg1/071.htm.

17. Dr. Gerald North, "Opening Statement," Surface Temperature Reconstructions for the Last 2,000 Years, National Academy of Sciences, 2006, http://www.nationalacademies.org/onpinews/newsitem.aspx?RecordID=6222006.

18. Ibid.

19. James Hansen, Makiko Sato, Reto Ruedy, Ken Lo, David W. Lea, and Martin Medina-Elizade, "Global Temperature Change," *Proceedings of the National Academy of Sciences* 103 (2006): 14288–14293. See also Barry Saltzman, *Dynamical Paleoclimatology: Generalized Theory of Global Climate Change* (New York: Academic Press, 2002), fig. 3-4. For a discussion of changes of temperature during the last 65 million years, which includes a commentary on the above citations, see John Baez, "Temperature," October 1, 2006, http://math.ucr.edu/home/baez/temperature/temperature.html.

20. All the data in this paragraph are reported in Baez, "Temperature."

21. IPCC, Climate Change 1, Working Group 1, "Third Assessment Report: Summary for Policymakers," 2007, 3.

22. Ibid., 1–5.
23. Ibid., 2–5.
24. Ibid., 2.
25. Ibid., 2–5.
26. Hansen cites the 385 ppm in his 2008 congressional testimony, indicating CO_2 concentration is rising about 2 ppm per year. Hansen, "Global Warming Twenty Years Later," 2.
27. IPCC, "Third Assessment Report: Summary for Policymakers," 2007, 2–6.
28. Ibid. For a citation and summary of the 2007 IPCC data on methane and CO_2 concentrations, see the discussion on GreenFacts. "Scientific Facts on Climate Change," 2007 digest, http://www.greenfacts.org/en/climate-change-ar4/l–3/1-human-natural-causes.htm.
29. IPCC, "Third Assessment Report," 3.
30. Ibid., 3.
31. IPCC, "Third Assessment Report" Working Group 2: Summary for Policy Makers," 2001, http://www.ipcc.ch/ipccreports/tar/vol4/english/108.htm. Working Group 2 focuses on "impacts, adaptation and vulnerability." For the 2007 Working Group 2 report, see http://klima.hr/razno/news/IPCCWG2_0407.pdf. See tables SPM.1 and SPM.2 for explicit discussion of these impacts; and see accompanying commentary in the text. See also the discussion of impacts by Hansen, "Global Warming Twenty Years Later." For a comprehensive summary of climate impacts on nature and people, reviewing many different scientific studies, see George Monbiot, *Heat: How to Stop the Planet from Burning* (Boston: South End Press, 2007).
32. IPCC, "Third Assessment Report, Working Group 2," table SPM.2.
33. Ibid.
34. Ibid.
35. Ibid.
36. Ibid.
37. Ibid.
38. Ibid.
39. Ibid.

Notes for Chapter 3

1. Schneider, a participant in the IPCC, was a pioneer in climate change research, publishing important articles as early as 1972. See Stephen H. Schneider, "Cloudiness as a Global Climate Feedback Mechanism: The Effects of Radiation Balance and Surface Temperature of Variations in Cloudiness," *Journal of Atmospheric Sciences* 29 (1975): 1413–1422. Schneider's popular discussion of frightening scenarios is cited in Dan Vergana and Patrick O'Driscoll, "Is Earth Near Its 'Tipping Points' from Global Warming?" *USA Today*, August 3, 2008, 1–2, http://www.usatoday.com.
2. Ibid., 2.
3. Ibid.
4. The leading spokesperson for this view is NASA's chief climate scientist, James Hansen, who has published scores of influential scientific articles on climate change. For a recent popular discussion of his thinking, see James Hansen, "Global

Warming Twenty Years Later: Tipping Points Near" testimony to Congress, June 23, 2008, 2.

5. Hansen's scientific publications can be found on his cv published online at http://www.columbia.edu/~jeh1/. Just one of the many important recent papers is J. Hansen, M. Sato, P. Kharecha, D. Beerling, R. Berner, V. Masson-Delmotte, M. Pagani, M. Raymo, D. L. Royer, and J. C. Zachos, "Target Atmospheric CO_2: Where Should Humanity Aim?" *Open Atmospheric Science Journal* 2 (2008): 217–231, doi: 10.2174/1874282300802010217.

6. Hansen, "Global Warming Twenty Years Later," 2.

7. Malcolm Gladwell, *The Tipping Point* (Boston: Back Bay Books, 2002).

8. Hansen, "Global Warming Twenty Years Later," 2.

9. This is one of many alarming statistics on sea-level change cited by John Holdren, now chair of President Obama's Office of Science and Technology. See Holdren's discussion in Roger Harribin, "Top Scientist's Fear for Climate," *BBC News*, August 31, 2006, http://news.bbc.co.uk/2/hi/science/nature/5303574.stm.

10. Peter D. Ward, *Under a Green Sky* (New York: HarperCollins, 2007), 183.

11. Proceedings of the National Academy of Sciences, February 2009, cited in "Threat from Global Warming Now Closer Than Thought," *Boston Globe*, February 24, 2009, A2, sourced from Associated Press.

12. Christopher Field cited in Tom Friedman, "Mother Nature's Dow," *New York Times*, March 28, 2009, http://www.nytimes.com/2009/03/29/opinion/29friedman.html.

13. Ibid.

14. Ibid.

15. This National Academy of Sciences 2007 report is edited by William Clark (Harvard University), "Global and Regional Drivers of Accelerating CO_2 Emissions," April 17, 2007, http://www.pnas.org/content/104/24/10288.abstract.

16. Scientists have recorded a variety of many other very recent changes that document the overconservatism of the IPCC and the plausibility of the revisionist new story. The Westminster Report, delivered to the British House of Commons in June 2007, states that "monitoring of the effects of global warming in virtually every parameter now shows a rate of acceleration that is outside the range of the ensemble of climate models underlying the IPCC Fourth Assessment Report." A few examples:

The rate of thinning of Arctic ice, and consequent predictions of the date of an ice-free North Pole

Intensification of drought conditions in Sub-Saharan Africa, North Mediterranean areas of Europe, Eastern Australia, etc.

Increase in the melt-rate of the Greenland ice-cap, evidence of surface-melt in areas of the Antarctic ice cap, more rapid retreat of glaciers around the world, with implications for the acceleration of sea-level rise

Slow-down in the Gulf Stream (the thermo-haline circulation) with far reaching consequential changes in the climate

Increased energy, wind-speed and damage in tropical storms whether in the typhoons and cyclones of the Pacific or the hurricanes of the Atlantic

Increased rate of extinction of species of fauna and flora in vulnerable habitats

Acceleration in the rate of drying, die-back, burning and carbon-release from tropical forests

Increased rate of thawing of tundra permafrost and acceleration in release of methane—Start of release of methane from the vast stores of ocean-floor "clathrates" far earlier than expected

See Westminster Briefing, "Feedback Dynamics and the Acceleration of Climate Change," presented to the British House of Commons, June 2007. The report, including the Summary for Policy-Makers, is reproduced at http://www.apollo-gaia.org/BaliandBeyond.htm.

17. Ibid.

18. Ibid., Summary for Policy-Makers.

19. Ibid.

20. Ibid.

21. For one of many of Hansen's and his collaborators' articles on feedback cycles, see J. Hansen, M. Sato, P. Kharecha, G. Russel, D. Lea, M. Siddall, "Climate Change and Trace Gases," *Philosophical Transactions of the Royal Society* 365 (July 15, 2007): 1925–1954.

22. Ibid.

23. Westminster Briefing, "Feedback Dynamics," Summary for Policy-Makers.

24. Ibid.

25. Gladwell, *The Tipping Point.*

26. Hansen, "Global Warming Twenty Years Later."

27. T. M. Lenton, H. Held, E. Kriegler, J. W. Hall, W. Lucht, S. Rahmstorf, and H. J. Schellnhuber, "Tipping Elements in the Earth's Climate System," *Proceedings of the National Academy of Sciences* 105 (2008): 1783–1785.

28. Hansen et al., "Target Atmospheric CO_2." See Hansen's presentations of these tipping point arguments at http://www.columbia.edu/jeh1/2008/TargetCO2_20080407.pdf and at http://www.columbia.edu/jeh1/RoyalCollPhyscns_Jan08.pdf.

29. Hansen, "Global Warming Twenty Years Later."

30. Bill McKibben, "Civilization's Last Chance," *Los Angeles Times,* May 11, 2008.

31. Hansen, "Global Warming Twenty Years Later," 3; emphasis added.

32. Robin Bell, "The Unquiet Ice Speaks Volumes on Global Warming," *Scientific American* (February 2008), http://www.sciam.com/article.cfm?id=the-unquiet-ice. See also the discussion of Bell's piece on Earthtalk, "Are Arctic Sea Ice Melts Causing Sea Levels to Rise?" *Scientific American,* June 13, 2008, http://www.sciam.com/article.cfm?id=arctic-ice-melts-cause-rising-sea.

33. Bell, "The Unquiet Ice."

34. For a popular account summarizing scientific research on methane burps, see Nicholas Kristof, "The Big Burp Theory of the Apocalypse," *New York Times,* April 18, 2006, http://query.nytimes.com/gst/fullpage.html?res=9D00EEDA173FF93BA25757C0A9609C8B63&sec=&spon=&pagewanted=all.

35. Westminster Briefing, "Feedback Dynamics," Summary for Policy-Makers.

36. Ward, "Under a Green Sky," 202ff.

37. The most readable of these is ibid.

38. Ibid., 138.

39. Ibid., 132–140.

40. For a discussion of the ice core research and the contribution of Hans Oeschger and Willi Dansgaard, see ibid., 149–151.

Notes for Chapter 4

1. Charles Reich, *The Greening of America* (New York: Bantam Books, 1971).
2. Ibid.; emphasis in original.
3. Ibid.
4. Paul Hawken, *Blessed Unrest: How the Largest Movement in the World Came into Being and Why No One Saw It Coming* (New York: Viking Press, 2007).
5. Public opinion polling on global warming has been extensive. I rely heavily here on a comprehensive review of the most important polling data during the last twenty years, summarized in a research article by Matthew C. Nisbet and Teresa Meyers, "The Trends—Twenty Years of Public Opinion in Global Warming," *Public Opinion Quarterly* 71, no. 3 (2007): 3, http://poq.oxfordjournals.org/cgi/content/full/71/3/444–470; doi:10.1093/poq/nfm031.
6. Al Gore, *Earth in the Balance* (New York: Plume, 1992).
7. Nisbet and Meyers, "The Trends," 3.
8. "Concern Soars about Global Warming as Top Environmental Threat," *ABC News*, April 20, 2007. http://74.125.93.104/search?q=cache:o7erDYDLBJIJ:woods.stanford.edu/docs/surveys/GW_2007_ABC_News_Release.pdf+ABC+news+2006+survey+data+85%25+say+earth+global+warming&cd=2&hl=en&ct=clnk&gl=us&client=safari.
9. Gary Langer, "Poll: Public Concern on Warming Gains Intensity," *ABC News*, March 26, 2006, http://abcnews.go.com/prnt?id=1750492.
10. "Fuel Costs Boost Conservation Efforts: 7 in 10 Reducing Carbon Footprint," tab. 2, "Views on Global Warming," ABC/Planet Green/Stanford poll, August 9, 2008, http://abcnews.go.com/images/PollingUnit/1067a1Environment2008.pdf. Belief and interest in global warming seem particularly susceptible to the salience of other short-term political issues, such as terrorism and economic crisis. Andew Kohut, director of Pew Polling, has emphasized the dips in belief and salience of warming after 9/11. See his comments and discussion of 2008 poll results in Andrew Revkin, "Environmental Issues Slide in Poll of Public Concerns," January 23, 2009, http://www.globalclimatescam.com/?cat=23.
11. "Fuel Costs." See also Langer, "Poll: Public Concern on Warming Gains Intensity." *ABC News*, March 26, 2006. http/abcnews.go.com/prnt?id=1750492.
12. Nisbet and Meyers, "The Trends."
13. "Fuel Costs Boost Conservation Efforts: 7 in 10 Reducing Carbon Footprint," Figure 2, "Views on Global Warming," ABC/Planet Green/Stanford poll, August 9, 2008, http://abcnews.go.com/images/PollingUnit/1067a1Environment2008.pdf.
14. Nisbet and Meyers, "The Trends," 6.
15. Peter Novelli, "What Are Americans Thinking and Doing about Global Warming?: Results of a National Household Survey," Center of Excellence in Climate Change Research, George Mason University, survey of 12,000 adults in May and June 2007, 6. "Fuel Costs," tab. 2.
16. Pew Global Attitudes Project, "Global Public Opinion in the Bush Years," December 2008, http://pewglobal.org/reports/pdf/263.pdf.
17. "Fuel Costs." See also Novelli, "What Are Americans Thinking?" tab. 1, "Beliefs about Global Warming." See also "Little Consensus on Global Warming," tab. "Americans Less Concerned about Global Warming," July 12, 2006, http://people-press.org/report/280/little-consensus-on-warming.

18. Novelli, "What Are Americans Thinking?" tabs. 1 and 2, "Beliefs about Global Warming" and "Believing vs. Doing." See also "Fuel Costs."

19. Pew Research Center, "Deeper Partisan Divide over Global Warming," May 8, 2008, http://people-press.org/report/417/a-deeper-partisan-divide-over-global-warming.

20. "Fuel Costs," tab. 3, "Carbon Footprint: Conservation?"

21. Ibid.

22. Ibid.

23. Ibid., 10. See also Nisbet and Meyers, "The Trends," 9.

24. Nisbet and Meyers, "The Trends," 14.

25. Ibid.

26. Ibid., 22.

27. Ibid.

28. Ibid.

29. Ibid., 19.

30. "Fuel Costs."

31. Ibid.

32. Nisbet and Meyers, "The Trends," 21 (based on ABC polls in 2006 and 2007).

33. Ibid., 22.

Notes for Chapter 5

1. William Schwartz and Charles Derber, *The Nuclear Seduction* (Berkeley and Los Angeles: University of California Press, 1990).

2. See polling data on personal and gut truth in Chapter 4. See especially Matthew C. Nisbet and Teresa Meyers, "The Trends—Twenty Years of Public Opinion in Global Warming," *Public Opinion Quarterly* 71, no. 3 (2007): 1–27.

3. Ernest Becker, *The Denial of Death* (New York: Free Press, 1997 [1973]).

4. Cited in ibid., 15.

5. Ibid., 15ff.

6. Ibid., 11ff.

7. Ibid., 27.

8. Ibid., 26ff.

9. Becker's whole work is a reflection on Freud's theory of death, repression, and sublimation. Becker devotes his chapter 6 to Freud's own fear of death and ways of managing it.

10. Ibid.; see also 173ff.

11. Ibid., 1ff. Becker opens his book with a focus on heroism, later analyzing it as the human response to the inevitability and tragedy of death.

12. Ibid., 1ff and 173ff.

13. Ibid., 281ff.

14. Mitch Albom, *Tuesdays with Morrie* (New York: Doubleday, 1997).

15. Koppel's interviews with Morrie took place on ABC's *Nightline* during the periods of Morrie's illness in 1995 and 1996.

16. For vivid scenarios of what such "collective death" would look like, see Peter D. Ward, *Under a Green Sky* (New York: HarperCollins, 2007), 193–204.

17. See Chapter 3, where these dark edge catastrophes are discussed.

18. Polls show the majority of Americans respect science but reject it when it conflicts with their religious beliefs on matters such as evolution. See Pew Forum, "Science in America: Religious Beliefs and Public Attitudes," December 8, 2007, http://pewforum.org/docs/?DocID=275.

19. Barry Glassner, *The Culture of Fear: Why Americans Fear the Wrong Things* (New York: Basic Books, 2000).

20. Ibid.

21. Bill McKibben, *Deep Economy* (New York: Times Books, 2007).

Notes for Chapter 6

1. I have used these generational classifications because they are the cohorts typically used in survey research. See, for example, New Politics Institute, "The Progressive Politics of the Millennial Generation," June 20, 2007, http://www.newpolitics.net/node/360?full_report=1. See also Edward Cheung, *Baby Boomers, Generation X, and Social Cycles,* vol. 1, *North America Long Waves* (Toronto: Longwave Press, 2007) for a discussion of broad generational cohorts.

2. For a discussion of these dimensions of the boomer generation, see Doug Owram, *Born at the Right Time* (Toronto: University of Toronto Press, 1997). See also Wikipedia, "Baby Boom Generation," http://en.wikipedia.org/wiki/Baby_Boomers.

3. See Charles Derber and Yale Magrass, *Morality Wars* (Boulder, CO: Paradigm Publishers, 2008), chaps. 7–9. See also Tom Hayden, *The Long Sixties* (Boulder, CO: Paradigm Publishers, 2009).

4. Jimmy Carter, *The Virtues of Aging* (New York: Ballantine Books, 1998).

5. Erik Erikson, *Identity and the Life Cycle* (New York: Norton, 1994).

6. Nicholas Kristoff, "Geezers Doing Good," *New York Times,* July 20, 2008.

7. Ernest Becker, *The Denial of Death* (New York: Free Press, 1997 [1973]). For a discussion of baby-boomer denial of aging and death, see "Baby Boomers in Denial over Aging," *CBS News,* April 5, 2009, http://www.cbsnews.com/stories/2004/03/05/national/main604287.shtml (drawn from a story by Bootie Cosgrove-Maher, Portland, Oregon, March 5, 2004). See also Robert Mullins, "Baby Boomers Lag in Preparing Funerals, Estates, et al.," *Business Journal of Milwaukee,* December 18, 1998.

8. See, for example, EDF, "Environmental Poll Compares Attitudes of Boomers and Internet Generation," April 12, 2000, www.edf.org/presrelease.cfm?ContentID=1274. See also Harris Poll, "For Earth Day: Two-Thirds of Americans Believe Humans Are Contributing to Increased Temperatures," April 18, 2008, table 5, http://www.harrisinteractive.com/harris_poll/index.asp?PID=898.

9. Jack Whalen and Richard Flacks, *Beyond the Barricades: The Sixties Generation Grows Up* (Philadelphia: Temple University Press, 1990).

10. Paul M. Kellstedt, Sammy Zhran, and Arnold Vedlitz, "Personal Efficacy, the Information Environment, and Attitudes toward Global Warming and Climate Change in the United States," *Risk Analysis* 28, no.1 (2008): 1–17.

11. New Politics Institute, "The Progressive Politics."

12. EDF, "Environmental Poll," 1.

13. Ibid.

14. Ibid., 1–2.

15. All data in this paragraph are drawn from Harris Poll, "For Earth Day."

16. The most widely discussed popular narrative about Gen X is Douglas Coupland, *Generation X: Tales for an Accelerated Culture* (New York: St. Martin's Press, 1991).

17. New Politics Institute, "The Progressive Politics."

18. See, for example, Harris Poll, "For Earth Day," table 5.

19. New Politics Institute, "The Progressive Politics," 1–2.

20. Harris Poll, "For Earth Day," table 5.

21. New Politics Institute, "The Progressive Politics," 1–2.

22. Tom Brokaw, *The Greatest Generation* (New York: Random House, 1998).

23. Ibid. This article summarizes a series of major polls on political and social attitudes linked to different generations, including major Pew polls carried out between 2005 and 2007.

24. Ibid.

25. Ibid.

26. Ibid., 4ff.

27. Ibid., 5.

28. Gallop Poll cited in ibid., 5.

29. Ibid.

30. Peter Novelli, "What Are Americans Thinking and Doing about Global Warming?: Results of a National Household Survey," Center of Excellence in Climate Change Research, George Mason University, survey of 12,000 adults in May and June 2007, tab. 7.

31. Ibid., 16–17.

32. Mike Farrell, "Poll Shows That Nearly 60% of Young Americans Feel Strongly That the Government Should Be Doing More to Protect the Environment," *Youthography,* April 18, 2007, 1, http://youthography.com/news/uploads/MR_Earth_Release_041807.pdf.

33. Ibid.

34. Ibid.

35. Ibid.

36. Novelli, "What Are Americans Thinking?" 16ff.

37. Farrell, "Poll," 1–2.

Notes for Chapter 7

1. James Hansen, "Global Warming Twenty Years Later: Tipping Points Near" testimony to Congress, June 23, 2008, 3; emphasis added.

2. Ibid.

3. Alexander is cited in an influential article by Mark Hertsgaard, "While Washington Slept," *Vanity Fair* (April 2006): 11, http://www.commondreams.org/views06/0420–31.htm.

4. The original and best source on the denial industry is Pulitzer Prize–winning journalist Ross Gelbspan, *The Heat Is On* (Reading, MA: Perseus Books, 1998). See also Hertsgaard, "While Washington Slept."

5. Gelbspan, *The Heat.*

6. Quoted in Gelbspan, *The Heat,* 53.

7. Ibid.

8. Both quotes from Fred Seitz, "Global Warming Petition," http://www.oism .org/pproject/. Seitz writes a cover letter accompanying The Oregon Petition (also at the Web site just mentioned) in which he expands on this assertion. The Oregon Petition is discussed by George Monbiot, *Heat: How to Stop the Planet from Burning* (Boston: South End Press, 2007), 29ff.

9. Robinson cited in Monbiot, *Heat*, 30.

10. Arthur Robinson and Zachary Robinson, "Science Has Spoken: Global Warming Is a Myth," *Wall Street Journal*, December 4, 1997.

11. Monbiot, *Heat*, 36. See also Hertsgaard, "While Washington Slept," 9–10.

12. Hertsgaard, "While Washington Slept," 9–10.

13. For Exxon's annual funding of the Marshall Institute, see Exxonsecrets Fact Sheet, George C. Marshall Institute, http://www.exxonsecrets.org/html/orgfactsheet .php?id=36.

14. Monbiot, *Heat*, 29ff.

15. Gelbspan, *The Heat*, 46–49.

16. Kevin Mooney, "Natural Forces, not Man, Causing Global Warming, Scientist Says," *CNSnews.com*, March 5, 2008, http://www.studentnewsdaily.com/daily-news-article/natural_forces_not_man_causing_global_warming_scientist_says/.

17. Gelbspan, *The Heat*, 46–47.

18. Ibid.

19. Memo cited in "The Truth about Denial" *Newsweek.com*, April 29, 2009, http:// www.newsweek.com/id/32482/page/3.

20. A detailed discussion of the Exxon plan and the collaboration with Seitz, Singer, and others at the American Petroleum Institute is reported by Sharon Begley, "The Truth about Denial: Warming Deniers, a Well-Funded Machine," *Newsweek*, August 13, 2007, http://www.msnbc.msn.com/id/20122975/site/newsweek/page/0/.

21. Inhofe delivered these remarks in a speech to the Senate in 2003 called "The Science of Climate Change." Cited by Monbiot, *Heat*, 38. See also Michael Shnayerson, "A Convenient Untruth," *Vanity Fair* (May 2007), http://www.vanityfair.com/politics/ features/2007/05/skeptic200705.

22. This is reviewed in detail by Begley, "The Truth about Denial."

23. Ibid.

24. Ari Fleischer, White House Press Briefing, May 7, 2001, http://www.slate .com/id/1007638/.

25. Tim Dickinson, "The Secret Campaign of President Bush's Campaign to Deny Global Warming," *Rollingstone.com*, June 28, 2007, http://www.rollingstone .com/politics/story/15148655/the_secret_campaign_of_president_bushs_ administration_to_deny_global_warming/print.

26. Cited by Hertsgaard, "While Washington Slept," 1.

27. Dickinson, "The Secret Campaign."

28. This entire sordid tale is laid out in detail in ibid.

29. Gelbspan, *The Heat*. See also Ross Gelbspan, *Boiling Point* (New York: Basic Books, 2005).

30. Hertsgaard, "While Washington Slept."

31. Cited in Greg Wynn, "Exxon Says It Never Doubted Climate Change," *Reuters*, June 14, 2007, http://www.reuters.com/article/environmentNews/ idUSL1441452220070614.

32. Tillerson cited in Jeffrey Ball, "Prototype of Texas Oilman," *Wall Street Journal*,

March 8, 2006, B1, http://www.brandingstrategyinsider.com/2006/10/exxon_ vision_is.html.

33. David Adam, "Exxon to Discontinue Funding to (Some) Climate Change Denial Groups," May 28, 2008, http://www.commondreams.org/archive/2008/05/28/ 9259.

34. Ibid.

35. Ibid.

36. Hertsgaard, "While Washington Slept," 1.

37. Both quotes from Bob Ward of the Royal Society, "Letter to Nick Thomas," Corporate Affairs, Exxon, September 4, 2006, http://www.commondreams.org/ archive/2008/05/28/9259.

38. John Browne, "Climate Change Speech," May 19, 1997, dieoff.org/page106 .htm.

39. Ibid.

40. All quotes in this paragraph are from ibid.

41. Friends of the Earth, Greenwash Oscars, August 23, 2002. http://www.foe. co.uk/campaigns/economy/news/earth_summit_23_august.html.

42. See the offense of the leading corporate greenwashing Oscar winners in ibid.

43. Ibid.

44. TerraChoice Environmental Marketing, "Sins of Greenwashing: Greenwash- ing Report 2007," http://sinsofgreenwashing.org/findings/greenwashing-report–2007/. See also TerraChoice Environmental Marketing, "The Seven Sins of Greenwashing: Environmental Claims in Consumer Markets," April 2009.

45. TerraChoice, "Sins of Greenwashing"

46. Browne, "Climate Change Speech," emphasis added.

47. Ed Crooks, "Back to Petroleum," Financial Times.com, July 9, 2009, http:// www.ft.com/cms/s/0/b8626bf4-6b20-11de-861d-00144feabdc0.html?nclick_ check=1

48. Cited in Steve Mufson and Juliet Eilperin, "Energy Firms Come to Terms with Climate Change," *Washingtonpost.com,* November 25, 2006, http://www .washingtonpost.com/wp-dyn/content/article/2006/11/24/AR2006112401361 .htmls.

49. Cited at some length in Martin Lamonica, "Duke Energy CEO: Coal Not Going Away," *CNETnews,* April 13, 2008, http://news.cnet.com/8301–11128_3- 9917630-54.html.

50. Ibid.

51. Ibid.

52. Cited in Martin Lamonica, "ConocoPhillips CEO: The US Needs Carbon Regulations," *CNETnews,* February 13, 2008, http://news.cnet.com/8301-11128_ 3-9871161-54.html.

53. The Republican Party discussion, including McCain's quote, is discussed in Kim Chipman, "Bush Faces Growing Dissent from Republicans on Climate Change," *Bloomberg,* April 24, 2007, http://www.bloomberg.com/apps/news?pid= washingtonstory&sid=aiUC2JB2UcGA.

54. For a discussion of McCain's evolving and contradictory speeches on climate change during the 2008 campaign, see "McCain Breaks with Bush on Climate Change," *Washingtonpost.com,* May 13, 2008, http://voices.washingtonpost.com/44/2008/05/12/ mccain_breaks_with_bush_on_cli.html.

Notes for Chapter 8

1. A large majority of Americans (85 percent) say global warming is probably happening, according to a new *Time* magazine/ABC News/Stanford University poll. An even larger percentage (88 percent) think global warming threatens future generations. More than half (60 percent) say it threatens them a great deal, 38 percent feel that global warming is already a serious problem, and 47 percent feel that it will be in the future. "Americans See a Climate Problem," *Time,* March 26, 2006, www.time.com/time/nation/article/0,8599,117696,00.html.

2. Barack Obama, "New Energy for America," Lansing, Michigan, August 4, 2008.

3. Charles Derber, *Regime Change Begins at Home* (San Francisco: Berrett-Koehler, 2004).

4. Michael Tanzier and Stephen Zorn, *Energy Update: Oil in the Late Twentieth Century* (New York: Monthly Review Press, 1985).

5. Harvey Wasserman, *Harvey Wasserman's History of the United States* (New York: Harper & Row, 1972).

6. Charles Morris, *The Tycoons: How Andrew Carnegie, John D. Rockefeller, Jay Gould, and J. P. Morgan Invented the American Supereconomy* (New York: Holt, 2004).

7. Larry Tye, *The Father of Spin: Edward L. Bernays and the Birth of Public Relations* (New York: Holt, 2002).

8. Stuart Ewen, *Captains of Consciousness: Advertising and the Social Roots of the Consumer Culture* (New York: Basic Books, 2001).

9. David Kyvig, *Daily Life in the United States, 1920–1940: How Americans Lived through the Roaring Twenties and the Great Depression* (Chicago: Ivan Dee, 2004).

10. Daniel Gross, *Forbes' Greatest Business Stories of All Times* (Hoboken, NJ: Wiley, 1996).

11. Arthur Schlesinger Jr., *The Age of Roosevelt,* vol. 2, *The Coming of the New Deal, 1933–1935* (New York: Mariner, 2003), 321, 338.

12. Yale Magrass, *Thus Spake the Moguls* (Cambridge, MA: Schenkman, 1981). William Leuchtenburg, *Franklin D. Roosevelt and the New Deal* (New York: Harper, 1963).

13. Robert Lekachman, *The Age of Keynes* (New York: Penguin, 1969).

14. Magrass, *Thus Spake the Moguls,* 221–232.

15. Charles Siegel, *The Politics of Simple Living* (San Francisco: Preservation Institute, 2008), 19.

16. Lekachman, *The Age of Keynes,* 151.

17. T. R. Reid, "The Superhighway to Everywhere," *Washington Post,* January 28, 2006.

18. Alexei Bayer, "Good for GM?" Researchmag.com, August 31, 2008, http://www.researchmag.com/Issues/2008/9/Pages/Good-for-GM-.aspx.

19. Magrass, *Thus Spake the Moguls,* 55; Siegel, *The Politics of Simple Living,* 19.

20. Herbert Gans, *The Levittowners* (New York: Columbia University Press, 1982).

21. Jonathan Grossman, "Fair Labor Standards Act of 1938," United States Department of Labor, 2009, http://www.dol.gov/oasam/programs/history/flsa1938.htm.

22. Siegel, *The Politics of Simple Living,* 10–11. Julie Schor, *The Overworked American: The Unexpected Decline of Leisure* (New York: Basic Books, 1993).

23. Will Bunch, *Tear Down This Myth: How the Reagan Legacy Has Distorted Our Politics and Haunts Our Future* (New York: Free Press, 2009). William Kleinknecht, *The Man Who Sold the World: Ronald Reagan and the Betrayal of Main Street America* (New York: Nation Books, 2009).

24. Thomas Friedman, "The Power of Green," *New York Times*, April 15, 2007.

25. "The Military's Impact on the Environment: A Neglected Aspect of the Sustainable Development Debate," a briefing paper for states and nongovernmental organizations, International Peace Bureau, Geneva, August 2002.

26. Alexandra Twin, "Stock Crushed; Approximately $1.2 Trillion in Market Value Is Gone after the House Rejects the $700 Billion Bank Bailout Plan," *CNN Money*, September 29, 2008.

27. Paul Krugman, "Partying Like It's 1929," *New York Times*, March 21, 2009.

28. Stephen Castle and James Kanter, "Huge Fight Looms in EU over Climate Change," *International Herald Tribune*, October 14, 2008.

29. Thomas Friedman, "Seeds for a Geo-green Party," *New York Times*, June 16, 2006.

30. Chant during vice presidential candidate Sarah Palin's acceptance speech, Republican National Convention, Saint Paul, Minnesota, September 3, 2008.

31. *The Money Pit*, produced by Steven Spielberg and directed by Richard Benjamin, 1986.

32. Jeremy Rifkin, *The European Dream* (New York: Jeremy P. Tarcher, 2004).

33. Will Durant, *The Life of Greece* (New York: MJF Books, 1993).

34. Al Gore, *An Inconvenient Truth: The Planetary Emergency of Climate Change and What We Can Do about It* (Emmaus, PA: Rodale Books, 2006).

Notes for Chapter 9

1. *Boston Globe*, February 9, 2009, A14.

2. For an excellent discussion of externalities, see Herman E. Daly and John B. Cobb, *For the Common Good* (Boston: Beacon Press, 1989), 52–57.

3. The concept of the tragedy of the commons has been widely discussed in recent environmental literature. The idea in its modern form was developed in Garrett Hardin, "The Tragedy of the Commons," *Science* 162, no. 3859 (December 13, 1968): 1243–1248. See also Francisco Dionisio and Isabel Gordo, "The Tragedy of the Commons, the Public Goods Dilemma, and the Meaning of Rivalry and Excludability in Evolutionary Biology," *Evolutionary Ecology Research* 8, (2006): 321–332.

4. Adam Smith, *The Wealth of Nations* (New York: Modern Library, 1994).

5. Adam Smith, although identified with free-market ideology and the invisible hand, actually presumed the existence of a strong moral community to steward the economy and society. See Adam Smith, *The Theory of Moral Sentiments* (New York: Book Jungle, 2009).

6. Daly and Cobb, *For the Common Good*, 55.

7. For an excellent discussion of how to design cap-and-trade arrangements, see Peter Barnes, *Climate Solutions* (White River Junction, VT: Chelsea Green, 2008), 56.

8. See Joseph Stiglitz, *Making Globalization Work* (New York: Norton, 2006), 181ff.

9. Thomas Friedman, "(No) Drill Baby, Drill," *New York Times,* April 12, 2009, 8.

10. Charles Derber, *Hidden Power* (San Francisco: Berrett-Koehler, 2005).

11. Much of my analysis of the dynamics, contradictions, and dangers of capitalism is based on Paul M. Sweezy and Paul Baran, *Monopoly Capital* (New York: Monthly Review Press, 1966).

12. Ibid. See also John Bellamy Foster and Fred Magdoff, *The Great Financial Crisis* (New York: Monthly Review Press, 2009).

13. Sweezy and Baran, *Monopoly Capital.* See also Charles Derber, *Corporation Nation* (New York: St. Martin's Press, 2000).

14. See Kevin Phillips, *Bad Money* (New York: Viking Press, 2008).

15. Ibid.

16. Phillips tracks the correlation of growing household, government, and bank debt in ibid.

17. Foster and Magdoff, *The Great Financial Crisis.*

18. Ibid. For the classic treatment of these issues, see Sweezy and Baran, *Monopoly Capital.*

19. Tom Wolfe, *The Bonfire of the Vanities* (New York: Dial, 2001).

20. David Harvey, *The Condition of Postmodernity* (Oxford, UK: Blackwell, 1991), 240ff.

21. Ibid., 240.

22. Ibid., 240ff.

23. Yale Magrass, *Thus Spake the Moguls* (Cambridge, MA: Schenkman, 1981).

24. Ibid.

25. Derber, *Hidden Power.*

Notes for Chapter 10

1. For a brief summary of the dangers of excessive executive power, see John P. MacKenzie, *Absolute Power: How the Unitary Executive Theory Is Undermining the Constitution* (New York: Century Foundation Books, 2008).

2. Jane Mayer, *The Dark Side: The Inside Story of How the War on Terror Turned into a War on American Ideals* (New York: Doubleday, 2008).

3. United States Code Annotated, Title 50: War and National Defense, Chapter 35: International Emergency Economic Powers, http://74.125.95 .132/search?q=cache:fH72YUXpcTAJ:www.treas.gov/offices/enforcement/ofac/ legal/statutes/ieepa.pdf+statute+IEEPA&cd=1&hl=en&ct=clnk&gl=us&client= safari.

4. Ibid.

5. "A History of Executive Orders," http://209.157.64.201/focus/f-bloggers/ 1607403/posts.

6. George Monbiot, *Heat: How to Stop the Planet from Burning* (Boston: South End Press, 2007). Charles Siegel, *The Politics of Simple Living* (Berkeley, CA: Preservation Institute, 2008).

7. "The Never-Ending Bailout," *New York Times,* March 3, 2009, A26.

8. Cited in Krishna Guba and Edward Luce, "Greenspan Backs Bank Nationalization," *Financial Times,* February 18, 2009, 1.

9. See David Korten, *Agenda for a New Economy* (San Francisco: Berrett-Koehler, 2009).

10. Andrew Carnegie, *The Gospel of Wealth* (Bedford, MA: Applewood Books, 1998).

11. "Government May Convert Bank Bailouts to Equity," *New York Times,* April 20, 2009, A16.

12. Paul Krugman, "Money for Nothing," *New York Times,* April 27, 2009, A21.

13. This is a central argument in Charles Derber, *Corporation Nation* (New York: St. Martin's Press, 2000), esp. chap. 6.

14. Warren Buffet, letter to shareholders of Berkshire and Hathaway, 2002, http://www.nytimes.com/2009/03/01/business/01buffett.html.

15. Robert Reich, "Corporate Welfare," speech delivered in 1994, cited by Jacob Weisberg, "Corporate Welfare NIMBY'S," *Slate.com,* http://www.slate.com/id/2264/.

16. Paul Krugman, "Bailouts for Bunglers," *New York Times,* February 1, 2009, http://www.nytimes.com/2009/02/02/opinion/02krugman.html.

17. Both quotes from Joseph Stiglitz, "Nationalized Banks Are the 'Only Answer,'" *Deutsche Welle,* reprinted in *Truthout,* February 6, 2009, http://www.truthout.org/020609R.

18. This argument has been made by President Obama, as discussed in Chapter 14. Obama has been influenced by several important books, including by Van Jones, now a top Obama energy adviser, who makes the case that creating green jobs is the key to economic recovery. See Van Jones, *The Green Collar Economy: How One Solution Can Fix Our Two Biggest Problems* (San Francisco: HarperOne, 2008).

19. Michael Renner, "Jobs in Renewable Energy Expanding," WorldWatch Institute, July 8, 2008, http://www.worldwatch.org/node/5821.

20. Charles Derber, *Regime Change Begins at Home* (San Francisco: Berrett-Koehler, 2004). See also Charles Derber, *Hidden Power* (San Francisco: Berrett-Koehler, 2005).

21. See the discussion of Obama's thinking and plan fleshed out in Chapter 14.

22. Cited in Steve Hargreaves, "The Green Jobs Boom," *CNNMoney.com,* October 7, 2007, http://money.cnn.com/2007/10/04/news/economy/green_jobs/index.htm. See also Apollo Institute Admin., "Green Collar Jobs Generated by the Senate Stimulus Plan," February 4, 2009, http://apolloalliance.org/uncategorized/green-collar-jobs-generated-by-the-senate-stimulus-plan/.

23. Paul Krugman, "Depression Economics Returns," *New York Times,* November 14, 2008, http://www.nytimes.com/2008/11/14/opinion/14krugman.html?_r=1. See also Paul Krugman, "Fighting Off Depression," *New York Times,* January 4, 2009, http://www.nytimes.com/2009/01/05/opinion/05krugman.html.

24. Keith Bradsher, "Green Power Takes Root in China," *New York Times,* July 3, 2009, B1.

25. William Leuchtenburg, *Franklin Roosevelt and the New Deal* (New York: Harper Torchbooks, 1963).

26. This was the notorious quote by Sarah Palin during the 2008 campaign, referring to Obama's association with 1960s radical Bill Ayers. Beltway Blips, "Palin Criticizes Obama's 'Terrorist' Connection," video http://beltwayblips.dailyradar.com/video/palin_criticizes_obama_s_terrorist_connection.

27. William Leuchtenburg, *Franklin Roosevelt and the New Deal.*

28. Ibid., chap. 13. See also Thom Hartmann, *Unequal Protection* (Ennasui, PA: Rodale Press, 2004).

29. Charles Derber, *People before Profit* (New York: Picador, 2003), chaps. 7–9.

30. Hartmann, *Unequal Protection*.

31. Hazel Henderson and Simran Sethra, *Ethical Markets: Growing the Green Economy* (White River Junction, VT: Chelsea Green, 2009).

32. Derber, *Corporation Nation*, chap. 13.

33. Marjorie Kelly, *Divine Right of Capital: Dethroning the Corporate Aristocracy* (San Francisco: Berrett-Koehler, 2001).

34. Michael Useem, *Investor Capitalism* (New York: Basic Books, 1999).

35. Bill McKibben, *Deep Economy* (New York: Times Books, 2008).

Notes for Chapter 11

1. Charles Derber, *Hidden Power* (San Francisco: Berrett-Koehler, 2005). See also Charles Derber, *Regime Change Begins at Home* (San Francisco: Berrett-Koehler, 2004).

2. Annie Leonard, "The Story of Stuff," *YouTube,* http://www.youtube.com/watch?v=gLBE5QAYXp8.

3. Derber, *Hidden Power*. See also Charles Derber and Yale Magrass, *Morality Wars* (Boulder, CO: Paradigm Publishers, 2008).

4. Jeremy Rifkin contrasts these American values with those of Europeans in Jeremy Rifkin, *The European Dream* (New York: Jeremy P. Tarcher, 2004).

5. My discussion in much of this section draws on the thinking of Charles Siegel. See Charles Siegel, *The Politics of Simple Living* (Berkeley, CA: Preservation Institute, 2008).

6. Derber and Magrass, *Morality Wars,* chaps. 2, 3. See also Katherine Adam and Charles Derber, *The New Feminized Majority* (Boulder, CO: Paradigm Publishers, 2008), chap. 2.

7. Frederick Jackson Turner, *The Frontier in American History* (New York: Dover, 1996). Derber and Magrass, *Morality Wars,* chap. 2.

8. Derber and Magrass, *Morality Wars,* chaps. 2, 4, 6.

9. For the classic work on the cultural antipathy toward American cities and the cultural effort to transform urban American into a land of "garden communities and suburbs," see Jane Jacobs, *The Death and Life of Great American Cities* (New York: Modern American Library, 1994).

10. This has been a traditional view of rurally based conservative movements, not just in the Bible Belt in the U.S. New Right but traditionally in European right-wing movements, most notably German fascism. Derber and Magrass, *Morality Wars,* chap. 4. See also Jacobs, *The Death and Life of Great American Cities*.

11. Charles Derber, *Corporation Nation* (New York: St. Martin's Press, 2000).

12. Siegel, *The Politics of Simple Living,* chap. 3. See also Jacobs, *The Death and Life of Great American Cities*.

13. Jacobs, *The Death and Life of Great American Cities*. See also Siegel, *Politics of Simple Living*; and Charles Siegel, "Unplanning" (unpublished ms., 2008).

14. Siegel, *The Politics of Simple Living*.

15. Bradford Snell, "The Street Car Conspiracy: How General Motors Deliberately

Destroyed Public Transit," *New Electric Railway Journal* (Autumn 1995), http://www
.lovearth.net/gmdeliberatelydestroyed.htm.

16. Cited in Siegel, *The Politics of Simple Living*, chap. 3.

17. For an elegant historical analysis of the role of urban planners in this process, see especially Siegel, "Unplanning." See also Jacobs, *The Death and Life of Great American Cities*.

18. Siegel, "Unplanning."

19. Jacobs, *The Death and Life of Great American Cities*.

20. Siegel, "Unplanning."

21. Juliet Schor, *The Overworked American* (New York: Basic Books, 1993). See also Siegel, *The Politics of Simple Living*, chap. 2.

22. Schor, *The Overworked American*.

23. Ibid.

24. Ibid.

25. Siegel, *The Politics of Simple Living*, chap. 2.

26. Ibid.

27. Shaila Dewan, "More Time for You: Furloughed in LA," *New York Times*, March 1, 2009, 1, 4, http://www.nytimes.com/2009/03/01/weekinreview/01dewan
.html?pagewanted=all.

28. This case for a choice of work time law has been made forcefully to me by Charles Siegel, and I thank him for his contribution. See Siegel, *The Politics of Simple Living*, chap. 2.

29. David Rosnick and Mark Weisbrot, "Are Shorter Work Hours Good for the Environment?" (London: CEPR, 2006).

30. This argument is implicit in the classic work by Paul M. Sweezy and Paul Baran, *Monopoly Capital* (New York: Monthly Review Press, 1966).

31. For a related argument, see John Bellamy Foster and Fred Magdoff, *The Great Financial Crisis* (New York: Monthly Review Press, 2009).

32. Siegel, *The Politics of Simple Living*, chap. 2.

33. Ibid.

34. Derber, *Hidden Power*.

35. Ibid., 34ff.

36. Charles Derber, *The Wilding of America: Money, Mayhem, and the New American Dream*, 4th ed. (New York: Worth, 2006), 14ff.

37. Ibid. See also Derber, *Hidden Power*.

38. Derber, *Corporation Nation*, chap. 8.

39. Brian Ross and Alice Gomysten, "Lehman Brothers Boss Defends $484 Million in Salary, Bonus," *ABC News*, October 6, 2008.

40. Julie Davis, "Lehman Sought Millions for Execs while Seeking Aid," *Huffington Post*, October 7, 2008, http://www.huffingtonpost.com/huff-wires/20081006/
meltdown-lehman/.

41. Derber and Magrass, *Morality Wars*, Conclusion.

42. Derber, *Corporation Nation*, chap. 8.

43. Sweezy and Baran, *Monopoly Capital*. Foster and Magdoff, *The Great Financial Crisis*.

44. Stewart Ewen, *Captains of Consciousness: Advertising and the Social Roots of the Consumer Culture* (New York: Basic Books, 2001).

45. Juliet Schor, *Do Americans Shop Too Much?* (Boston: Beacon Press, 2000).

46. Foster and Magdoff, *The Great Financial Crisis.*

47. This was all foreseen in Sweezy and Baran, *Monopoly Capital.* See also Foster and Magdoff, *The Great Financial Crisis.*

48. Juliet Schor, *Born to Buy* (New York: Scribner, 2005).

49. Peter S. Goodman, "A Shopping Guernica Captures the Moment," *New York Times,* November 30, 2008, http://www.nytimes.com'2008/11/30/weekinreview/30goodman.html?pagewanted=print.

50. Ibid.

51. Ibid.

52. David Kessler, *The End of Overeating* (New York: Rodale Press, 2009).

53. Cited in Lindsey Layton, "Crave Man," *Washington Post,* April 27, 2009, http://www.washingtonpost.com/wp-dyn/content/article/2009/04/26/AR2009042602711.html.

54. This argument is made by Bill McKibben, who emphasizes the pleasures of simpler living. See McKibben, *Deep Economy* (New York: Times Books, 2008), chap. 1. See also Siegel, *The Politics of Simple Living.*

55. Dewan, "More Time for You."

56. See Friends of the Earth, "The Happy Planet Index: An Index of Human Well-Being and Environmental Impact," http://www.happyplanetindex.org/.

57. David Korten, *Agenda for a New Economy* (San Francisco: Berrett-Koehler, 2009).

58. Karl Marx, *Capital,* vol. 1: *A Critique of Political Economy* (New York: Penguin Classics, 1992).

59. Ibid.

60. Ibid.

61. Riane Eisler, *The Real Wealth of Nations* (San Francisco: Berrett-Koehler, 2007).

62. See McKibben, *Deep Economy,* chap. 1.

63. Derber, *The Wilding of America,* chap. 1.

64. Ibid. See also Derber, *Hidden Power*; and Derber and Adam, *The New Feminized Majority.*

65. Cited in Derrick Jackson, "Outside Things Are Looking Righter," *Boston Globe,* January 24, 2009, A11.

66. Ibid.

67. Ibid.

Notes for Chapter 12

1. Turner has become a passionate environmentalist and has been encouraging young people to take green jobs as the most secure and meaningful work they can do. Quotes here are from a talk to journalism students at the University of Arizona in February 2009.

2. Numerous works refer to the growing economic power and potential hegemony of China and East Asia. One of the most interesting is Giovanni Arrighi, *Adam Smith in Beijing* (London: Verso Books, 2009).

3. Thomas Friedman, *Hot, Flat, and Crowded* (New York: Farrar, Straus and Giroux, 2008).

4. This is the central argument being made by President Obama himself in his forceful argument for new energy and climate change legislation, embodied in his 2009 stimulus and 2010 budget plans. For discussion and quotation of Obama's views, see Chapter 15.

5. Friedman, *Hot, Flat, and Crowded*.

6. Ibid., 365ff.

7. Ibid., 244ff.

8. Ibid., 244.

9. See Chapter 15 for a detailed discussion of Obama's treatment of energy independence.

10. Select Committee for Energy Independence and Global Warming, http://globalwarming.house.gov/.

11. Michael Klare, *Blood for Oil* (New York: Owl Books, 2007).

12. Ibid.

13. Ibid.

14. Bob Woodward, *The Commanders* (New York: Simon and Schuster, 2002).

15. Charles Derber and Yale Magrass, *Morality Wars* (Boulder, CO: Paradigm Publishers, 2008), chap. 2.

16. Ibid. See also Andrew Bacevich, *American Empire* (Cambridge, MA: Harvard University Press, 2002). Noam Chomsky has written the most decisive critiques and explanations of U.S. hegemony. See Noam Chomsky, *Hegemony or Survival* (New York: Holt, 2004). See also Paul M. Sweezy and Paul Baran, *Monopoly Capital* (New York: Monthly Review Press, 1966).

17. Linda Bilmes and Joseph Stiglitz, *The Three Trillion Dollar War* (New York: Norton, 2008).

18. Paul Kennedy, *The Rise and Fall of the Great Powers* (New York: Vintage Books, 1989).

19. Sweezy and Baran, *Monopoly Capital*.

20. Arguments about the centrality of military Keynesianism have been made repeatedly by Noam Chomsky. See Noam Chomsky, "The Pentagon System," *Z Magazine* (February 1993), http://www.thirdworldtraveler.com/Chomsky/PentagonSystem_Chom.html.

21. Bacevich, *American Empire*. See also Derber and Magrass, *Morality Wars*, chap. 2.

22. Chuck Collins and Felice Yeskel, *Economic Apartheid in America* (New York: New Press, 2005).

23. Ibid. See also Charles Derber, *Hidden Power* (San Francisco: Berrett-Koehler, 2005).

24. For an early discussion of the anxious class, see Charles Derber, *Corporation Nation* (New York: St. Martin's Press, 2000), chap. 5.

25. Collins and Yeskel, *Economic Apartheid in America*.

26. Kevin Phillips, *Bad Money* (New York: Norton, 2008).

27. Derber, *Hidden Power*, chap. 2.

28. Ibid.

29. Charles Derber, *The Wilding of America: Money, Mayhem, and the New American Dream*, 4th ed. (New York: Worth, 2006).

30. See especially Derber, *Hidden Power*; and Charles Derber, *Regime Change Begins at Home* (San Francisco: Berrett-Koehler, 2004).

31. This is detailed in the brief history of the environmental movement by Van Jones, *The Green Collar Economy: How One Solution Can Fix Our Two Biggest Problems* (San Francisco: HarperOne, 2008), 36ff.

32. Cited in Megan Rowling, "Report Estimates Deaths by Warming," *Boston Globe*, May 29, 2009, 8.

33. Cited in ibid.

34. Ibid.

35. Rachel Carson, *Silent Spring* (New York: Mariner Books, 2002).

36. See Jones, *The Green Collar Economy*, 53.

37. Ibid., 51.

38. Ibid., chap. 3.

39. Ibid., chap. 4.

40. Ibid.

41. Ibid., frontispiece.

42. Ibid., chap. 4.

43. Jennifer A. Diouhy, "Energy Lobby Ready to Fight Obama's Plan," *Energy Tribune*, March 9, 2009, http://www.energytribune.com/articles.cfm?aid=1417.

44. Jones, *The Green Collar Economy*, 108ff.

45. For a discussion of corporate regimes and populist movements, see Derber, *Corporation Nation*, chaps. 13–14. See also Derber, *Hidden Power*, chap. 7.

Notes for Chapter 13

1. U.S. Energy Information Administration, "United States Country Analysis Brief," 2005, http://web.archive.org/web/20061012181146/http://www.eia.doe.gov/emeu/cabs/Usa/Full.html.

2. Noam Chomsky, *Hegemony or Survival* (New York: Metropolitan Books, 2003). See also Andrew Bacevich, *The Limits of Power* (New York: Metropolitan Books, 2008).

3. For a discussion of the morality of hegemony, as exemplified through the course of European empires down to the current U.S. hegemonic era, see Charles Derber and Yale Magrass, *Morality Wars* (Boulder, CO: Paradigm Publishers, 2008).

4. Giovanni Arrighi, Beverly Silver, and Iftikhar Ahmad, *Chaos and Governance in the Modern World System* (Minneapolis: University of Minnesota Press, 1999).

5. For more extensive discussion, see Andrew Bacevich, *American Empire* (Cambridge, MA: Harvard University Press, 2002). See also Chomsky, *Hegemony or Survival*; and Derber and Magrass, *Morality Wars*.

6. See Richard Falk, *The Costs of War: International Law, the UN, and World Order after Iraq* (New York: Routledge, 2007). See also Richard Falk, Balakrishnan Rajagopal, and Jacqueline Stevens, eds., *International Law and the Third World: Reshaping Justice* (Abingdon, UK: Routledge-Cavendish Research in International Law, 2008). See also Charles Derber, *People before Profit* (New York: Picador, 2003), chaps. 6, 10.

7. Derber, *People before Profit*, chaps. 1–3.

8. See Chomsky, *Hegemony or Survival*. See also Bacevich, *The Limits of Power*; and Derber and Magrass, *Morality Wars*, chap. 2.

9. Derber and Magrass, *Morality Wars*, chaps. 2–3.

10. Obama's speech and the alignment with the views of Kissinger and Nunn

have been widely reported. See "White House Says Nuclear-Free World Achievable," *CBS News,* April 4, 2009, http://www.cbsnews.com/stories/2009/04/04/ap/politics/main4919530.shtml.

11. For a discussion of the new diplomatic initiatives, both in the United States and globally, for a nuclear-free world in which traditional hegemonic claims are abandoned, see Steve Andreasen, "A Joint Enterprise: Diplomacy to Achieve a World without Nuclear Weapons," Arms Control Association, April 2009, http://www.armscontrol.org/act/2009_04/Andreasen.

12. For an overview of views of relative responsibilities of developed and developing nations on climate change, see P. R. Shukla, "Development and Climate: A View from the South," Indian Institute of Management, 2002, http://www.iddri.org/Activites/Conferences/shukla.pdf.

13. For another discussion of the South's perspective on this, as expressed at the Kyoto Accords and subsequently, see Joseph Stiglitz, *Making Globalization Work* (New York: Norton, 2007), chap. 6.

14. Derber, *People before Profit.*

15. Stiglitz, *Making Globalization Work,* esp. chap. 6.

16. Derber, *People before Profit.*

17. Lori Wallach and Michelle Sforza, *The WTO* (New York: Seven Stories Press, 1999). See also Stiglitz, *Making Globalization Work*; Joseph Stiglitz, *Globalization and Its Discontents* (New York: Norton, 2002); and Derber, *People before Profit.*

18. Wallach and Sforza, *The WTO.*

19. Ibid. See also Stiglitz, *Globalization.*

20. For a discussion of the positive role of government, see Robert Kuttner, *Obama's Challenge* (White River Junction, VT: Chelsea Green, 2008). See also Stiglitz, *Making Globalization Work.*

21. George Soros, *George Soros on Globalization* (New York: PublicAffairs, 2002). See also Stiglitz, *Globalization*; and Derber, *People before Profit.*

22. Wallach and Sforza, *The WTO.*

23. Stiglitz, *Globalization.* See also Derber, *People before Profit.*

24. This is the central argument of George Soros, a financier who understands both the virtues and the dangers of global financial flows and makes a strong case against the Washington consensus for not regulating international finance. See Soros, *George Soros on Globalization.* See also Derber, *People before Profit,* chap. 8.

25. Robert Kuttner, *Everything for Sale* (New York: Knopf, 1997).

26. Soros, *George Soros on Globalization.* See also Stiglitz, *Globalization.*

27. Stiglitz, *Globalization.* See also William Grieder, *One World: Ready or Not* (New York: Simon and Schuster, 1998); and Derber, *People before Profit,* chap. 8.

28. Derber, *People before Profit.* See also Derber, *Hidden Power,* chap. 2; and Stiglitz, *Making Globalization Work,* chap. 10.

Notes for Chapter 14

1. The American penchant for technological change as the solution to social problems has deeply permeated the climate change discussion here, even among the most influential advocates for a green revolution. A classic example is Thomas Friedman, *Hot, Flat, and Crowded* (New York: Farrar, Straus and Giroux, 2008).

2. Joseph Stiglitz, *Globalization and Its Discontents* (New York: Norton, 2002).

3. Kevin Phillips, *Bad Money* (New York: Norton, 2008), chap. 7.

4. Ibid. Chap. 7 and appendix on global public opinion toward the United States after the 2008 Wall Street crisis.

5. Joseph Stiglitz, *Making Globalization Work* (New York: Norton, 2007), esp. chap. 6.

6. Immanuel Wallerstein, *The Decline of American Power* (New York: Norton, 2003).

7. Stiglitz, *Making Globalization Work*, chaps. 3, 6, 10.

8. Andrew Bacevich, *The Limits of Power* (New York: Metropolitan Books, 2008).

9. Ibid.

10. Linda Bilmes and Joseph Stiglitz, *The Three Trillion Dollar War* (New York: Norton, 2008).

11. Paul Kennedy, *The Rise and Fall of Great Powers* (New York: Vintage, 1989).

12. Elitsa Vucheva, "'Laissez-Faire Capitalism Is Finished,' Says France," *Euobserver.com,* September 26, 2009, http://euobserver.com/9/26814.

13. Phillips, *Bad Money,* chap. 7.

14. Stiglitz, *Making Globalization Work,* 175.

15. Ibid.

16. Megan Rowling, "Report Estimates Deaths by Warming," *Boston Globe,* May 29, 2009.

17. Bacevich, *The Limits of Power.*

18. Noam Chomsky, *Profit over People: Neo-liberalism and Global Order* (New York: Seven Stories Press, 2003).

19. Bacevich, *The Limits of Power.* See also Chalmers Johnson, *Blowback,* 2d ed. (New York: Holt, 2004).

20. Joshua Partlow, "A Protected Forest's Fast Decline," *Washingtonpost.com,* February 6, 2009, http://www.washingtonpost.com/wp-dyn/content/article/2009/02/05/AR2009020503199_pf.html.

21. This Tobin tax idea was proposed a decade ago by William Greider to slow down destructive global speculative finance flows. See William Greider, *One World: Ready or Not* (New York: Simon and Schuster, 1998). The idea of using a tax on speculative global finance to support green global development is becoming an initiative passed in progressive U.S. communities, such as Arcata, California. See "Arcata, CA Resolution Supporting the Tobin Tax," http://www.greenpolicy.us/index.php?title=Arcata%2C_CA_Resolution_Supporting_the_%22Tobin_Tax%22.

22. Stiglitz, *Making Globalization Work,* chap. 8.

23. Ibid.

24. Lori Wallach and Michelle Sforza, *The WTO* (New York: Seven Stories Press, 1999).

25. "Playing with Fire," *China Environmental Law,* 2009, http://www.chinaenvironmentallaw.com.

26. Stiglitz, *Making Globalization Work,* chap. 6.

27. Ibid.

28. Lester Brown, *Plan B 3.0: Mobilizing to Save Civilization,* 3d ed. (New York: Norton, 2008).

29. Peter Barnes, *Climate Solutions* (White River Junction, VT: Chelsea Green, 2008), 75ff.

30. Ibid.

31. Gong Ying, "Summary of China's Policies and Actions for Addressing Climate Change" (unpublished ms., October 29, 2008).

32. Friedman, *Hot, Flat, and Crowded.*

33. Phillips, *Bad Money,* esp. the appendix on global attitudes toward the United States and U.S. market rules.

34. Greider, *One World.* See also Charles Derber, *People before Profit* (New York: Picador, 2003), 149–151.

35. Stiglitz, *Globalization.*

36. David Sanger and Mark Landler, "In Europe, Obama Calls for Rules on Finances," *New York Times,* April 1, 2009, http://www.nytimes.com/2009/04/02/world/europe/02prexy.html?ref=economy.

37. Stiglitz, *Making Globalization Work,* chaps. 1–3.

38. Barack Obama, talk at Columbia University, September 2008, http://www.nypost.com/seven/01042009/postopinion/opedcolumnists/obama_the_real_yes_man_147104.htm.

39. Karl Marx, *Capital,* vol. 1: *A Critique of Political Economy* (New York: Penguin Classics, 1992), chap. 1.

40. See Hazel Henderson, *Beyond Globalization* (West Hartford, CT: Kumarian, 1999), 24ff.

41. Ibid.

42. Jeremy Brecher and Tim Costello, *Global Village or Global Pillage* (Boston: South End Press, 1994).

43. Stiglitz, *Making Globalization Work,* chaps. 6, 10. See also Derber, *People before Profit.*

44. Derber, *People before Profit,* chap. 8.

45. David Korten, *Agenda for a New Economy* (San Francisco: Berrett-Koehler, 2008).

46. Loretta Napoleoni, *Rogue Economics* (New York: Seven Stories Press, 2008).

47. Christopher Chase-Dunn and Thomas Hall, *Core/Periphery Relations in Pre-Capitalist World* (Boulder, CO: Westview Press, 1991).

48. Korten, *Agenda for a New Economy.* Bill McKibben, *Deep Economy* (New York: Times Books, 2008).

49. McKibben, *Deep Economy,* chap. 2.

50. Ibid.

51. Jeremy Brecher and Tim Costello, *Globalization from Below* (Boston: South End Press, 2000), 42–43.

52. McKibben, *Deep Economy,* chap. 2.

53. Ibid.

Notes for Chapter 15

1. Barack Obama, "Inaugural Speech," *CNN*.com, January 20, 2009, http://www.cnn.com/2009/POLITICS/01/20/obama.politics/index.html.

2. John M. Broder, "Obama, Who Vowed Rapid Action on Climate Change, Turns More Cautious," *New York Times*, April 11, 2009, A10.

3. Carl Hulse, "In Climate Change Bill, What May Become an Election-Year Issue," *New York Times*, June 28, 2009, 18.

4. Bryan Walsh, "Obama's Move on Fuel Efficiency: A Clear Win for Greens," *Time*, January 26, 2009, http://www.time.com/time/health/article/0,8599,1874106,00.html.

5. Barack Obama, "Energy Independence and the Safety of Our Planet," April 3, 2006, http://obamaspeeches.com/060-Energy-Independence-and-the-Safety-of-Our-Planet-Obama-Speech.htm; emphasis added.

6. Obama, "Inaugural Speech." See also http://www.whitehouse.gov/agenda/energy-and-environment.

7. Council on Foreign Relations, Essential Documents, "Obama-Biden New Energy for America Plan," January 21, 2009, http://www.cfr.org/publication/18306/obamabiden_new_energy_for_america_plan_january_2009.html.

8. Seph Petta, "Comparing Energy Plans," *Apollo News Service*, September 8, 2008, http://apolloalliance.org/data-points-nap/comparing-energy-plans/.

9. Joe Klein, "Why Barack Obama Is Winning," *Time*, October 22, 2009, http://www.time.com/time/politics/article/0,8599,1853025-4,00.html.

10. Ibid.

11. Obama, "Inaugural Speech."

12. Al Gore, *Assault on Reason* (New York: Penguin, 2007).

13. Chris Mooney, *The Republican War on Science* (New York: Basic Books, 2005).

14. Barack Obama, "The Search for Knowledge, Truth and a Greater Understanding of the World," December 20, 2008, http://change.gov/newsroom/entry/the_search_for_knowledge_truth_and_a_greater_understanding_of_the_world_aro/.

15. Barack Obama, "From Peril to Progress," January 26, 2009, http://www.whitehouse.gov/blog_post/Fromperiltoprogress/.

16. Cited in Jim Tankersly, "California Farms, Vineyards in Peril from Warming," *Los Angeles Times*, February 4, 2009, http://articles.latimes.com/2009/feb/04/local/me-warming4.

17. Ibid.

18. Steven Chu, "Coal Is My Worst Nightmare," *Wall Street Journal*, December 11, 2008.

19. Stacy Feldman, "Energy Secretary Pick Steven Chu on Climate Change, in His Own Words," *Solveclimate.com*, December 12, 2008, http://solveclimate.com/blog/20081212/energy-secretary-pick-steven-chu-climate-change-his-own-words.

20. Cited in "Obama Announces Chu as Next US Energy Secretary," Copenhagen Climate Council, December 17, 2008, http://www.copenhagenclimatecouncil.com/get-informed/news/video-obama-announces-steve-chu-as-next-u-s-energy-secretary.html.

21. John Holdren, "The Future of Climate Change Policy," *Scientific American* (October 2008), http://www.sciam.com/article.cfm?id=the-future-of-climate-change-policy.

22. Cited in Jeff Jacoby, "Questions for Obama's Science Guy," *Boston Globe*, January 18, 2009, http://www.jeffjacoby.com/2337/questions-for-obamas-science-guy.

23. Both quotes from Barack Obama, "Obama Speaks about the Economy,"

CNN.com, January 16, 2009, http://politicalticker.blogs.cnn.com/2009/01/16/happening-now-obama-speaks-about-the-economy/.

24. Barack Obama, "Official Announcement of Presidential Candidacy," February 10, 2007, http://www.americanrhetoric.com/speeches/barackobamacandidacyforpresident.htm.

25. Brian Merchant, $60 Billion for Green in the Stimulus Bill: Where the Money Will Go," treehugger.com, February 16, 2009, http://www.treehugger.com/files/2009/02green-stimulus-bill-60-billion.phptreehugger.com.

26. C. Wright Mills, *The Sociological Imagination* (New York: Oxford University Press, 2000).

27. Ibid.

28. Thomas Ferguson, *Golden Rule: The Investment Theory of Party Competition and the Logic of Money-Driven Political Systems* (Chicago: University of Chicago Press, 1995).

29. Mark Trumbull, "Rebuilding the Economy," *Christian Science Monitor,* January 21, 2009, http://features.csmonitor.com/economyrebuild/2009/01/21/geithner-pledges-swift-bold-fix-to-financial-system/; emphasis added.

30. David Leonhardt, "A Broken Economy," *New York Times,* August 24, 2008, http://www.nytimes.com/2008/08/24/magazine/24Obamanomics-t.html?pagewanted=all.

31. Cornelia Dean, "Emissions Cut Won't Bring Quick Relief, Scientists Say," *New York Times,* January 26, 2009, http://www.nytimes.com/2009/01/27/science/earth/27carbon.html.

32. Felicity Barriner, "U.S. Given Poor Marks on the Environment," *New York Times,* January 23, 2009, http://news.cnet.com/U.S.-given-poor-marks-on-the-environment/2100–13836_3–6227224.html.

Notes for Chapter 16

1. Paul Hawken, *Blessed Unrest: How the Largest Movement in the World Came into Being and Why No One Saw It Coming* (New York: Viking Press, 2007).

2. Ibid., 174.

3. Ibid., 141–142.

4. Ibid., 145.

5. Ibid., 19.

6. Ibid., 151.

7. Bill McKibben, *Fight Global Warming Now: The Handbook for Taking Action in Your Community* (New York: Holt, 2007).

8. Charles Derber, *Hidden Power* (San Francisco: Berrett-Koehler, 2005).

9. Howard Zinn, *A People's History of the United States* (New York: HarperCollins, 2003).

10. Tom Hayden, *The Long Sixties* (Boulder, CO: Paradigm Publishers, 2009), chaps. 1–2. See also Derber, *Hidden Power,* chap. 7.

11. Zinn, *A People's History.* See also Richard Flacks, *Making History* (New York: Columbia University Press, 1988).

12. Henry David Thoreau, *Civil Disobedience and Other Essays* (New York: Dover, 1993).

13. Derber, *Hidden Power*, chaps. 2, 5.

14. Charles Derber, *Corporation Nation* (New York: St. Martin's Press, 2000), chap. 9. See also Derber, *Hidden Power*, esp. chap. 5.

15. Hayden, *The Long Sixties*, chaps. 1–2. See also Charles Derber and Yale Magrass, *Morality Wars* (Boulder, CO: Paradigm Publishers, 2008), chaps. 6–7.

16. Derber and Magrass, *Morality Wars*, chap. 6.

17. Erving Goffman, *Stigma: Notes on the Management of Spoiled Identity* (New York: Penguin, 1990).

18. Todd Gitlin, *The Twilight of Our Common Dreams* (New York: Holt, 1996).

19. Naomi Klein, *Fences and Windows* (New York: Picador, 2002).

20. Derber, *Hidden Power*, chaps. 2, 5, 7.

21. Flacks, *Making History*.

22. All quotes in this paragraph are from Wendell Barry and Bill McKibben, "Call for Civil Disobedience against Coal-Fired Power Plants," *Yes Magazine*, February 7, 2009, http://www.commondreams.org/view/2009/02/27–10.

23. Cited in ibid.

24. See polling data summarized in Chapter 4.

25. These efforts can be seen in the growth of multi-issue "movement" groups such as Moveon.org, Progressive Democrats for America, and the Campaign for America's Future. We are also witnessing calls by labor movements, including the AFL-CIO, for broad European-style agendas, including universal health care, better education, and climate change legislation.

26. See Klein, *Fences and Windows*.

27. Hayden, *The Long Sixties*.

28. Hawken, *Blessed Unrest*.

29. California Green Stimulus Coalition, http://californiagreenstimulus.org/.

30. The term is used by Jeremy Brecher, Tim Costello, and Brendan Smith, "Labor's War on Global Warming," *The Nation*, March 10, 2008, http://www.thenation.com/doc/20080324/brecher.

31. Cited in ibid.

32. All quotes in this paragraph are cited in ibid.

33. Van Jones, *The Green Collar Economy: How One Solution Can Fix Our Two Biggest Problems* (San Francisco: HarperOne, 2008).

34. Brecher et al., "Labor's War."

35. Ibid.

36. Cited in ibid.

37. Van Jones emphasizes this point in Jones, *The Green Collar Economy*, chap. 4.

38. Derber, *Corporation Nation*, chap. 10.

39. Jones, *The Green Collar Economy*, 104ff.

40. Ibid.

41. The workshop took place in Cambridge, Massachusetts, in February 2009 and included many community activists who were dedicated to building a movement to green the planet.

42. Flacks, *Making History*.

43. Ibid.

44. The carbon diet group is part of a national project based on the guide by David Gershon, *Low Carbon Diet: A 30-Day Program to Lose 5,000 Pounds* (San Francisco: Empowerment Institute, 2006).

45. C. Wright Mills, *The Sociological Imagination* (New York: Oxford University Press, 2000).
46. Charles Siegel, *The Politics of Simple Living* (Berkeley, CA: Preservation Institute, 2008).
47. Mills, *The Sociological Imagination*.
48. Hayden, *The Long Sixties*, chaps. 1–2.
49. Derber, *Hidden Power*, chaps. 7–9.

Notes for Chapter 17

1. Richard Flacks, *Making History* (New York: Columbia University Press, 1988).
2. For a discussion of the mushrooming number of green jobs, see Van Jones, *The Green Collar Economy: How One Solution Can Fix Our Two Biggest Problems* (San Francisco: HarperOne, 2008).
3. Flacks, *Making History*.
4. Vivian Gornick, *The Romance of Communism* (New York: Basic Books, 1979). See also Flacks, *Making History*.
5. Katherine Adam and Charles Derber, *The New Feminized Majority* (Boulder, CO: Paradigm Publishers, 2008).
6. Most of the information on Peter is based on two extended interviews I conducted with him in 2008 and 2009.
7. Alexis de Tocqueville, *Democracy in America* (New York: Penguin Classics, 2003).
8. Robert Putnam, *Bowling Alone* (New York: Simon and Schuster, 2001).
9. Bill McKibben, *The End of Nature* (New York: Random House, 2006).
10. This section draws heavily on the account by McKibben and his students of their Step It Up campaign. See Bill McKibben, *Fight Global Warming Now: The Handbook for Taking Action in Your Community* (New York: Holt, 2007).
11. Ibid.
12. Ibid.
13. The Noah Principles are outlined in Jones, *The Green Collar Economy*.
14. Paul Hawken, *Blessed Unrest: How the Largest Movement in the World Came into Being and Why No One Saw It Coming* (New York: Viking Press, 2007).
15. McKibben, *Fight Global Warming Now*.
16. Charles Derber, *Hidden Power* (San Francisco: Berrett-Koehler, 2005). See also Charles Derber, *Regime Change Begins at Home* (San Francisco: Berrett-Koehler, 2004).
17. For details on McKibben's 2009 Copenhagen campaign, go to his Web site, http://www.350.org/oct24.

Index

Acknowledgments

Let me first thank Dean Birkenkamp, the founder and publisher of Paradigm, who understands the threat to the planet and the inhumanity of our economic system. Paradigm does crucially important work, and it is a pleasure to work with Dean and his colleagues. I want to thank them for all their help to me and for working tirelessly to make the world a better place.

I am grateful to Yale Magrass, who coauthored one chapter and offered key historical insights on the relation between capitalism and climate change. I also want to thank Charles Siegel, who sensitized me to the issues of work time, suburban life, and urban planning. I am very grateful to my colleague and friend David Karp, for reading the manuscript and supporting me at every step. And many thanks also to my colleague and friend John Williamson, who offered his own unflagging support.

I want to thank other colleagues at the Boston College Sociology Department and Leadership for Change, for their writing and/or conversations on sustainability, consumerism, and social justice. These include Juliet Schor, Anders Hayden, Mike Cermak, Peter Crawley, Ken Mirvis, Rebecca Rowley, Sandra Waddock, and others.

Thanks also to activist colleagues who are trying to link the environmental, labor, and peace movements. These include especially Paul Shannon, Suren Moodler, and Chuck Collins, all of whom do amazing political work.

My friends and neighbors in the Clothesline Gang and in the Dedham environmental community have inspired me. They include Elena Kolesnikova, Linda Wilkins, Steve MacAusland, Charlotte MacAusland, Hanna Heald, Linda Grenfell, Jonathan Briggs, and, of course, Ginny LeClair.

And, finally my deepest thanks go to Elena, for her activism on climate change issues, for her endurance of my obsessions and long work hours, and for her courage and steadfastness. She saves me, just as we must now all save each other and the earth.

BASEMENT

About the Author

Charles Derber is Professor of Sociology at Boston College and former director of its graduate program on social economy and social justice. He is a prolific scholar in the fields of politics, economy, international relations, and U.S. culture, with thirteen internationally acclaimed books and several major research grants. Derber's most recent books include *The Wilding of America*, fifth edition (W. H. Freeman, 2010) and *Morality Wars: How Empires, the Born-Again, and the Politically Correct Do Evil in the Name of Good*, revised and updated (Paradigm Publishers, 2010). Other recent books include *Hidden Power: What You Need to Know to Save Our Democracy* (Berrett-Koehler, 2005); *People Before Profit: The New Globalization in an Age of Terror, Big Money, and Economic Crisis* (Picador, 2003), which has been translated into Chinese, German, Arabic, and British English; as well as *Corporation Nation* (St. Martin's, 2000), a widely discussed analysis of the growing power and responsibilities of corporations in the United States, recently translated and published in China. Three other works of note are *The Pursuit of Attention* (Oxford, 2000), *The Nuclear Seduction* (with William Schwartz, University of California Press, 1989), and *Power in the Highest Degree* (with William Schwartz and Yale Magrass, Oxford, 1990).

Derber espouses a public sociology that brings sociological perspectives to a general audience. Derber lectures widely at universities, companies, and community groups, and appears on numerous media outlets. His op-eds and essays appear in *Newsday, The Boston Globe*, and other newspapers, and he has been interviewed by *Newsweek, BusinessWeek, Time*, and other news magazines. He speaks frequently on National Public Radio, on talk radio, and on television. His work has been reviewed by *The New York Times, The Washington Post, The Boston Globe, Boston Herald, Washington Monthly*, and numerous other magazines and newspapers.

Derber is a lifelong social activist. He is now working to help unify the labor, peace, and environmental movements as an unstoppable force for social justice.

268